CW01501968

We have worked in the area of chronic illnesses – mainly cancer and HIV/AIDS – for close to 20 years. Then again, so have many others. However, what we feel we can contribute is the lessons we have learned from working with PNI (and other methods) in an African context, where there is often little knowledge of (Western) psychology, and where medical structures are often weak or absent. In many ways, this has forced us to abandon Western concepts of the mind and focus on concepts and methods that are easy to understand and use.

The methods we present in this book can be used for a large range of chronic illnesses. Our main area of interest and experience, though, is in suppressed immune conditions, such as cancer, chronic fatigue immune deficiency syndrome and AIDS.

A hard lesson to learn – at least for us – is that people in general are not particularly interested in research, statistics, control groups and all the technical details of PNI research. However, what does grab people's attention are the real-life stories of people who have dealt with their chronic illness and managed to bring it under some measure of control.

So we have structured this book as a story – a true story – of how people have successfully coped with their life-threatening illnesses. Each chapter includes a part of someone's story, how it relates to PNI research findings, and how you can apply the principle to your own health.

For further information, the authors can be contacted at:
P O Box 13043, Nelspruit North, 1209, Republic of South Africa.
tel: (South Africa) 083-226-9466
e-mail: neil_orr@yebo.co.za / drp@mweb.co.za

THE HEALER INSIDE YOU

THE HEALER INSIDE YOU

Using PNI, a mind–body science, to help heal your body

Neil Orr (MA Psych)
& David Patient (MHT)

DOUBLE
STOREY
a juta company

First published 2004 by Double Storey Books, a division of Juta & Co. Ltd,
Mercury Crescent, Wetton, Cape Town, South Africa

© 2004 David Patient and Neil Orr

ISBN 1-919930-56-6

Illustrations by Adam Carnegie
Cover design by Toby Newsome
Editing by Sandy Shepherd
Text design and layout by Jenny Sandler
Printing by Creda Communications, Epping, Cape Town

CONTENTS

INTRODUCTION

PNI (psychoneuroimmunology) is a relatively new area of science, which connects health psychology and medicine. Its main focus is to look at the relationship between social, mental and emotional factors, and your body's immune system.

In terms of its development, PNI has only recently been declared a 'mainstream' area of research by international institutions such as the US National Institutes of Health. A measure of its growing recognition was a statement by the American Medical Association a few years back, which declared the treatment of heart disease without some form of psychological (PNI-based) intervention to be 'unethical'.

However, for many orthodox medical and other health professionals, PNI is a new kid on the block, and there is still some scepticism. In our experience, this scepticism is rapidly resolved when such professionals read the hundreds of studies in this area.

The results of this research are slowly but surely having a profound effect on how we view the development of illnesses and also how we treat them – heart disease, cancer, HIV and AIDS, arthritis and diabetes, to name a few.

However, when you are personally dealing with a chronic illness, your priorities are a little different. You want to *do* something about the illness, not just read fascinating research.

In this book we take you on a journey of methods that can perhaps help you lessen illness and pain, using mental and emotional methods. The need to *do* something is the main priority of this book. For those who want more detailed information about PNI and the wealth of research it contains, we have created a bibliography of references at the end of the book.

DAVID'S STORY

Neil Orr – the 'scientist' – is the guy who did all the research on PNI for this book. He has an MA in Research Psychology, in which he focused on PNI and HIV/AIDS and cancer. If you ask him questions, he'll give you facts and figures … boring stuff. So that's the end of his story as far as this book is concerned.

David Patient, on the other hand, is one of the longest-surviving people living with HIV in the world today (21 years since diagnosis, and about 23 years since infection, in March 2004). He's regarded as one of the top motivational speakers in Africa today, particularly in the light of his background and the way he's retained his health despite being told almost 21 years ago that he had only six months to live.

Nowadays, with new antiretroviral treatments, David's longevity – although unusual – is not unique. However, David is not on antiretrovirals (ARVs) – he's dealing with his illness in another way. And that 'other way' is a lot more interesting than PNI statistics, because it shows what can actually be done with PNI.

The problem child

David was a problem child (some would say he's still a bit of a problem). He was born in Zambia (previously Northern Rhodesia), parents unknown, in March 1961. Records of his birth were destroyed by fire when Zambia gained its independence. He was adopted soon after birth by a British couple, and he spent the first years of his life in Zambia, before his family emigrated to South Africa.

It wasn't too long before his parents discovered that their newly acquired 'bundle of joy' had a few problems: hyperactivity, attention deficit disorder, dyslexia, to name a few. Needless to say, educating David was not exactly an easy task, as a series of headmasters discovered, and he started school life by being expelled from pre-primary kindergarten. The Boy Scouts refused to give him his fire badge, even though he displayed great enthusiasm in burning down a section of their meeting hall.

A panel of psychiatrists diagnosed him as mentally bright but a social misfit. They predicted that he would end up in prison or at the gallows. He did, however, manage to complete primary school. After three disastrous years at high school, he finally left school and moved to Johannesburg in the late 1970s to seek his fortune. It wasn't too long before he attracted the interest of the Bureau of State Security for making anti-apartheid statements, and at the tender age of 18 he was hastily shipped off to Europe to escape arrest. He soon ran out of money and was left stranded in the US, on his way to Australia.

Happy birthday, David

Somehow David managed to sort out work and temporary residency, and went about making a life for himself in Las Vegas. Although it was the end of the disco era, it was still the age of sexual freedom and experimentation, and David literally had a permanent party. That meant plenty of anonymous sex and tons of drugs.

In February 1983, a friend of his was diagnosed with pneumonia, and died in the operating theatre with what was then called GRIDS (Gay Related Immune Deficiency Syndrome), the precursor to the term AIDS. Several cases had been reported in the year prior to this, all characterised by either a rare form of cancer called Kaposi's sarcoma or an equally rare form of pneumonia, called PCP (pneumocystis pneumonia). While waiting for the autopsy results of his friend, the doctor described some of the typical symptoms of GRIDS, and David realised that he had some of the same symptoms, which he had dismissed as recurrent flu or glandular fever.

At that time there was no HIV test, because medical researchers had not even discovered what was causing GRIDS. What they did know was that it was characterised by a severely depressed immune system, typically in relation to the Helper T-cells (also called CD4 cells). So David had his T-cells checked, and the test confirmed that as his T-cell count was very low he probably had GRIDS. He received his diagnosis on his 22nd birthday.

As a matter of record, blood drawn for this 1983 test was frozen and retested in 1985, after the development of the first HIV antibody test. It confirmed David's HIV-positive status. He has had more than 35 HIV tests of various kinds since then, at institutions ranging from private laboratories to the National Institutes of Health and various universities, all of which have confirmed his HIV status.

David is not entirely sure when he became infected. The most likely period was 1980 – a particularly active party period – which would explain why his symptoms had developed by 1983. At the time of his diagnosis he had muscle pains, had lost about 20 kilograms, had night sweats, chronic fatigue, and several other typical AIDS symptoms. His doctor told him to go home and get his affairs in order, since he had about six months to live. He was also told not to return to the doctor's office, because his doctor was afraid other patients would discover that he was treating a GRIDS victim. Happy birthday.

David then did something rather unusual. He went to a funeral company, bought a coffin and a funeral policy, and to the horror of the funeral director, insisted on testing the coffins by lying inside them. He also wrote his eulogy, chose the funeral hymns and wrote his will. That afternoon, he also went to purchase a house, with a 30-year mortgage. He figured – in the days before insurance companies had HIV-exclusion clauses – that he might as well leave something to his family when he died.

David was not a happy young man, long before his diagnosis. He had been hospitalised several times for suicide attempts, and had been heavily involved in drugs for a few years since arriving in the US. As a result, his diagnosis was actually a bit of a relief. So he simply went home and commenced the party to end all parties.

However, the party was not exactly very successful. First, within a day or two of his diagnosis the local newspaper published his name and address, under the headline *Gay Plague Reaches Las Vegas!* Several things happened rather rapidly: bomb threats, bricks thrown through windows, pets poisoned, and all his so-called 'friends' were suddenly nowhere to be found. He also lost his job as a direct result of the newspaper article.

Epiphany on the mountain

In absolute desperation, he resorted to his old-time favourite avoidance method, suicide. And, being a rather flamboyant young man, he decided to climb to the top of Mount Charleston outside Las Vegas and jump off a cliff. It was a rather melodramatic (and potentially messy) plan. However, the climb to the top was more tiring than he had anticipated, and he had to sit down to catch his breath before the final jump. It was those few moments that changed his life.

For reasons unknown, he closed his eyes for a few seconds and began to talk to this 'thing' that was inside his body killing him. He figured it had to be something like a virus, so he called it Mr Virus. Years of anger spilled out, which was thrown in the general direction of Mr Virus. What David had not anticipated was that Mr Virus would talk back! It told him that it too wanted nothing more than to survive. In what seemed like a very long time, but which in reality took only a few seconds, David and Mr Virus had a heart-to-heart chat, which culminated in David telling Mr Virus that he was quite willing and able to kill himself, and thus Mr Virus too. So, if Mr Virus wanted to survive it had better think about keeping itself under control and not making David's body ill. If they were both to survive, they would have to agree to a truce. Mr Virus agreed, and David walked back down the mountain. This occurred on July 4, Independence Day in the US, and David repeats this chat with Mr Virus every year on the same day.

After the aborted suicide attempt David moved to Florida, where no-one knew about him, and started a series of part-time jobs to fund his drug habit, with crack cocaine being a particular favourite. During this time, he also participated in the very first human AZT trials (in 1986), along with several hundred other men infected with HIV. He used to travel 400 km every week to get his medications, and at the same time collect his other, illicit, drugs. However, things did not work out very well with this cosy arrangement. The initial trials of AZT used high doses and David rapidly became ill from the side effects. So he – and one other person – dropped out of the trials. Of interest is that the only two people left alive of all those in this initial trial are the two who dropped out. This is not a criticism of the medication, but rather a reflection of the fact that the doses were so high that death was inevitable from the side effects. Nowadays, much lower and safer doses are used.

The turning point in David's self-destructive behaviour occurred rather unexpectedly. He returned home one day to find that a few pieces of crack cocaine which he had dropped on the carpet had been discovered by his dogs, who were running around wild-eyed and frantic. He recognised that they were acting exactly as he must have been, and vowed to stop taking the drugs immediately. It is one thing to hurt yourself, but another to hurt those you love. So he stopped, cold turkey, without any counselling or support.

The long-term non-progressor

Over the next year or two, he slowly began the process of trying to repair the damage to relationships caused by years of drug abuse, and started to apply himself to learning to be a chef and getting a regular job.

He also began attending support groups for people living with HIV and AIDS, and was soon counselling others himself. He broke through a major psychological barrier by going to college and obtaining certification as a hypnotherapist, which he used to great effect in pain control and easing people's suffering as they died from AIDS.

By 1992 he had buried literally hundreds of his friends and many more clients. He had also nursed his lover until his death and helped set up the first AIDS agency in Florida. In 1994 he received a commendation from President Clinton for his work in AIDS.

It was also during this time that he was a regular visitor to research laboratories, as part of studies of 'long-term non-progressors'. Until the late 1980s, it was simply assumed that everyone who was infected with HIV eventually developed AIDS and died. However, researchers (especially those working on the Los Angeles Men's Study, LAMS) began to notice that there was a small group of men who – although they had been infected for many years, some since 1976 – were simply not getting ill. It is not commonly known that in 1976 a US government-funded hepatitis study collected thousands of blood samples in the main cities of the USA. Many of the people who were tested for hepatitis also happened to be gay. Funding was withdrawn when there was a change in government, and the blood was frozen. Many years later – after 1985, when the HIV test was developed – a researcher remembered this large sample of blood and decided to test the samples to see if HIV was present in those communities before 1980. Indeed it was, and the men who donated the blood were traced, and informed of their HIV status. It was during this tracing process that it was discovered that some of the men simply did not know they had HIV, because they had never become ill. That is how researchers discovered the presence of these 'long-term non-progressors'.

A 'long-term survivor' is technically someone living with HIV whose immune system gets weaker much more slowly than normal. It does, however, get weaker. A 'non-progressor' is someone with HIV whose immune system simply does not get weaker, even after 20 years of infection.

Technically, David does not fit the health profile of the 'standard' non-progressor because his immune system first went down (the lowest point was when his CD4 count was 364), but then it came back up to normal levels again. In this respect, he is a rare phenomenon. His is one of the few cases in which the immune decline has actually been reversed in HIV/AIDS without medication. Nowadays, this kind of reversal is fortunately common with the use of antiretroviral medicines.

Later research in the late 1980s and early 1990s showed that there was a consistent percentage of HIV-infected people (3–7 percent) who, regardless of where in the world they were, were simply not getting sick with AIDS.

In 1991 David moved to California, where he had a part-time job as the chef for a wealthy newspaper owner and a part-time counselling therapy practice. It was also at this time that word began to spread of the political changes happening in South Africa, and David eagerly awaited the day he would be removed from the banned list and could return home.

In the interim, he had connected with a group of people in San Francisco who were sending various AIDS medications – including antiretrovirals – to agencies in South Africa. In San Francisco, people living with AIDS were provided with free medication. If and when these people died, their unused medications were collected quietly, repackaged and sent to doctors in South Africa. It is rather ironic that David is sometimes accused of being opposed to antiretrovirals, when he was one of the first to bring them into South Africa at great personal risk.

Many people confuse his advocacy of health-maintenance methods, such as PNI and nutrition, with a rejection of orthodox medical treatment. He is adamant that this is not the case. As far as he is concerned, when you are seriously ill you need to use everything at your disposal to regain your health, including medications.

He also makes it clear that maintaining your health with PNI and nutrition is just as important as dealing with AIDS illnesses with medication. 'Do whatever it takes' is his motto.

The prodigal son returns

In 1994, when it was clear that apartheid was at an end and his ban was lifted, David returned to South Africa to meet the people he had been supplying with medications and to give talks to patients at their clinics.

At one of these clinics he met Neil, who was conducting his MA research there. David began to relate his story – and those of other long-term non-progressors – and Neil in turn began to tell David about PNI research. It wasn't long before they both realised that what David and other long-term non-progressors had done coincided with what PNI research had been suggesting for several years, in terms of how to deal with viral infections. And thus the collaboration began that led to this book.

After several months of rather expensive trans-Atlantic communications, Neil went to California to interview other long-term survivors, via the research networks that David was participating in at the time. About a year later, the first PNI therapy protocol was produced and they decided to return to South Africa to present it to a conference of people living with AIDS in Cape Town.

When the workshop on the common psychological factors of long-term progressors, and the therapy protocol, was presented, only 20 people arrived. By the second day word had spread and there were 100 people. One of the most moving experiences at this conference was that there were people who had lived healthily with HIV for almost as long as David, but who had been telling friends they had not been infected very long. They had felt guilty for being survivors while their friends had died. When the PNI explanations for their longevity were presented, many cried, finally understanding why they were still alive and they were finally able to help others do the same.

Despite their enthusiasm, PNI took a long time to succeed in South Africa, at least in terms of HIV and AIDS. The time was simply not right. Public apathy was widespread and most people did not want to know anything about HIV or AIDS, a situation that has changed only recently.

So David and Neil modified the PNI protocol and applied it in private therapy practice, working with people who had cancer, multiple sclerosis and a host of other chronic illnesses. In many ways, this was necessary to develop the protocol to the point it is at today, making it useful to a broad range of chronic conditions.

The protocol was further adapted and developed within the corporate setting, as a motivational process, and has worked superbly in rural and urban settings. The greatest test of the process – in conjunction with various nutritional and physical measures – has been in poverty-stricken regions, such as Mozambique.

Today, David is still healthy. His immune system is well within normal range, and his viral load is still low. Yes, he does occasionally get ill with either shingles or chest infections. However, these are rare, and when necessary he treats them with the appropriate medication.

David is by no means unique. There are many other people who have reversed cancer or AIDS, as well as a wide range of other serious illnesses. What is interesting, however, is that these people all have a similar psychological profile (in terms of attitude and coping styles), which we intend to explain step by step throughout this book.

PNI and you

When David's story is told in conferences and workshops, people react in one of two ways: ninety percent say *'Wow – aren't you amazing!'* (i.e., they place him on a pedestal and miss the fact that they can do the same thing). Ten percent ask *'How did you do that?'*

In which category do you place yourself? The issues of *'Is it possible, generally?'* and *'Is it possible for me?'* are the first areas we examine in the PNI therapy process.

There are several crucial points to keep in mind when beginning your PNI journey:

- **Be realistic about how much time you have to do the work.** It is theoretically possible to accomplish amazing things in a very short span of time, even in quite advanced stages of disease. However, the body is sometimes quite weak and devastated and this must be factored into what you do, how much you can do, and whether it's worth doing. Sometimes, a person is just plain tired and has had enough. Death is something you have to confront at some point, either now or later, whether through illness, being run over by a bus, or old age. And healing is not always in the direction of health … it can also be healing into death.

  PNI is not an escape from death and dying, it is simply an option with a range of methods that can, under certain conditions, extend physical life by enhancing the immune system. That is all it can do.

- **Ask yourself why you want to extend your physical existence.** Think seriously about this. Do not come up with unconvincing statements such as *'Well – doesn't everyone?'* No, not everyone wants to live and this is also a valid choice. More to the point, what 'everyone else' wants is (a) irrelevant to your healing process, and (b) none of your business. You have more than enough to deal with, so stop avoiding the real question.

- **Clearly understand that your logic and reason are not going to be sufficient to get you through.** 'Understanding' PNI is not the same as doing the work required. PNI intervention means that you have to deal with a bunch of 'yuck' stuff – death, anger, guilt, painful memories and more. You will not be the same afterwards and life will not be the same as before. Your sense of what is important, what you are willing to tolerate from others and what you want from life will be affected. That is part of the package deal. As Sharron, one of our clients, said: *'I stopped worrying about what people thought about me and started putting myself first.'*

If you are clear that this is what you want, then read on and do the various exercises.

If this is not what you want, acknowledge that it is your right to choose not to do this and that this choice is just as valid and 'right' for you. Guilt and obligation, as forms of motivation, go nowhere. Don't waste your time.

If there is any lesson we have learned that rises above all others in terms of importance, it is that you must want to live if you intend to live. And no, you don't have to be a saint to heal – we all have our own paths to healing.

WHAT IS PNI?

Psychosomatics

People have long believed that emotions, beliefs and attitudes can affect physical health. More than two thousand years ago the Greek philosopher Aristotle stated that there was a connection between melancholy (or depression) and cancer. Naturally, people have investigated this phenomenon, and the field of psychosomatics (psycho-soma = mind–body) developed. However, because there was no real way of proving that thoughts or emotions could cause disease or contribute one way or the other to illness or health, this field of research did not carry much weight in the medical profession.

This scepticism is justified, because even if you can prove that there is a connection between, for example, cancer and depression, this does not mean that the depression 'caused' the cancer. You could logically argue that people with cancer are more depressed than people without cancer, because cancer is frightening and painful, and its victims naturally have thoughts about possible death, surgery, chemotherapy and so on. It could also be argued that something about the cancer cells causes chemicals to be released which cause the depression. The point is this: psychosomatics, in a general sense, could not prove anything more than the fact that certain diseases are associated with certain characteristic thoughts, emotions and coping styles. Fortunately, with new technology and PNI research methods these associations can now be tested to see what comes first, the illness or the emotion.

The emergence of PNI

Beginning in the late 1970s, a new approach to the mind–body dynamic slowly emerged and was called PsychoNeuroImmunology (PNI). This has now replaced psychosomatics. It examines how your coping styles, emotions, attitudes and the events of your life affect your body's nervous system, hormones, immune system and, ultimately, your health.

Frustrated with the 'soft' approach to mind–body research until that point, a number of researchers – mostly medical and psychiatric researchers – began to investigate the nitty-gritty of the biological mechanics of how, if at all, psychological states impact on the body. Instead of using disease as the measurement, they began to look at the body's immune system and all the various cells and systems that determine when, how and whether disease forms and how physical healing occurs.

This was initially difficult. For example, the technology and equipment necessary to count the number of specific cells in a millilitre of blood was slow and very expensive.

By the mid-1980s, this all changed dramatically, largely due to research into cancer and then AIDS. Millions of dollars began to be invested in the area of immunology. A direct outcome of this unprecedented funding was the development of equipment to rapidly – and relatively cheaply – test and measure the finer details of what occurs in the body from moment to moment. An example is the flow cytometer, which can accurately count the number of a wide range of cells in a matter of a few minutes.

This explosion of technology and funding had a direct impact on PNI research. For the first time, it became possible to do large controlled studies over time, with detailed information of exactly what happens at the level of immune system cells. It was also possible to determine whether specific psychological states were present before, during or after changes in the immune system, and exactly how such psychological factors translated into chemical and cellular changes in the body.

Finally, it became possible to talk about cause and effect, and how this happens at a physical level. No longer would we merely speculate about whether there are such mind–body connections. Today, we can categorically state that such connections are substantial, measurable and follow logical biochemical pathways.

The debate of whether there are such mind–body connections is over. For the adventurous reader who wants to see hard-core scientific evidence, you are referred to *Psychoneuroimmunology* by Robert Ader and colleagues *[1]* and Candace Pert's *Molecules of Emotion [2]*.

For an introductory summary of the profound complexity of these biopsy-chological pathways, excellent overviews are included in the bibliography *[3 to 6]*, (page 262).

Your body

The biggest problem people have in understanding and accepting PNI therapy is that they cannot see how 'thoughts' can lead to changes in their body. And – in our opinion – the reason they cannot understand this is that they do not know very much about the body itself.

People tend not to give their bodies much thought except when they are hurt, sick or tired, when they don't look the way they want to look, and when they are having sex.

Your body is not just a pile of meat and fat. It is probably one of the most complicated and extraordinary creations on this planet. Your brain, by itself, is so complex that scientists cannot even imagine ever building a computer that can do what it does.

Because the body is such a complex organism, the professionals who study it – doctors, biologists, immunologists, to name a few – have developed a huge range of terms and names for its various parts and systems. It is a language in itself, which is what makes it so difficult to learn more about the body. We believe that it is this terminology that prevents most people from understanding their own bodies.

We will discuss the immune system in greater detail in the next chapter. However, here follows a brief introduction to some of the parts of your body that we focus on in PNI.

Cells and chemicals

Your body is mainly made up of water (about 80 percent). The rest of it is made up of cells and various chemicals. Cells are the building blocks of your body. They are like the bricks of a house. There are many kinds of cells, each type doing a specific and special function. For example, the cells in your heart are different from the cells that make up your lungs and the cells of your bones and blood.

Like everything else in life, cells are born, do what they need to do, then die. The body makes more of all these cells all the time. Every single cell in your body is replaced at some point. However, because cells are so small and this process of growth and death happens all the time, we tend to think of our bodies as staying the same, except to get a little older every year.

Apart from cells, there are also hundreds of different chemicals that float around your body – in your blood, muscles, stomach, lungs and brain. We are not going to list them all, except to mention a few that are important to PNI:

NEUROTRANSMITTERS: Chemicals produced in the brain, such as dopamine and serotonin.

HORMONES: Chemicals released by various glands, such as adrenaline and cortisol.

ANTIBODIES: Chemicals released by immune system cells, which attack germs. Some antibodies attack specific diseases only, whereas others attack a range of illnesses. When you are vaccinated against an illness, such as measles, you are in fact being injected with the antibodies to that illness.

The immune system

The immune system is really all about the several systems your body uses to stay healthy and to fight any disease. As you read the more detailed explanations in the next chapter, you will realise that all the different cells work together as a system, and that these cells 'talk' to each other with chemicals.

Most people believe that their immune system comprises just certain special cells in their blood. This is not true. The immune system includes all and every defence method against germs and poisons, including the wax in your ears, saliva in your mouth, hairs in your nose, plus all the cells in your blood, various glands, neurotransmitters and so forth.

Your body is designed to deal with disease. The really important question is why it sometimes does not succeed in this task. Often, it is not the germs or cancer cells that are the 'problem', but rather the fact that your immune system is not dealing with them properly. This is why we speak of 'strengthening the immune system'.

For example, why does the body sometimes attack itself? This is what happens in autoimmune (or self attacking self) illnesses, such as multiple sclerosis, rheumatoid arthritis and systemic lupus erythematosus.

And why does the body not send the necessary fighter cells to cancer tumours even when those cells exist? This is an example of a suppressed immune system illness.

These two examples illustrate why the immune system has been described as the physical expression of your body's ability to tell the difference between self and non-self. In other words, the immune system, when working properly, should be able to tell which cells and chemicals belong to you and which do not. It is supposed to protect your body and attack anything that is not 'yours'.

As you will discover in the following chapters, there is a fascinating connection between the psychological sense of self, and your body's sense of self. In effect, when the psychological aspect is not balanced or strong, this has a direct effect on the physical aspect too.

The mind–body connection

PNI looks at the connection between your psychology (mind, emotions, attitudes) and the immune system. It examines a range of effects that psychosocial events (personal thoughts and feelings, plus social situations) have on health. Here are some of the questions it seeks to answer:

■ What does 'stress' actually do to your body, in terms of hormones, cells and your health?

■ Are there different attitudes and coping styles in people who get cancer or heart attacks? If so, how do these coping styles contribute to the development of the illness?

■ Do people who recover from serious illness (or who survive longer than average) have specific coping styles that make them different from other people? If so, how do these coping styles impact on their bodies' ability to deal with the illness?

- Can specific psychological methods, such as visualisation, hypnosis or writing letters to release emotions, actually produce changes in the immune system? Can these methods be used for people with illnesses such as cancer and AIDS? Do they work in these situations? How?

- Do major events in our lives – moving home, losing a job, divorce, death in the family – affect our health? If so, how?

- Why is it that, even when a large group of people receive the same medical treatment, the same basic diet and exercise routines, only some pull through whereas others don't?

These are just a few of the areas that PNI research has examined and it has produced some interesting and useful conclusions. It does these investigations by focusing on the details of health and illness, namely the immune system.

It is this specific focus that makes PNI different from other types of psychology. PNI is not interested in anything except the physical, measurable changes and events in the body that are produced by psychological and social events.

For example, a counsellor may be pleased to hear a client with cancer say: *'Oh, I feel so much better today!'* However, a practitioner of PNI would be interested only in what physical changes have occurred to the cancer cells and the immune cells that control them. Success or failure in PNI concerns physical measurements, not emotional measurements.

Strictly speaking, PNI is an area of research. But, when we apply the results of this research and try to improve people's health, it is called Applied PNI.

The basic findings of PNI

Germs and cancer cells exist, regardless of what you think and feel. PNI research does not say that psychological factors **cause** disease to exist. All it says is that specific psychological and social factors **contribute** to the development of disease, and also to the healing of that disease. For instance:

- How you feel about yourself has an affect on whether you will say 'yes' or 'no' to taking the risk of being exposed to certain types of germs. HIV is an example.

- How you cope with life in general also affects your immune system to the degree that your body will either fight or fail to fight germs when you are first exposed to them.

- Once a germ or cancer cell has started to affect your body, psychological factors make a difference in how well or not your body deals with it.

- Genetic predispositions to certain illnesses – i.e., vulnerabilities inherited from parents – can be either lessened or strengthened by how you cope with life.

Please do not make the mistake of jumping to the conclusion that every illness has a psychological cause or component. Sometimes, you just ate the wrong things, or breathed dirty air, or something went wrong in your physical environment.

Applied PNI has never been – and should never be – viewed as a stand-alone intervention. It should always be conducted alongside proper orthodox medical treatment, nutritional assistance, exercise, and whatever else is appropriate for your illness.

In other words, PNI is not about 'mind over matter', or 'mental power'.

We wish to caution you about assuming that PNI methods are in any way a replacement for standard medical treatment. This assumes that PNI is a non-medical, alternative therapy. We state quite categorically that **PNI is not an alternative therapy – it is a complementary approach that works best together with orthodox treatment and monitoring.**

How are you going to know whether your T-cells are increasing if you do not have a medical blood test? How will you know if your tumour is shrinking if you do not have a scan? Ensure that your health is monitored and treated with orthodox medicine. But it is also a good idea to consult a professional therapist to help with your psychological issues. You may even ask him or her to help you work through the issues and methods in this book.

What PNI is not

PNI is not faith healing. It is not spiritual healing. It is not 'New Age' either.

It is understandable that practitioners of these various healing methods feel somewhat supported by PNI research. However, rarely do these people know what PNI is, nor do they know the research or the biological pathways involved.

It is not our intention to criticise non-medical modes of healing or to comment on religious belief, faith, chakras, the aura, the existence of the soul or universal love. But until any of the above can be scientifically demonstrated to have an impact on the immune system, and the biological mechanisms of the method can be explained, that method of healing cannot refer to itself as PNI-related. This does not mean that other psyche-based methods of healing do not exist, nor that they are somehow less real or valid. It simply means that they are not PNI.

A good example of the dilemma of what is and what is not PNI is prayer. Controlled scientific studies have demonstrated that group prayer has an influence on a person's healing process, even when the sick person does not know that people are praying for him or her. Does this make prayer an Applied PNI method of intervention? In our opinion, it does not, because the actual mechanisms involved cannot be explained in terms of the immune system, nor how prayer translates across time and space to affect the brain–immune system. Does this mean that prayer does not work? Of course not – the evidence clearly states that it does. It simply cannot be explained scientifically ... yet.

And yes, sometimes we do things because they work, even when we don't know how they work. Every day, millions of people take Aspirin for pain, even though we still don't know how it works!

You do not have to believe in PNI to apply it and benefit from it. You do, however, have to do some work.

Can psychological factors affect the immune system?

It is all well and good discussing whether psychological factors can affect the immune system. For those with a serious disease, a more important question is: '*Can I positively affect my immune system or illness by using psychological methods?*' The answer is an unequivocal '*yes*', based on a large body of research.

The following psychological factors have been clearly demonstrated to weaken the immune system:

Anxiety and depression
Absence of social support
Unemployment
Exam-related distress
Loneliness
Bereavement
Miscarriage
Retirement
Fear
Suppressed anger and other emotions
Denial coping
Stressed power
Stressed control
Living in a dangerous place
Taking care of someone with a serious disease
Low marriage quality, divorce and separation
Insomnia
Low self-worth

Examples of research findings:

- Robert Ader and Nicholas Cohen clearly demonstrate that the immune system can be behaviourally conditioned. It is clear that the mind–immune connection works both ways *[7]*.

- Social contact and relaxation have been shown to increase natural killer cell activity *[8]*. The same result can be achieved with visualisation *[9]*.

- Viral conditions, such as warts, respond well to hypnosis *[10]*. Hypnosis reduces susceptibility to the exposure of viruses such as tuberculin *[11]*.

- Imagery and music can increase antibody secretions, such as immunoglobulin A *[12]*.

- Watching pleasant movies can increase antibodies and increase T-cell activity *[13]*. Similar effects have been obtained with humour *[14]*.

- Disclosing traumatic events boosts the immune system *[15, 16, 17, 18]*.

These are just a few of the many studies demonstrating that the immune system can be enhanced through psychological intervention. There are hundreds more.

One example that demonstrates the reality of such interventions is the study regarding the effects of confronting past traumas (Pennebaker, Kiecolt-Glaser and Glaser, 1988). The study involved 50 healthy students, half of whom wrote about some superficial topic (such as 'How I decide which vegetables to buy in a large supermarket'), while the other half wrote about a personally traumatic past experience (such as relationship break-ups, loss of loved ones, car accidents, failing an important exam). All students wrote for 20 minutes per day for four consecutive days. The idea was to determine the immunological effects of confronting past upsets and traumas.

Several significant results were obtained, including the fact that those students who wrote about past painful upsets had stronger immune responses immediately after the experiments and had fewer subsequent health-related visits to the college clinic. Three months later, the students who wrote about personal traumas were significantly happier than the others in the study.

Another interesting result of this study concerned the benefits derived by the students who wrote about personal traumas. It was found that those students who had previously held back from talking to others about the traumatic experiences – before writing about them – benefited more than those who had previously discussed their past traumas with someone. The researchers concluded that this study supported the idea that suppressing personal traumas is stressful. Also, talking (or writing) about such events – getting it off your chest – removes some of that stress, hence the immunological benefits.

What is important to note about this release is that it did not require 'therapy' in the conventional sense – the students simply wrote about their experiences. In other words, Applied PNI methods can be used by ordinary people, at home.

The mechanisms of how this mind–immune connection may occur are discussed in Chapter 3.

Passive and active Applied PNI methods

There are many PNI methods. You will probably develop your own after a while. However, you will notice that we do not spend much time discussing 'passive' methods, such as meditation or relaxation exercises. The reason is simple. Research indicates that – with some exceptions – the benefits of such approaches are variable and mainly in terms of buffering, or reducing, the effects of daily stress. In other words, these methods help the immune system by reducing the impact of stress. However, they do not generally prevent the emotional stress from occurring because they don't address the cause. There are of course exceptions to this general rule, and we have included a few specific visualisation processes which are not aimed at general relaxation, but are rather targeted at confronting fears or building internal resources.

We have decided to focus on methods that have more direct benefits to the immune system, in terms of enhancing – not just maintaining – immune function as far as possible. This involves focusing on sources of chronic stress.

We therefore strongly recommend any form of physical exercise, relaxation or imagery work as a maintenance programme, but not as the central or only focus of intervention.

Ready to begin?

MIND–BODY CONNECTIONS

Uh-oh ... technical stuff. At this point, you probably want to put the book down and run for cover. If this is the case, take a deep breath and relax. You do not have to understand or memorise any of this information in order for the methods in the following chapters to work. In fact, if technical information scares you, skip this chapter until you have the time to read it. Not understanding how these things work is not going to stop you from actually doing the processes in the following chapters.

Then why do you need to read this chapter? If you're reading this book to see if PNI can offer you some assistance in your disease management, this chapter shows that a slight knowledge of how your body works can go a long way in determining what will work for your own process and what is less likely to work.

The intellect itself can only lead you to the door, but it cannot do the healing itself. Healing lies in the area beyond the door of intellect, in the realm of feelings and emotions. This chapter can help you find that door, that's all.

Of course, the intellect also provides impressive conversation at parties and support groups. And when you want to explain why you are doing things differently after working through some of the processes – such as being honest about what you are thinking and feeling – it is so much easier to say, '*Oh, it's because I need to control my HPAC system, which is messing around with my T-cells.*' Case closed, walk away. Alternatively, give this chapter to the person asking for an explanation, to read and study, and this should give you plenty of time to get on with more important things.

But seriously ... without some basic understanding of how PNI works, this book would be nothing more than asking you to trust the opinions of strangers who say: '*Do this, do that, and don't ask why – we're the experts!*' This kind of blind faith in 'authority' and 'experts' may be a large part of the psychological coping style that has created problems with your immune system. Give it a go, and don't stress about not understanding everything.

The purpose of this chapter is to introduce the lay person to a simple, but logical, explanation of why and how PNI is scientifically understandable, and not a matter of 'faith' or sheer belief. It is purposely simplistic and overgeneralised. We ask expert readers (such as biochemists, psychologists and medical doctors) to take a deep breath and consider for whom this information is primarily targeted – the person with the disease and non-medical caregivers, such as counsellors and therapists. Our objective is to make the methods accessible, and to this end we have consciously sacrificed theoretical and technical detail by generalising complicated concepts. If you are a medical professional or psychologist, please forgive the generalisations. Read between the lines – there is ample reference material cited for this purpose.

Some important terms and definitions

Acute   Short-term, ranging from a few seconds to a few days.

Chronic   Long-term, ranging from a week to months, even to years.

Autoimmune An illness caused by the body attacking a part of itself.

Suppressed   Weakened, lower than normal activity.

Pathways   Channels, mechanisms, ways in which something happens.

Perception   The way you see things.

Conscious   Thoughts you are aware of. If someone asked you 'What are you thinking?', you could tell them only your conscious thoughts.

Unconscious   Memories and thinking activities you are not aware of.

The focus of this book is chronic diseases, such as cancer, AIDS, multiple sclerosis and arthritis. All these are primarily immune system failures. Certain questions need to be asked. First, do specific psychological states contribute towards such immune system disorders? There is ample evidence to this effect, as listed in the previous chapter.

The next question is: can this be scientifically explained in terms of PNI biological pathways? Again, the answer is yes. This chapter aims to explain, as simply as possible, the 'why' and 'how' of this interaction between your thoughts, feelings, attitudes and your health.

Here we go. Mental seatbelts fastened, please ...

THE THREE PARTS OF PNI (PSYCHONEUROIMMUNOLOGY)

P = Psycho   **Mental–emotional factors**

Emotions, thoughts, beliefs, attitudes, coping styles, fear, stress, loneliness.

N = Neuro   **The brain and the nervous system**

Also included is the endocrine system – the system of glands in your body that produces and controls various hormones.

I = Immunology   **The Immune System**

The system of cells and chemicals in your body largely responsible for detecting and dealing with bacteria, viruses, cancer cells, parasites and any other living or non-living particles that can lead to illness.

PNI is strictly speaking the area of research that investigates how all these things are connected, and Applied PNI (or PNI therapy) is about taking this research and using it to help people with illnesses, and also to prevent illness.

The 'P' part of 'PNI' = psycho (mind)

Psycho: This is the 'mind' part of the puzzle. You may interpret this as simply referring to thoughts, attitudes and beliefs, but it is not that simple. Included in the 'psycho' part are emotions and feelings, such as guilt, anger, fear, depression, anxiety, joy and excitement. In addition, there are your perceptions – the way you view or interpret the world and what is happening – and all your memories from birth onwards. Some would even say that you have memories from conception and the womb. Then there are also your attitudes, skills, beliefs, values and morals.

Conscious – Subconscious – Unconscious

Most of what is contained in an individual's psyche is not easily accessible. Most of us are aware of only a very small part of what is stored there. For example, when you forget where you put your keys, the memory of where you put your keys down is simply not available. However, after a period of thinking, you may remember where you put them. In the same way, most of what you've learned and experienced in your life is 'forgotten', i.e. it becomes 'unconscious'. Not remembering doesn't mean that it's not stored somewhere in your psyche. Sigmund Freud was the first person to name these aspects of the psyche (conscious, subconscious and unconscious levels of the mind), and most psychology is based on his work, directly or indirectly.

CONSCIOUS MIND

- All the thoughts and memories of which you are currently aware, and which you can quite easily remember.
- Logic and reason.

SUBCONSCIOUS MIND

- Things that are difficult to remember, but which you can remember with a little effort and concentration.

UNCONSCIOUS MIND

- Past memories that you can't remember.
- Attitudes and beliefs which you have but which you are unaware of.
- Requires special methods (e.g. hypnosis) to access.

There is often confusion about the words 'subconscious' and 'unconscious' because they are often used interchangeably. Strictly speaking, the correct word for all memories and beliefs which you are not aware of, and which are stored deeply in your mind, is 'unconscious'.

The term 'subconscious' more accurately describes thoughts and feelings which are temporarily just under the surface of conscious awareness, and which can be remembered fairly easily. Forgetting your keys, and then remembering where you put them a few minutes later, is an example of the subconscious level of awareness – a temporary forgetting that is easily remembered.

The subconscious may be viewed as the thin top layer of the unconscious, or the layer between the conscious and unconscious layers of your mind.

A good example of the difference between conscious and unconscious parts of your psyche involves the formation of habits and skills. When you first learned to ride a bicycle, you were very aware of putting your feet in the right place and keeping your balance while simultaneously pedalling and steering properly. This felt very complicated at first, and it probably took quite a few attempts before you coordinated all the various actions, after several falls and scraped knees. However, if we were to ask you now to tell us how you know to ride a bicycle, you would probably not remember how difficult it was to learn the skill.

The same could be said for learning to drive a car. How many times have you driven from one place to another and realised that you could not remember the journey because you were day-dreaming? Yet there was a part of your mind that knew exactly what to do, when to change the gears, apply brakes, stop, start, change speed, and a wide range of other activities – all of which you had no conscious memory of performing. In a very similar manner, the memories of the important and unimportant events of our lives slide into the unconscious part of our mind and continue to influence us all the time, even when we are unaware of this influence.

Just as you automatically know how to drive even when you are thinking about something else, the challenge in working with the psyche lies in past decisions and events that influence present-day feelings, thoughts, attitudes, beliefs, values and actions, without your necessarily being aware of them.

This is why it is fundamentally important to consider and explore the possibility that, for example, **a conscious decision to recover from illness may not be supported by some unconscious belief.** Some powerful forces that block healing lie in the unconscious, which is discussed in a later chapter.

However, as you begin to ask questions such as '*What must I believe about myself to behave this way?*', you begin the process of bringing these unconscious beliefs into awareness. Initially, you may just have a feeling about what it is, or dream about it. When it is just at the tip of your tongue, it has reached the subconscious level. Soon thereafter, you will become consciously aware of the belief.

This is why it takes time to work through issues. You have to first assume that there may be something in your mind that is causing some behaviour. You may have no idea what it is, because it may be unconscious. By persistent focusing and effort, the thought or belief surfaces, first into the subconscious level of your mind, and then into conscious awareness.

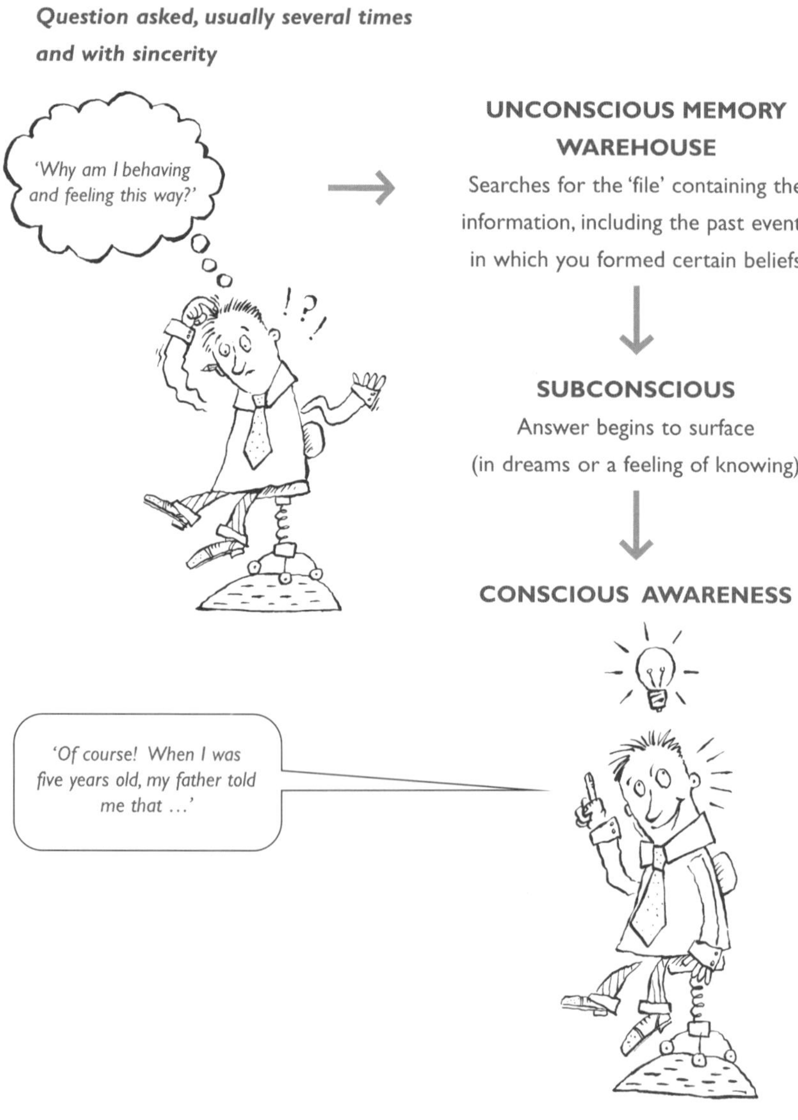

Question asked, usually several times and with sincerity

'Why am I behaving and feeling this way?'

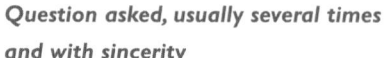

UNCONSCIOUS MEMORY WAREHOUSE

Searches for the 'file' containing the information, including the past events in which you formed certain beliefs

SUBCONSCIOUS

Answer begins to surface
(in dreams or a feeling of knowing)

CONSCIOUS AWARENESS

'Of course! When I was five years old, my father told me that …'

Sometimes the presence of unconscious beliefs is obvious, such as when you sincerely want to stop smoking, start a diet or exercise, but you cannot seem to get it right, no matter how hard you try. In these cases, you are aware of the effects of the unconscious beliefs but do not know what these beliefs are or how to deal with them.

However, most of the time these unconscious beliefs are not at all obvious or they present themselves as rational and reasonable 'reasons' why something is not possible. A typical example is when someone is 'too busy' to take care of her health, or 'forgets' her appointment with a doctor or therapist. People are truly unaware of how their unconscious beliefs influence their actions.

'But,' you say, 'how do I know that there is something in my so-called unconscious mind – how do I know that it exists in the first place? It is just as easy to say that there is no such thing as the unconscious, and that my behaviour and feelings are just natural!'

Excellent question! The example of forgetting your keys, someone's name, or some object and then remembering soon afterwards seems to indicate that your memory of something does not just dissolve when you forget. It seems to indicate that it temporarily 'goes somewhere' – almost like a filing system – until you 'find' it again.

You may also have noticed that certain smells, images and sounds can spontaneously bring back a memory of the past – even memories from your childhood. Where were these memories before you remembered? The only logical answer we can offer is that they are stored in the unconscious mind.

Are all memories stored away? Surely some things are permanently forgotten? Apparently not. There is fascinating research which indicates that even conversations that occur when you are in a coma are stored away in the unconscious mind, and that these memories can be recalled with special techniques, such as hypnosis. The facts of the event can then be checked with the people who were there at the time.

The 'N' part of 'PNI' = Neuro (brain)

Neuro: This refers to the brain and the nervous system. Have you ever wondered how you can think of, for example, lifting your finger, and then your

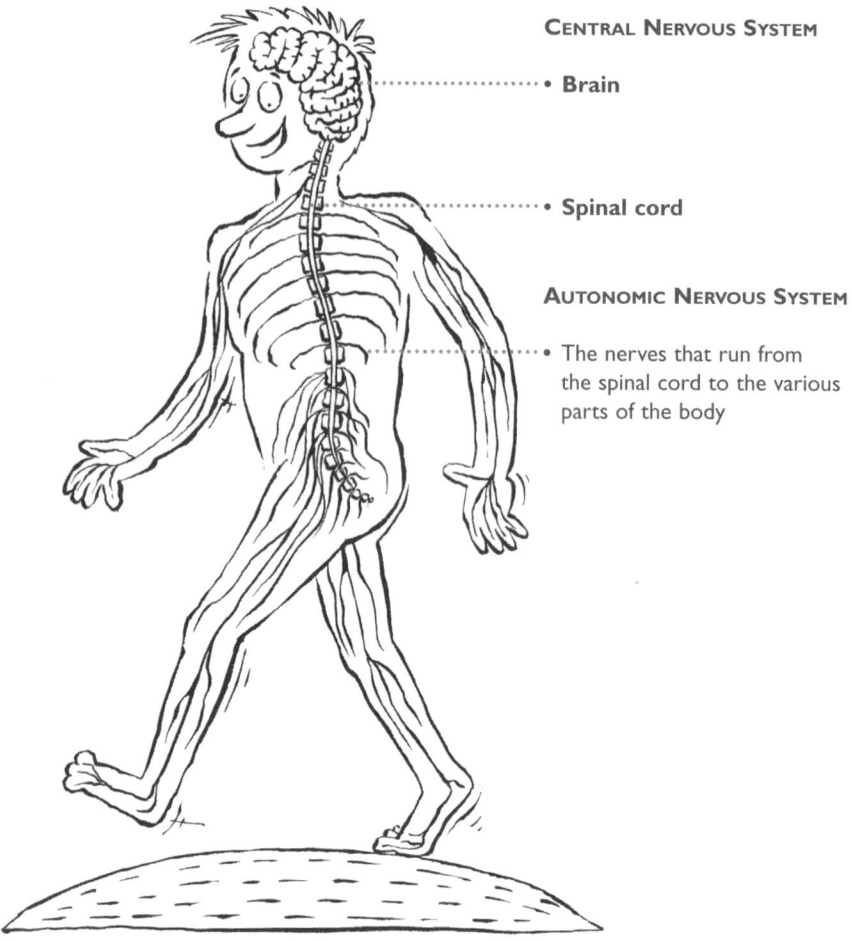

CENTRAL NERVOUS SYSTEM

• **Brain**

• **Spinal cord**

AUTONOMIC NERVOUS SYSTEM

• The nerves that run from the spinal cord to the various parts of the body

THE BRAIN AND NERVOUS SYSTEM

finger moves? How does your thought travel through your body and instruct your body to do things?

The most obvious mechanism is the brain and nervous system, which is a highly intricate system of 'wiring' that sends electrical signals back and forth from your brain to your body through nerve 'wires', with your brain being the main 'switchboard'. So, for example, you think '*Finger – lift!*' (although rarely does this happen consciously – it is usually unconscious), and the brain translates this instruction into an electrical impulse that races through your nerves to your finger, which then obeys the instruction and causes the finger muscles to 'lift'!

The brain is connected to the rest of the body by means of the spinal cord, which runs through the centre of your spine, and from which nerves extend into the rest of the body. Together, the brain and the spinal cord are called the central nervous system (CNS). The major nerve system that connects the spinal cord to the rest of the body, especially the various organs of your body, is called the autonomic nervous system (ANS).

The autonomic nervous system has two types of nerves – the sympathetic nervous system (SNS), which, for example, causes your heart to beat faster, and the parasympathetic nervous system (PNS), which, for example, slows your heart rate down.

Most people believe that the brain and nervous system are the primary control mechanism of the human body. In reality, there are two equally powerful control systems – the brain–nerve system, and the endocrine system.

The endocrine system of glands and hormones

Throughout your body there are a number of organs called endocrine glands, whose primary function is to produce chemicals called hormones. These hormones have the ability to control other cells in your body.

For example, the pancreas (an endocrine gland located beneath your stomach) secretes the hormones insulin and glucagon, which control the level of blood sugar in your body, which in turn affects your metabolism and energy levels.

Another well-known gland is the thyroid gland (located in your throat), which also releases hormones that affect the metabolic rates of your cells. The ovaries in women, and testes in males, are endocrine glands that release sex hormones such as oestrogen and testosterone.

Other important glands – in terms of PNI – are the adrenal glands, which are located on top of the kidneys. These glands have two parts, namely the adrenal medulla, which secretes adrenaline, and the adrenal cortex, which secretes cortisol. These hormones are important in understanding the effects of stress.

Most importantly, the pituitary gland – the gland that controls all the other glands – is located inside the brain, and is connected to the hypothalamus by means of a tiny vessel called the hypophysial stalk. The hypothalamus is sometimes referred to as the 'seat of emotions'. Directly or indirectly, all emotions and thoughts pass through, and are processed by, the hypothalamus.

This connection between the pituitary gland and the hypothalamus is the most obvious of the connections between thoughts, feelings and what happens in the body.

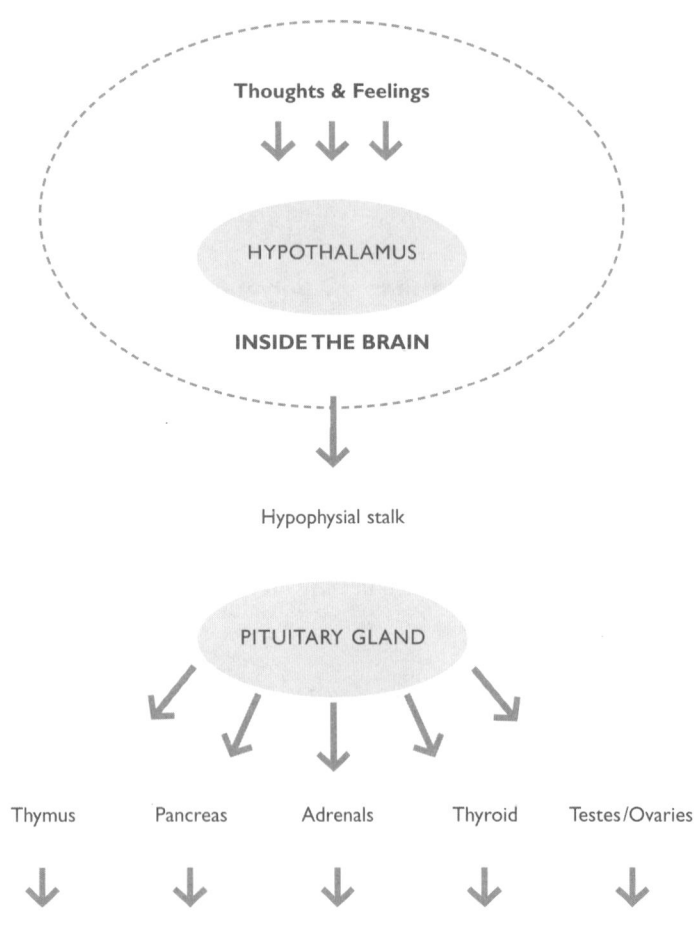

Thoughts & Feelings

↓ ↓ ↓

HYPOTHALAMUS

INSIDE THE BRAIN

↓

Hypophysial stalk

PITUITARY GLAND

↙ ↙ ↓ ↘ ↘

Thymus   Pancreas   Adrenals   Thyroid   Testes/Ovaries

↓   ↓   ↓   ↓   ↓

Hormones affect the rest of the body

When we discuss PNI, most people can relate to the aspects regarding the psyche. However, the chemicals and processes of the brain that influence the immune system are not as simple to understand. A central component of this brain influence is the group of substances called 'neuropeptides'. Originally, it was thought that these chemicals – made up of smaller chemical compounds called amino acids – were found only in the brain. However, we now know that they are found everywhere in the body, including the immune system.

Some neuropeptides – like dopamine, serotonin, Substance P, encephalin and melatonin – are chemical messengers of emotions. It's not that there is a specific chemical for each emotion. Each emotion, such as anger, is accompanied by a release of a group of neuropeptides. These chemicals attach themselves to cells, and cause the cells to react in various ways that can strengthen or weaken immune responses.

Low levels of the neuropeptide dopamine, for example, are associated with depression, and also with lower numbers of natural killer cells, an important part of your immune response. When you feel love, this is accompanied by a rush of dopamine, which in turn increases natural killer cell numbers. Serotonin appears to act in very similar ways.

The 'I' part of 'PNI' = Immunology

Immunology: the final piece of the PNI puzzle. Most people understand the immune system as the cells that attack cancer cells, bacteria and viruses. However, the immune system is much more complicated than this and includes other areas of the body.

Imagine that your body is a city full of people. Around this city is a huge wall (your skin) which prevents most intruders (bacteria, viruses and parasites) from getting inside your body. There are also a number of gates into this city – your ears, mouth and nose. All these gates are protected. Your ears have wax, your eyes have tears, and your nose has hairs and mucus, all of which prevent intruders from entering your body. If the intruders get past these body defences, the acid in your stomach will usually kill them or the chemicals in your saliva will destroy most of them. All these parts of your body, and the substances they produce, form part of your immune system as well. This system of defence is called the non-specific immune defence system.

NON-SPECIFIC IMMUNE DEFENCE SYSTEM

Protective mechanisms	Coughing germs out
	Sneezing germs out
	Wafting of cilia (hair-like things) lining the
	trachea and bronchi (throat and lungs)
Secreted substances	Hydrochloric acid in your stomach
	Wax in your ears
	Enzymes in your tears
Cells that attack as soon	Macrophages
as something enters	Neutrophils
the body	
Circulating substances	Complement
	Interferon
Special cells	Natural killer cells

It is only when the intruders get beyond these barriers that the second line of defence kicks in, namely the cells in your blood which are like the army waiting inside the walls of the city. This is called your specific immune defence system, which has two main components – the humoral system (which deals mainly with bacterial and parasite infections) and the cell-mediated system (which deals mainly with cancers and viral infections).

SPECIFIC IMMUNE DEFENCE SYSTEM

Humoral system	Deals mainly with bacteria and parasites
	Produces antibodies/immunoglobulins
	B-lymphocytes
	Plasma cells
Cell-mediated system	Deals mainly with cancers and viruses
	T-cells (T-lymphocytes)

'White blood cells' include a group of cells from the non-specific immune defence system (macrophages and neutrophils), cells from the humoral system (B-lymphocytes and plasma cells) and some from the cell-mediated system (T-lymphocytes).

'Red blood cells' are erythrocytes. They transport oxygen through the blood, with molecules of haemoglobin. These cells are not directly involved in the immune system.

Summary of the body's immune defence mechanisms

The outer wall (non-specific immunity)

- Coughing and sneezing action – expels germs that have entered the body.
- Acid in your stomach, wax in your ears, chemicals in your tears – these destroy germs.
- Neutrophils and macrophages, cells that kill germs as soon as they enter the body.

Defence inside the walls (specific immunity)

a. **The police** (humoral system)
- B-cells – these identify the germ (antigen) and produce an identikit (or memory) of the germ.
- Antibodies (also called immunoglobulins) – these are produced by plasma cells, based on the identikit provided by the B-cells. These antibodies 'arrest and lock onto' the germ, so that other cells can recognise it as an invader. As a result, other cells (such as macrophages) can kill the 'arrested' germs. This system works well for bacterial infections.

b. **The army** (cell-mediated immunity)
- T-cells (another name for T-lymphocytes) – these specialise in germs that are already inside tissue and cells (such as viruses and tumours). They recognise the germ in the cell or tissues, attach themselves to it, and kill it.

How cells talk to each other

How do all these tiny cells communicate with each other? How does the liver know when to release glucose when needed? How does the heart know when to pump more blood than normal and when to slow down?

There are two forms of communication – the nervous system and the chemical system including hormones.

Imagine the complicated process that must occur when one cell discovers a virus or cancerous cell in some location within the body. First, it must know that what it has found is not normal – it has to have some kind of memory. Second, it must somehow let someone know that this problem has been identified and located. Third, the 'authorities' must send troops out to the site. Fourth, they must destroy the 'abnormal' organism and, finally, dispose of it. Every second of our lives, these incredible processes occur inside our bodies without our being aware of them.

Although this is an extraordinarily complicated process, it could be described as a chemical version of sending an SMS, a fax or an e-mail, which also happens within a split second.

There are many identified chemical messengers, making it possible for all the various kinds of cells to know what is happening, where to go, what to do and when to stop:

- Various interleukins, interferon, and TNF (tumour necrosis factor).
- A wide range of hormones that activate or slow down cellular activities.
- Neuropeptides – chemicals released by the brain, which flow through the blood and affect cell activities.

There are receptors on the surface of many cells, which can be compared to satellite dishes, each one designed to pick up different chemical messages.

A great deal of current medical research concerns why the chemical messages are either not sent from the site of cancerous growths (for example), and why the cells meant to receive the messages and act on them may not respond. Yes, believe it or not, defective communication is often the cause of many diseases, even when all the cells necessary to remove the problem are ready and waiting for instructions.

Autoimmune and suppressed immune system illnesses

It is not possible to do the immune system any justice in a few pages. But then again, it isn't necessary to know every kind of cell, how it does what it does, and how the whole system links together. It is, however, necessary to understand something about how certain kinds of immune responses can lead to specific kinds of diseases, in particular chronic diseases.

Autoimmune diseases, such as rheumatoid arthritis, systemic lupus erythematosus and multiple sclerosis, are the result of the immune system mistakenly attacking 'normal' parts of the body. In arthritis, the immune system destroys the tissue in the joints, whereas in multiple sclerosis it attacks the 'insulation' around the nerves (the myelin sheathing) causing a 'short-circuit' of nerve impulses to the limbs.

If the immune system can be understood as the body's ability to distinguish 'self' from 'non-self', then autoimmune diseases can be understood as 'self' attacking 'self' at an immunological level. Another way of viewing these diseases is to see them as the result of an overactive immune system.

Suppressed immune system diseases include cancer, AIDS and CFS (chronic fatigue syndrome, sometimes called 'yuppie flu' or ME – myalgic encephalomyelitis). In all these diseases, the immune system is not reacting as it should – it is apathetic and lazy, or not responding the way it could, for some or other reason.

For example, cancerous cells develop as a matter of course in every person. A cancer cell is a cell which refuses to die and just carries on growing. These cells accumulate and use blood and resources, thus starving the adjacent tissue. They also put pressure on neighbouring organs and tissues. The usual job of the various white blood cells is to identify cancerous cells and destroy them. However, when the immune system is suppressed, this does not occur and tumours develop.

In HIV/AIDS, the virus attacks and occupies the very cell responsible for sending out the chemical messages that something is 'wrong', and so the virus effectively hijacks a very important part of the immunological communication service. However, other cells, such as natural killer cells, do not require such prompting and should clean up the virus but, in most cases, they don't. Once again, the immune system is not responding as it should (or could). In about 95 percent of cases, this failure to destroy virally infected cells continues over several years, gradually weakening the immune system, allowing various bacteria and other viruses to wreak havoc with little resistance.

Most people assume that all cases of HIV infection lead to this weakening or suppression of the immune system. We now know that this does not occur in all cases. In fact, about three to seven percent of HIV infections don't result in AIDS, and the immune system retains its strength throughout [1]. Studies indicate that as many as 10 percent of HIV-infected people do not have immune system declines for up to 78 months from infection [2]. Such people are called 'long-term non-progressors'.

For reasons still unclear, the immune system in people with CFS crashes. This appears to be quite sudden and the system remains weak for quite some time, even years. One theory is that this is caused by the immune system not recovering properly from a previous viral infection.

In both autoimmune and suppressed immune system diseases, we have not stated what sets off the exaggerated or underactive trend. Whether the cause was a virus or bacteria is not the point – the point is that the immune system, as a whole, fails to identify the problem correctly, either acting against itself or failing to act when it should. This may be viewed as an immunological identity crisis.

The role of hormones in immune functioning

Various hormones, such as cortisol and adrenaline (also known as epinephrine), are able to profoundly affect immune system functioning. However, these profound effects are often unappreciated.

Cortisol is a powerful suppressor of the immune system. There are receptors on the surfaces of most white blood cells for cortisol, and it is cortisol that effectively slows down cell activity. This is most clearly seen in tissue transplant procedures (such as bone marrow, heart and lung transplants), in which the patient is infused with great quantities of corticosteroids (cortisol-like hormones), specifically to ensure that the immune system does not respond to the 'foreign' organ being transplanted into the body by rejecting it. One of the most astonishing facts about these artificially high levels of cortisol is that the side effects closely mimic AIDS in almost all respects, including anxiety, depression and susceptibility to all and any bacterial and viral infection. However, unlike AIDS, the immune system normalises when the cortisol treatment is stopped.

Furthermore, the addition of cortisol to HIV and CD4 white blood cells increases viral ability to infect these cells by up to 70 percent *[3, 4]*. **Most physiology textbooks clearly identify psychological 'stress' as the major cause for cortisol secretion.**

Are the connections between things to do with the psyche (e.g. stress) and immune function (e.g. cancer) starting to make a little sense?

Connecting the dots: P + N + I = PNI

At this point it is appropriate to pull the various components together, and show how thoughts and feelings can affect the immune system. There are many biological pathways connecting psychological processes and immune functioning. The release of chemicals in the brain (neuropeptides) is one of those.

However, the easiest mechanisms to understand and relate to are called the SAM (sympathetic nervous system, adrenal medulla) and HPAC (hypothalamus, pituitary, adrenal cortex) systems.

Hello!
My name is Trog.
I'm going to show you how thoughts and emotions affect the immune system.

Imagine that a person called Trog lived 100 000 years ago, before towns and cities existed, and the content of his (or her) daily life was largely survival-based. In this environment, the SAM and HPAC mechanisms make a great deal of sense.

Trog had to go out and hunt for food. Meat was important, as this protein was critical for the evolution of the human brain. This was a dangerous venture that had to be performed regularly, and nature ensured that Trog had the best possible physical mechanisms for all eventualities, to ensure survival as far as possible.

As you read the following section, keep in mind that our (modern) bodies are still genetically programmed according to the life and times of Trog, no matter how sophisticated and clever we think we are.

The SAM system – fight or flight

If Trog encountered a large and dangerous animal, such as a lion, he would have had a split second in which to decide to fight or run away. This is referred to as the fight-or-flight response. For this to occur, the SAM system evolved.

OPTION 1 *Fight!*

OPTION 2 *Run!* (Flight)

In other words, Trog first perceived a situation involving either challenge or danger. ('*Ahah! Fur-wrapped food with teeth and claws! Somebody get the fire stoked*', or '*Uh-oh! Trouble! Run!!*')

By means of the sympathetic nervous system, the brain sends a signal into a part of the adrenal gland called the adrenal medulla, which is responsible for secreting the hormones adrenaline and noradrenaline. These hormones rapidly circulate throughout the body.

When someone swerves in front of you while you are driving on the highway, you get a fright that wakes you up. It probably feels like a combination of shock treatment and some seriously strong coffee. This is the effect of the hormone adrenaline. You've just had a Trog fight-or-flight moment.

Adrenaline causes your body to stop digestion in the stomach so that all energy and blood can be redirected to the muscles, assisting you in either doing the 'macho' thing, by fighting (in the case of being cut off in traffic, this can take the form of swearing, hooting, or extending a central digit to the offending driver), or mustering enough energy to get out of there. Energy (in the form of glucose) is released for rapid action. Your heart rate increases and the pupils in your eyes dilate. Simultaneously, your sinuses and other mucous membranes stop secreting mucus. Adrenaline causes your entire body to focus on one thing and one thing only – fighting or running away as fast as possible. You literally feel 'wide awake' when adrenaline is racing through your body. It's nature's caffeine …

It is important to keep in mind that when the fight-or-flight mechanism evolved in humans it was designed to deal with immediate and physical threats and challenges, such as wild animals. Today, the same mechanism works when we believe or perceive there to be challenge or danger, even though it may not be physical. Think about the average high-powered business executive, who lives with constant challenge, which results in the over-activation of the SAM system and wear-and-tear on the heart.

Normally, the surge in adrenaline has only a temporary boosting effect on the immune system. One of the interesting effects of adrenaline is that it reduces the secretion of mucus. Theoretically, if you have a head cold with a runny nose, a good adrenaline-producing roller-coaster ride should sort out the runny nose and clogged sinuses. Now you know why so many people feel fine until they relax on the weekend or go on holiday! Quite literally, their body slows down the fight-or-flight system when they relax, so the symptoms of the cold or flu they might have had, but which their adrenaline-inducing lifestyle was masking, suddenly appear in the form of a runny nose.

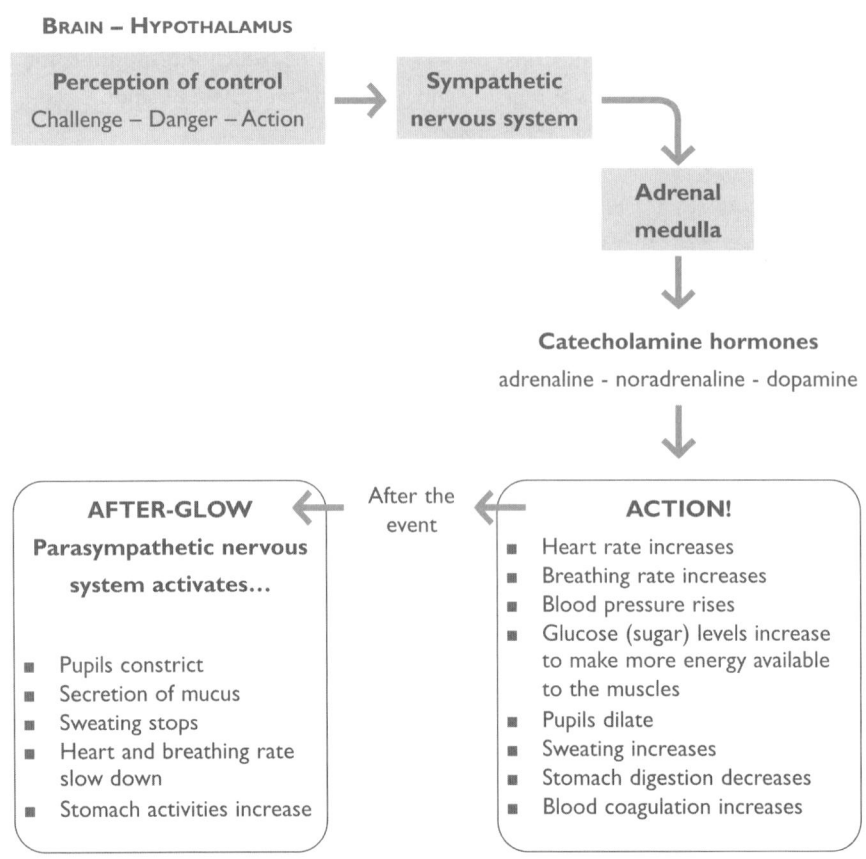

SAM SYSTEM (FIGHT-OR-FLIGHT)

If you remain in the fight-or-flight mode for too long, your immune system invariably weakens, almost as a form of burn-out, and this includes:

- Decreased natural killer cell activity (cells of the T-cell group that destroy tumours and virally infected cells).
- Decreased T-cell activity and ability to multiply, so the numbers drop.

These symptoms are important to keep in mind when considering the causes of some suppressed immune system conditions such as CFS. It is not uncommon to find that people with CFS were high-powered 'go-go-go' people, whose world crashed due to some failure. They were producing too much adrenaline for too long.

Other consequences of chronic activation of the SAM system include:

- High blood pressure.
- Overstressed heart, leading to possible heart attacks, strokes and similar chronic diseases.
- Burn-out: chronic fatigue (no energy resources left to access).

After the challenge or danger is over, your brain switches from the sympathetic nervous system to the parasympathetic nervous system. The secretion of mucus returns, your heart rate and breathing slow down, and digestion kicks back into operation. Interestingly enough, sexual arousal, orgasm and post-orgasmic 'glow' involve the same process, switching from the sympathetic to parasympathetic nervous systems. There is a direct biological connection between the physical arousal related to danger and sexual arousal, and it is not surprising that some people confuse the two!

What is also important to keep in mind is that your body can be stimulated to produce adrenaline for too long, causing the control of this hormone to fail. Long after you have been 'stressed', your body keeps pumping out adrenaline. This happens when you have simply failed to rest after each fight-or-flight incident.

It is essential to keep in mind that the SAM system was designed for single short-term events – such as Trog facing the lion. When any situation becomes chronic (i.e. continues for some time), the SAM mechanism starts to backfire and produce negative health effects, as listed above.

The problem with our civilised way of life is that most of the challenges and threats are now experienced inside ourselves, such as our need to be the best, to win at all costs, and to prevent failure at all costs.

How many movies or television shows portray people 'climbing to the top' of their profession by working long hours, day in and day out, ignoring family and relaxation? In real life, such people are admired and selected for promotion. No one seems to notice that these people also don't last very long in that profession, because they simply burn out, get sick with a chronic illness, or have heart attacks. Generally speaking, the high need to avoid failure and to win at all costs is called the 'stressed power syndrome'.

When you perceive a challenge or threat (regardless of whether it exists or not), the SAM system activates. Bear in mind that the SAM system is based on your perception of control over the threat or challenge. Read this paragraph one more time ...

The absence of challenge, however, can have the reverse effect, such as low levels of human growth hormone, HGH (the hormone responsible for cell and muscle tissue growth, among other functions). For example, the wasting away of muscle tissue in some AIDS cases, known as the HIV wasting syndrome, is partially a result of abnormally low levels of HGH.

How do we know this happens in real life?

In a fascinating study [5], Stanislav Kasl and colleagues examined a specific type of military cadet. These cadets had overachieving fathers (defined as fathers who achieved more than their education suggested they would), high levels of motivation, and were not performing as well as they thought they should. This is a classic stressed power syndrome situation, where expectations exceeded abilities. It is interesting to note that first-born children often have this stressed power syndrome, because first-time parents tend to put all their hopes and dreams on this first child and create the impression that they approve of (or love) the child only when she or he achieves something good.

Kasl and colleagues found that this group of cadets were more likely to develop clinical symptoms of infectious mononucleosis (also called glandular fever or 'kissing disease') compared to other cadets who did not have this '*I must succeed, but I might fail*' motivation.

In other words, although two people can be infected with the same virus, the one with stressed power syndrome is more likely to get ill as a result. This indicates that his or her immune system is less effective in dealing with the virus than the person with lower levels of stressed power syndrome.
This does not mean that only people with stressed power syndrome get glandular fever! Anyone can get it. However, your psychological make-up can affect how ill you get when you are infected with it.

People with stressed power syndrome are driven to succeed by fear of failure as their primary motivation force. This is not the same as being driven to succeed by a desire to experience or attain the objective. Consequently, the person with stressed power syndrome is constantly on the lookout for any threats to his or her success and therefore experiences a chronic activation of the SAM system. Failure is devastating to them and they usually see it as a clear indication of little or no self-worth. This becomes a major problem when their expectations are higher than their abilities to achieve, as witnessed with the military cadets.

It is not surprising that Type A Personalities with the 'must succeed' (versus 'want to succeed') motivation drives are attracted to competitive environments, such as the corporate world. In this environment, their drive to succeed can cause a constant overactivation of the SAM system, leading to heart conditions, high blood pressure and other SAM-related conditions.

For further information and research regarding stressed power syndrome and the so-called Type A Personality, particularly in terms of its associations with heart disease, the research by David McClelland (cited in Henry Dreher's book *Immune Power Personality [6]*) is useful. For example, he found in a study of 76 men that measures of what he calls 'inhibited power motives' (stressed power syndrome in other words) predicted high blood pressure and heart disease 25 years later.

In the same book, research by Meyer Friedman and Ray Rosenman showed that the '… *vast majority of … patients with heart disease exhibited Type A behaviour – a pattern of hostility, impatience, and hard-driving competitiveness*'.

The HPAC system – 'I am wounded'

The next important system covers the possibility that poor old Trog did not run away from the lion fast enough and got wounded somewhere in the encounter. Poor Trog.

For this possibility, Mother Nature evolved the second important PNI pathway, the HPAC system. We refer to it as the 'Hopeless – Helpless' system or, alternatively, the 'I am wounded' system.

Oddly enough, the HPAC system is specifically designed to suppress the immune system. This makes no sense until you understand the paradox. A slightly suppressed immune system is beneficial for a more rapid healing of wounds. In other words, when you hurt yourself, a wide range of immune system cells rush to the scene of the wound. If this 'rushing to the scene' is not controlled or slowed down, the swelling caused by all those eager little cells can cause even more damage to the tissue than the original wound. For example, some people are highly allergic to bee stings or pollen. If they are not careful, they can die from being exposed to such substances, not because the pollen or bee sting is 'poisonous' but because their throats swell due to the 'rushing in' of eager-to-help cells, which closes the windpipe, and they die from suffocation. This swelling is nothing more than an over-eager immune system.

To control such swelling, the body sets off a chemical domino effect, called a 'hormonal cascade'. When the person realises that he or she is hurt, the hypothalamus secretes a chemical called CRF (corticotropic releasing factor). In turn, this activates the pituitary gland to secrete ACTH (adreno-corticotropic hormone), which races through the blood system to the adrenal cortex, secreting cortisol (a corticosteroid), which, in turn, is released into the blood system and slows down the immune system.

Cortisol – as previously mentioned – is a powerful hormone that suppresses the immune system. This is why many allergy medications contain cortisone (a variation of cortisol) as their main ingredient. Incidentally, many ointments for rashes, insect bites and allergies that contain cortisone are topical creams, i.e. they're applied externally and their effects are limited to the area to which they are applied. These creams are not of concern if used for a limited time by people with suppressed immune systems (such as cancer and AIDS).

The effects of cortisol on the immune system are very powerful, particularly when this hormone is continually secreted over a long period of time (six months or longer).

Cortisol is the classic stress hormone. In the past, the HPAC system (and cortisol) evolved to deal with wounds and external situations when control was lost. Nowadays, however, the internal perception of loss of control or wounding (i.e. emotional distress) produces the same effects. Read the previous sentence one more time, and you will understand the immense danger of viewing yourself as a 'victim'.

In other words, chronic emotional distress – upset, fear, worry, anxiety, depression – directly results in chronic increases in cortisol. This in turn leads to long-term suppression of the immune system.

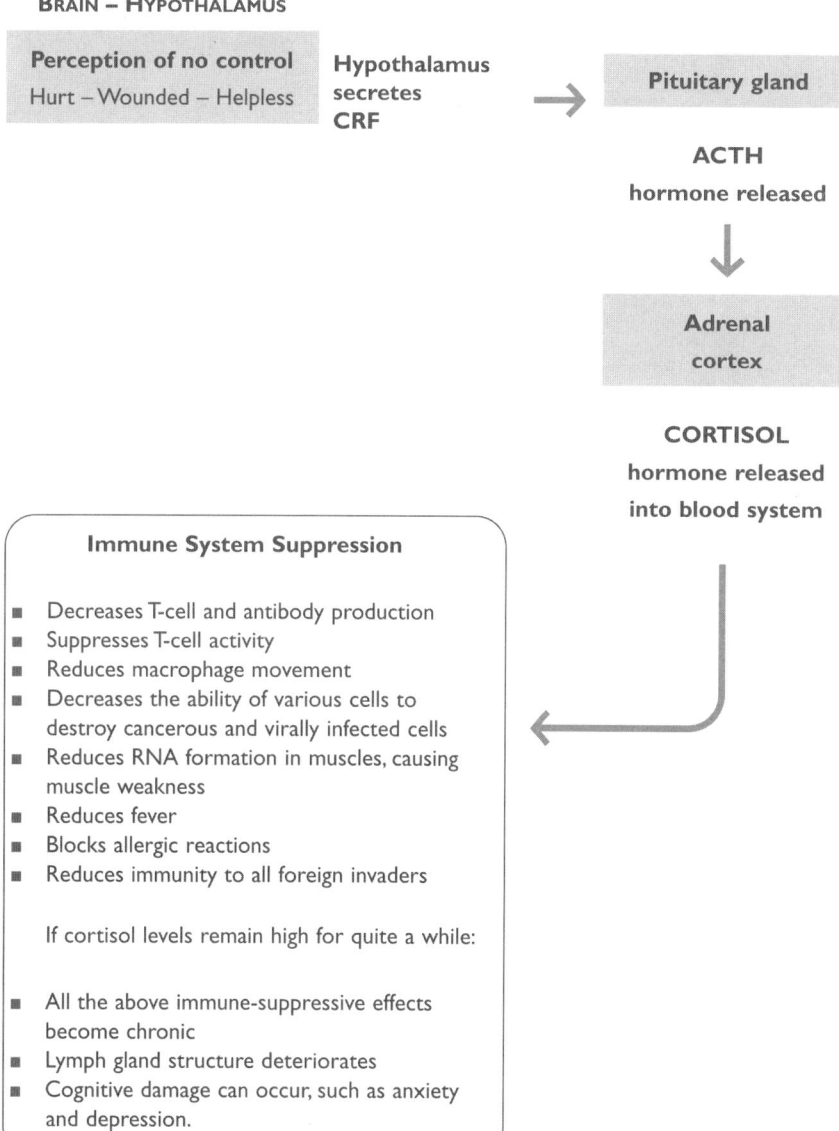

BRAIN – HYPOTHALAMUS

Perception of no control
Hurt – Wounded – Helpless

Hypothalamus secretes CRF

→

Pituitary gland

ACTH
hormone released

↓

Adrenal cortex

CORTISOL
hormone released
into blood system

Immune System Suppression

- Decreases T-cell and antibody production
- Suppresses T-cell activity
- Reduces macrophage movement
- Decreases the ability of various cells to destroy cancerous and virally infected cells
- Reduces RNA formation in muscles, causing muscle weakness
- Reduces fever
- Blocks allergic reactions
- Reduces immunity to all foreign invaders

If cortisol levels remain high for quite a while:

- All the above immune-suppressive effects become chronic
- Lymph gland structure deteriorates
- Cognitive damage can occur, such as anxiety and depression.

HPAC SYSTEM
(HELPLESS – HOPELESS – WOUNDED)

A glance at the HPAC diagram above – particularly the box containing the effects of cortisol on the immune system – reveals an astonishing range of effects, many of which can be directly linked to cancer, AIDS and other suppressed immune system disorders.

No, we are not saying that cortisol 'causes' these diseases. Instead, we are pointing out that cortisol – and the psychological stresses that cause this hormone to be released – can certainly contribute towards the development of such diseases.

The most important concept to keep in mind is that this hormonal effect is triggered by a perception of not having control, and a sense of 'being wounded'.

Of all the various statements made in this chapter, the previous one is the most important. Let us repeat: **The mere *perception* of control – or not having control – is sufficient to set off a range of profound chemical changes in your body, all of which can help or hinder your health.**

How do we know this happens in real life?

One of the earliest indicators that the hypothalamus is involved in immune functioning concerned research with rats. Researchers removed sections of their hypothalamus, and found that the production of germ-fighting antibodies was reduced. Production of T-cells by the body was also less. They also found that *'those regions of the hypothalamus which are cut, thereby creating the preconditions for a laboratory animal to be predisposed toward disease, are precisely the same regions of the brain which are most reactive to ... stress'* [7].

Does there have to be a dramatic change in the immune system to cause disease?

Kenneth Pelletier [7] 'makes it quite clear that we do not require a dramatic or large shift in the functioning of the immune system for problems to arise'. It appears that the immune system operates in 'surveillance mode' most of the time, checking to see if there is anything wrong (such as the formation of any cancer cells), and then destroying these abnormal cells on a daily basis. Even a small decrease in this surveillance activity can swing the balance, causing more and more cancer cells to slip through the net, eventually resulting in clinical cancer. He also states that people with cancer tend to have such suppressed immune systems.

It is important to keep in mind that the SAM and HPAC system mind–body effects are not dramatic or obvious in the short term. Most of the effects we have discussed occur as a result of a slight decrease in immune functioning over a long period of time, usually six months to two years.

This is one of the major reasons why research that focuses on the short-term effects of stress finds little evidence for such disease effects. However, studies conducted over several years clearly demonstrate these connections and effects. As a result, **the focus of Applied PNI is chronic stress and not short-term stresses.**

In this regard – and it is good news for those who are panicking about having a bad day – the research clearly shows that acute (short-term) stress does not have any lasting effect on the immune system. Rather, a slight drop in the immune system occurs, which then returns to normal levels within 15 minutes or so *[8, 9]*.

It is also worth restating that cortisol, which is the end-product of the HPAC system's mechanisms, has been shown to increase the ability of HIV to infect T-cells, largely by affecting the receptors on the surface of such cells. (Refer to the study by Markham, Salahuddin and colleagues cited in the bibliography *[4, 3]*). Another study *[10]* 'similarly found that administration of corticosteroids can reduce immune functioning in AIDS patients'.

It is important, too, to keep in mind that the explanations offered are highly simplified and generalised. If you are willing to undertake a serious study of how the mind affects the body and immune system, an excellent place to start would be the various overview articles and books cited in Chapter 2. It is beyond the intent and scope of this book to provide a more in-depth and accurate summary of this research.

Internal or external threats and wounds

As previously stated, the SAM and HPAC systems originally evolved as a mechanism for dealing with external threats in a world where dangerous animals and injuries were the major threats to survival. There were no supermarkets to buy food, so Trog had to hunt for food – there was no way round that reality.

Also, it was extremely unlikely that he could live without injuries, whether from animals, fights or simple cuts and scratches. The challenges and dangers in such a person's life were short-term and external. Therefore, the SAM and HPAC systems were ideal under these circumstances.

For the most part, however, today's world is a very different place. How many people do you know who – of necessity (not choice) – encounter wild and dangerous animals on a daily basis? How many still hunt wild animals for food? And no, an irritable cow does not qualify as a wild animal. Also, for the most part, injuries are much scarcer than they used to be. There are relatively few external dangers for most people. People have grouped together into large communities, an arrangement which offers protection for each community member, and we have largely eliminated dangerous animals and circumstances from our environment, except crime. Our food supplies are regulated to such an extent that, if you have the money to do so, you can basically buy anything you want. Getting a job to earn the money to buy the food is another issue.

There are still certain external dangers, including reckless driving and crime, but there are systems in place to regulate these as well. Many people also have some degree of choice regarding these matters, such as moving to a different neighbourhood or installing security systems. For many people nowadays, danger is no longer external. Instead, most of the dangers we face are internal, such as the fears and anxieties around failure and rejection. There are certainly people for whom and places where the dangers are still external, but even these are much less than they were 100 000 years ago.

Why should you respond to a fear of failure almost as if you were facing a hungry and dangerous lion? How is that possible? Surely we know the difference between real (or external) danger and imaginary (perceived) danger?

There are two parts to the answer to this question:

- First, your Conscious Mind may know the difference, but your Unconscious Mind may not. It is useful to keep in mind that the Unconscious Mind does not distinguish between real situations and imaginary ones. Have you ever had a nightmare and woken up dripping with sweat and your heart pounding? Realistically (logically) you were safe in bed, and yet your body responded to the images in the nightmare as if they were real. Similarly, according to the Unconscious Mind, the thought is as real as if you were really facing a life-and-death threat outside yourself. **Your body responds largely to your Unconscious Mind, more than to your Conscious Mind.**

- Second, there is plenty of evidence to demonstrate the phenomenon of behavioural conditioning. The first person to document and research this was Ivan Pavlov, in 1928. He developed a method called 'conditioned response' in dogs by ringing a bell when he fed the dogs. After doing this for a while, he could get the dogs to salivate (as if there was food on its way) just by ringing the bell. This is simply because the dogs became conditioned to associate the food with the sound of the bell. This association continued, even when the bell was rung without presenting food.

The point is that – since the time of Trog, our prototype cave person – we have been genetically conditioned through 'body memory' to respond to danger, challenges and wounds in a specific way. It is quite possible that, for example, failure has been linked to actual injury or pain, and this association has carried forward to today, despite the absence of real danger of injury if you fail. A long time ago, if you failed, you could die. Today, this is not likely, but it 'feels as if' it could happen. The same could apply to a wide range of emotional perceptions, such as fear of rejection, abandonment and feelings of 'being hurt' emotionally.

Perception of control

Studies of animals indicate that their perceived control (versus actual control) over pain is an important factor in determining which system – the SAM or HPAC – will be activated at any given moment in time *[11]*. Even when the control is not real, the SAM system is activated. When the animal believes it has no control (has a perception of being helpless or hopeless), the HPAC system kicks in.

For example, if a dog is trained to believe that by pushing a button in its cage it can prevent a mild electric shock, then the SAM system is activated so that the dog doesn't develop typical HPAC system diseases such as cancer. Even if the button is not actually connected to the electrical device and so pushing it has no effect on the frequency or strength of the electrical shocks, the dog does not develop cancerous tumours. However, if the animal believes that it can do nothing at all to prevent the electrical shocks from occurring (perception of no control), it typically develops HPAC-related diseases such as cancerous tumours. It needs to be clearly understood that these experiments were conducted over several weeks or months and were not short-term situations.

It is the perception (belief) of control or absence of control that determines which system – the SAM or the HPAC system – is activated in any circumstance.

This is an astonishing fact. What it means is that – as far as the body is concerned – it doesn't really matter what is real or imagined. If you believe you have control (or not) – even when this is not true – the SAM or HPAC systems activate. This is a crucial point to remember when considering whether your mind and emotions can make a difference to your body.

Short-term versus long-term stress

Ironically, for one simple reason, such internal threats and anxieties (the beliefs and perceptions) are more difficult to deal with than an external threat such as an angry and hungry lion. When you face a lion, you quickly discover whether you can fight and win or run away and survive. If neither option works, you won't notice, because you'll be dead! Regardless, the danger is resolved one way or the other in a very short space of time.

However, fear of rejection or failure can last for months, even years. The 'danger' is chronic and long-term. It is this fact that is the key to the problem. **Your body is not designed to handle long-term threats and dangers.** This is probably why your body responds so quickly and positively to dealing directly with your fears.

The SAM and HPAC systems work wonderfully for short-term events and circumstances but become destructive when chronically activated.

An overview of PNI studies clearly indicates that short-term events – such as watching a scary movie or experiencing a sudden fright – do indeed cause the immune system to dip. However, these 'dips' quickly return to normal within 15 minutes to half an hour or so (refer to *How do we know this happens in real life?* on page 52).

Also, certain life events – marriage, divorce, death of a spouse, moving to a new town, starting a new job or exams – can have a significant impact upon the immune system. This makes sense in terms of the SAM and HPAC systems.

Sometimes these events have a long-term effect, referred to as chronic stress. For example, if you divorce your spouse and, once it is over, you view the failed marriage as a simple mistake which does not reflect on your overall self-worth, then the effects of stress would probably be short-term. If, however, you perceive your divorce to be a reflection of some fundamental failure, or as indicating there is something wrong with you, or you worry about ever finding another person to love you, the effects will be different.

Stress is not an event – it is a perception or a thought or a decision about an event or circumstance.

Take another example. If you feel that you're 'trapped' in your job or marriage and that you can't leave, you are probably experiencing helplessness and hopelessness (long-term and chronic 'wounding'). Your immune system will probably become suppressed because of chronic activation of the HPAC system. However, if you change your perspective (belief) about your circumstances and choices in those circumstances, the HPAC system will probably not be chronically activated.

If you fully comprehend the implications of the previous paragraphs regarding the power of shifting perceptions, you are already in a strong position to utilise PNI to its fullest extent.

It bears repetition (for the third or fourth time) to state that it is the perception of the circumstance or event that influences which system (SAM or HPAC) the brain activates. There is no such thing as a 'stressful' event *per se*, simply because one person may experience it as positive and challenging while another may experience it as devastating.

An extreme example is the death of a loved one. If the death is sudden, then this loss is tremendous. However, if the person died after a long illness, then you may feel relief for both yourself and for the deceased.

STRESS IS A PERCEPTION OF AN EVENT
STRESS IS NOT THE EVENT ITSELF!

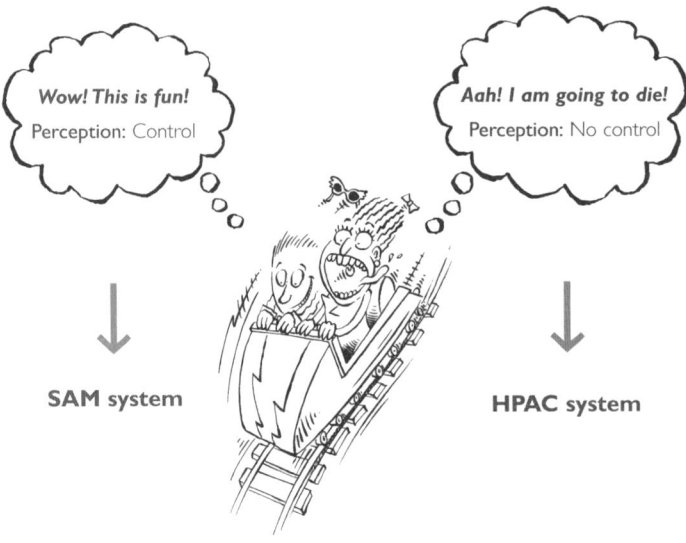

Same event, but with a change in perception …
different physical effects

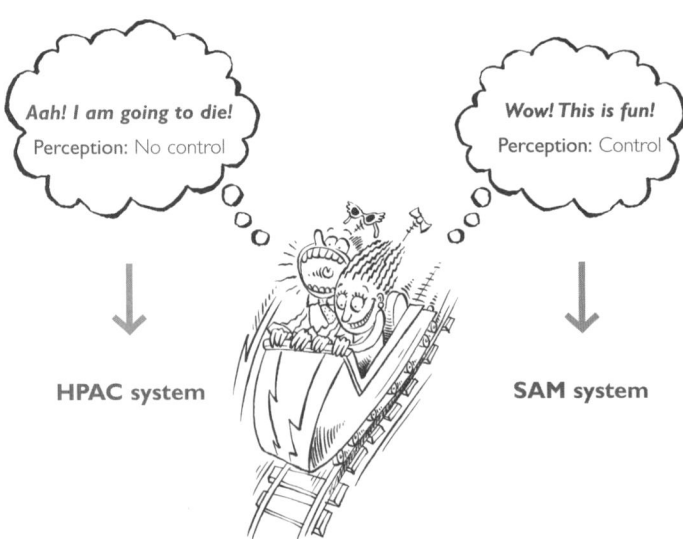

The big picture is by no means complete. However, scientific research clearly explains how a range of psychological states lead to a similarly wide range of immune dysfunctions. Furthermore, **when these psychological states are long-term and chronic, the associated immune system dysfunctions are equally chronic.**

In conclusion, we do not say that the HPAC or SAM systems and their hormones are the 'cause' of any and all disease, nor are we saying that these systems are the major or primary force acting on the immune system in these diseases. What we are saying is that, with a basic knowledge of these two systems, it is possible to begin a rational and focused examination of how specific psychological states can produce specific immunological conditions. How this happens and which psychological factors lead to such irregularities is another matter and the subject of another chapter.

WHERE DO I START?

All PNI-based processes start and end at the same place – the body. Yes, there will be many emotional and mental changes over the course of the programme, but all these are designed to do one thing, and one thing only – have a positive effect on your physical health.

Therefore, the very first thing that needs to be done – if you have not done it already – is to get a medical check and obtain as much information as possible about your present physical condition. For some, this involves having scans done for tumours. For others, it involves having blood tests to check for important immune markers. And for others still there may be various medical tests needed to determine exactly what the condition is of your body, focusing on the illness itself.

David has maintained a file of blood work, dating back to 1983. In this file, he has a record of each and every medical examination he has undergone, plus the CD4-cell and viral load levels of his blood over a period of 20-odd years. However, it was only a few years after his diagnosis that anyone – including doctors – knew what they were looking for, namely a virus. From the moment the basics became known, David read everything there was to read about the disease. In later years, AIDS activists in several cities began study groups.

One such project was called Project Inform, based in San Francisco. The project involved collecting – and studying – everything there was to know about HIV and AIDS, worldwide. It was an extraordinary project, because almost all the participants either had AIDS or were living with HIV. The rest – hairdressers, bank clerks, shop assistants, university students – had lost a friend or loved one to AIDS. Their expertise grew to such an extent that some of them were regarded as world experts on issues such as the direction of future research, how the virus impacts on the immune system, and the ethics of research.

One of the most vivid experiences Neil has had, was of being the only HIV-negative person in a lecture room full of people studying immunology. Each week, one or two people would not return, due to illness, but the rest carried on. These people really wanted to live and were determined to learn whatever they could to increase their – and other people's – chances of survival.

David is still one of the most knowledgeable people around regarding HIV/AIDS, and he continues his research, through the Internet, books and journals.

Why not leave all this in the hands of doctors? The reason is simple. It is your body and your life. It makes sense to know what is going on so that you can make informed decisions about it. It also makes it possible for you to make intelligent – and informed – decisions about treatment options, medical and complementary.

Become informed about your disease

When you consult your doctor, write down the actual medical term for the condition you have been diagnosed with. Sometimes, if you have a good doctor, she or he will explain what the term means in ordinary language. In other cases, it will be your responsibility to do some homework and research on your condition, using the medical terminology as your starting point. How? Probably the most rapid way to gather information is through the Internet. Slower methods involve going to your public library or asking your doctor to provide you with reading material.

The next step is to find out if there are any groups or organisations in your area that can provide more information or support. A great deal of anxiety can be lifted off your shoulders when you find out exactly what you are dealing with. More importantly, it is very useful to hear and read about how other people have dealt with the same condition.

Are you embarrassed to tell strangers – such as librarians or members of support organisations – what condition you are dealing with? Is your embarrassment more important than your need to learn and cope?

During your self-education process, begin to ask about what is considered to be the 'key marker' of the disease. In other words, what are the main measurements of the condition? For example, in certain forms of cancer, there are tests for levels of specific cells and chemicals, which give you an idea of how active the cancer is. There are also tests for cells that tell you how well your immune system is working. Use these markers as your main measurement of your health and the PNI process.

It is not possible to make a list of all possible medical tests and assessments. It all depends on your illness and condition. However, here are some basic guidelines (acknowledgements for this information go to Dr Margo de Kooker) for the most common chronic immune diseases.

CATEGORY 1: Suppressed immune system diseases

Cancer: There are many kinds of cancer, but they all share some basic characteristics. They are all considered to be diseases of the cell, in which normal mechanisms of control (such as growth, movement and multiplication) are disturbed. The term 'cancer' is therefore an umbrella term that includes a large variety of tumours of a malignant (harmful) nature, which are potentially lethal.

Cancer cells form in any body, at any age. They invade the tissue they find themselves in, or spread through the body through the blood or lymphatic system.

The detection and monitoring of cancer depend on the type of cancer. Cancers involving specific organs are monitored by checking the function of that organ, the tumour growth and the effects of the tumour on the body, such as pain and pressure on the surrounding tissues.

Tumours can release certain chemicals or hormones which can be measured, giving an indication of disease progression. Blood counts that measure specific organ functions (such as those for the liver) and general blood counts (such as those given by anaemia tests and tests that measure increases or decreases in white blood cells and changes in erythrocyte – red blood cells – sedimentation rates) give you an idea of how well the body is dealing with the cancer. These indicators are most useful in monitoring treatment, rather than for diagnosis.

Some types of cancer have specific indicators:

- Prostate cancer: levels of acid phosphatase in blood.
- Metastases and bone cancer: levels of alkaline phosphatase.
- Malignant myeloma: specific IgG (immunoglobulin G) levels.
- Cancer of the gut and digestive glands: CEA (carcino-embryonic antigen) and alfa fetoprotein levels.

HIV and AIDS: HIV (Human Immune Deficiency Virus) is a virus that is transmitted via sexual fluids, blood and breast milk. Its principal action – over time – is to decrease the level of CD4 cells (helper T-cells), which leads to profound immune suppression. When such immune suppression occurs, other diseases emerge (called opportunistic diseases), and this condition is referred to as AIDS (Acquired Immune Deficiency Syndrome). AIDS is also diagnosed if the CD4-cell count is at or below 200, with or without the presence of opportunistic infections.

Although it is commonly believed that HIV directly kills many CD4 cells, this appears not to be the case. Instead, it seems that most of the CD4 cells that die during infection do so as the result of a process called 'cell apoptosis' (meaning 'cellular suicide'). The theory is that this is caused by the immune system confusing certain parts of the CD4 cell's structure with that of HIV. It is therefore possible that HIV/AIDS has an autoimmune disease component, which leads to a suppressed immune system.

The principal treatment of HIV is antiretrovirals (ARVs), which are typically administered when the CD4-cell levels reach levels of 350 or less (in more affluent societies), or at or below 200 (in developing countries), or when serious opportunistic infections occur. ARVs are preferably administered in a combination of different types, to prevent the virus from mutating to a resistant form.

For pregnant HIV-positive women, the ARV called Nevirapine is administered within 72 hours prior to labour, and to the new-born infant within 72 hours after birth, to reduce the probability of infection of the infant.

Diagnosis of HIV is done by an HIV test, of which there are several types – ELISA, Western Blot and PCR. Important monitoring measures are viral load tests, CD4-cell counts, CD4-cell activity levels, and various tests to detect the presence of opportunistic infections (such as tuberculosis or cancer).

AIDS is treated by dealing with the opportunistic infection and using ARVs to reduce the levels of virus in the body.

Chronic fatigue syndrome (CFS): This disease has also been called 'yuppie flu', CFIDS (chronic fatigue immune deficiency syndrome), EBVIR (Epstein-Barr virus infection syndrome) and ME (myalgic encephalomyelitis). The disease is not fully understood, and some doctors do not accept it as an identifiable illness.

There are three main theories to explain CFS:

- Suppression of the immune system
- Depression
- The after-effects of a viral infection, specifically Epstein-Barr virus (the same virus that causes mononucleosis, the so-called 'kissing disease', or glandular fever).

Women seem to be affected far more than men, and it tends to affect people in the age range of 20 to 30.

Common symptoms include fatigue, mild fever or chills, sore throat, tender lymph nodes (neck, armpits and groin), muscle pain, headache, difficulty in sleeping and mental confusion. Many other diseases have similar symptoms, making diagnosis of CFS difficult. There is no specific treatment for CFS. Its symptoms tend to increase and decrease over time, in waves, but the disease does not seem to increase the risk of death.

Laboratory tests of viral loads and antibodies are sometimes used to monitor CFS. However, such tests show only whether the person has been previously exposed to a virus, or if the body is not clearing a virus very well.

CATEGORY 2: Autoimmune diseases

Multiple sclerosis (MS): MS is a chronic relapsing (or recurring) illness in which there is an immune response to the myelin sheath surrounding bundles of nerves. The myelin sheath is the 'insulation', just as an electrical wire is surrounded by plastic insulation.

The progression of MS is measured clinically according to the patient's neurological (brain and nervous system) signs.

In about 70 percent of patients, a lumbar puncture and analysis of cerebrospinal fluids reveal slightly raised IgG (immunoglobulin G) levels.

MS usually presents with some kind of neurological problem, such as weakness – especially in the legs – and numbness.

Rheumatoid arthritis (RA): Rheumatoid arthritis falls in the category of connective tissue illnesses. It usually presents with pain in the joints, restrictions in movement and deformity of the joints involved. It is usually diagnosed with X-ray evidence and analysis of blood and joint fluids.

In active RA, blood tests reveal increased white blood cell counts, decreased red blood cell counts and an elevation in erythrocyte sedimentation rates (ESR). Rheumatoid factor (RF) – an auto-antibody (one that attacks normal joint tissue) – is also present in most cases of RA.

Systemic lupus erythematosus (SLE): SLE is another type of connective tissue disease, and also involves autoimmunity. Its symptoms are usually fever, fatigue and joint pains, and it is possible that damage to the nervous system, liver, heart and blood vessels may occur.

Auto-antibodies to DNA, blood cells, thyroid tissue, liver tissue and blood vessels may be found in those with this disease. The detection of these auto-antibodies is a useful way to monitor SLE. In active SLE there is a decrease in platelets and red cells, and erythrocyte sedimentation rates are increased.

Other diseases that involve auto-antibodies, and which are grouped under the category of connective tissue diseases are:

- Progressive systemic sclerosis
- Giant cell arteritis
- Polymyalgia rheumatica
- Polymyositis
- Polyarteritis nodosa

Your relationship with your doctor

It is not unusual to be shocked when you receive your initial diagnosis, and you should not expect to be feeling bright and determined to tackle the condition for a few weeks.

It is also not unusual for doctors with specific preferences to urge you strongly to take specific measures, such as surgery or specific medications. When radical steps are suggested, always get a second opinion, if there is sufficient time. Take some degree of responsibility for your health programme and the decisions that need to be made.

Do not be afraid to ask '*Why?*' Also, don't hesitate to ask your doctor to explain what she or he is talking about. You are paying for the advice, so get your money's worth.

Do not for a moment forget that doctors are human. They make mistakes and sometimes have biases towards certain procedures. Again, always get a second opinion before doing anything drastic.

This does not mean that you 'shop around' from one doctor to the next, hoping to hear better news. Rather, this means checking that the diagnosis and treatment suggested are not only accurate but also the best for you. When you have a serious illness to deal with, it is always advisable to get more than one opinion on the matter. It is also preferable to obtain independent opinions and not simply accept the opinions of two (or more) doctors who happen to work together, or who belong to the same organisation.

If you have found support organisations, ask people there – those with the same or similar condition – who they have found to be the best doctors for your specific kind of condition.

Ask about the possible side effects of the treatment being proposed to you. Some side effects are mild and some are severe. Ask about how these side effects are treated. Also find out if there are ways to reduce or prevent them.

Complementary treatments

There is, in principle, no problem with pursuing complementary therapies. However, some people do indeed take advantage of desperate people. Just as you research the details of your medical condition, it is advised that you also research the alternative, complementary treatment you are considering. Make sure you search for the criticism of that therapy too, otherwise you will get a one-sided story. There is no such thing as a 'works-every-time' treatment, whether orthodox or complementary.

Be particularly cautious about some extremely enthusiastic alternative practitioner who tells you to stop any medical treatment, and to do only what he or she suggests. This is plain crazy.

We have known people who have had an irrational fixation on some or other 'miracle cure', who stubbornly stuck to it even although there were no positive physical results, and who eventually died because of it. At the same time, we have known people who have achieved amazing results with complementary therapies.

The bottom line is that you need to be careful – with both orthodox and complementary therapies – not to allow desperation to obstruct your common sense. That is why it is so important for you to learn about the markers that give you an idea of how well you are doing physically, and to have these checked regularly. If something is not working, then at least you can establish this in time to take corrective action.

The placebo effect

When considering various treatments, find out what the success rate is for that procedure, for your specific condition. Be careful not to get information about the 'success stories' only – that is a biased approach.

In general, about 35 percent of all treatments – orthodox and complementary – can be explained by the 'placebo effect', in which the benefits of a treatment can be explained purely as a result of belief in the treatment and not in the treatment action. So, when evaluating a treatment, check that it has a success rate of more than 35 percent, tested on a fairly large group of people.

Nutrition

Many treatments are designed to 'attack' the offending virus, cancer cell or whatever is perceived to be the principal cause of a specific illness. However, it is equally important to consider what your body – and your immune system – needs in order to cope with the disease and to stay strong.

Unfortunately, most medical professionals are not very familiar with nutritional methods, except in a basic sense. We urge you to do some homework on foods, food supplements and medicinal plants that may help your body, such as those that contain antioxidants and immune-enhancing substances. Examples include selenium – found to be very beneficial in suppressed immune conditions, Vitamin C, zinc and the following plants:

- *Aloe vera* and *Aloe ferox* – the juice of the inner leaf is rich in selenium and pectin
- *Lessertia frutescens* (previously *Sutherlandia*) – strong immune-strengthening effects
- African potato (*Hypoxis*) – proven immune-stimulating effects
- Carrots and sweet potatoes – they have exceptionally high levels of beta carotene, a safe form of Vitamin A
- Brazil nuts – have very high levels of selenium
- Morogo (*Amaranthus*) – the leaves and stalks have exceptionally high levels of zinc. It also contains high levels of many other vitamins and minerals
- Rooibos – the tea made from this plant contains flavonoids, is rich in several minerals including iron and zinc, and has particularly effective antioxidants

Be careful about 'immune-boosting' plants and remedies, however. The reason for this caution is simple. Rarely do such products tell you which part of the immune system they 'boost'. There is no such thing as a generic 'immune-boosting' remedy. Instead, such remedies boost either cellular immunity (the TH1 system, which deals with viruses and cancers) or humoral immunity (the TH2 system, which typically deals with bacteria). Strengthening one of these two systems tends to weaken the other.

For example, when you are dealing with a bacterial infection, the 'immune-boosting' plant echinacea is very effective. However, if you are dealing with a suppressed immune-system condition, this treatment can cause the chronic disease to get worse, even although your bacterial infection may benefit. In an otherwise healthy person, echinacea can still be used for some non-bacterial infections, such as colds and flu.

In our experience, it is preferable to utilise remedies that balance the immune system, not 'boost' it in one direction or the other. Examples of plants used in remedies that accomplish this are the African potato (*Hypoxis*) and *Lessertia* (previously called *Sutherlandia*). Because these remedies address the balance of the immune system, people with suppressed immune systems and autoimmune diseases benefit equally. However, it needs to be clearly stated that none of these remedies are replacements for proper medical treatment.

Conclusions

The point of these guidelines is that you need to learn more about what you are dealing with, so that you can make informed decisions about what you want to do and what you need to do about it. Applied PNI should never be viewed as the only intervention you engage in.

SMALL THINGS THAT MATTER

PNI is a treatment based on a collection of research studies and methods resulting from this research. We view the methods as the 'bricks' of Applied PNI. However, what is absent from all these amazing methods and principles is the 'cement' that holds it all together.

Let us illustrate. When David does a presentation to a group of people living with cancer or HIV, for example, a curious thing happens. Most of his audience ask him about his relationships, how he got infected, whether he has children, what his wife thinks, and basically anything except *how* he has managed to live healthily for so long. Yes, there are usually a few people that ask questions regarding *how*, but they are indeed few.

The conclusion we have arrived at is that most people want to find ways to make David 'different' or 'special'. More specifically, they want to make him 'different' from themselves. In some way, this makes it easier for them to put aside the possibility of their achieving what he has achieved themselves.

This is not unusual. Most people who have achieved something remarkable are placed on pedestals, not so much for the purpose of idolising and admiration, but more to create 'difference' and distance from those who place them there.

When we ask people if they believed it is possible to turn cancer, AIDS, MS or any other serious disease around, they usually say that 'it' is possible. What they rarely say is: '*It is possible for me?*' And that is the heart of the matter.

Do you honestly believe that it is possible for you personally to help heal your body? If you are not sure, or you actually don't believe you can, then you are not unlike many other people in your situation.

How 'special' do you have to be?

The first thing you need to know is that healing the body – with Applied PNI – is not a matter of mental intelligence or education. We don't mean to insult anyone, but you don't have to be a rocket scientist to do it. It is a simple matter of doing the exercises. What you need more than mental IQ, is 'emotional IQ'.

What is emotional IQ? It is the ability to allow yourself to feel what you are feeling, to know what you are feeling, to value and trust what you are feeling, and to be able to express what you are feeling. So, if you can feel angry or sad, or any other emotion, and you know that you are angry and you can express that feeling, you can benefit from Applied PNI. You do not have to understand how the various hormones, brain and nerve pathways do what they do in order to benefit from PNI yourself. But this understanding is useful when you are trying to explain PNI to someone else.

Be a rebel

The second thing you need is a rebellious streak. When David – and many others – were diagnosed with HIV in the 1980s, there was literally nothing known about HIV and AIDS. Zero. The only fact that was available was that when you get it, you die. There were no survivors. Yet, people like David somehow stepped out of that 'fact' and considered another possibility, namely that they could live.

When David was told by his doctor that he was going to die, his first internal response was: *'Maybe that's what you think, but maybe it is not so – maybe it is possible that I can live.'* In other words, he did not automatically trust the authority of science and medicine. He certainly heard it and respected it, but did not take it to be the whole story. This was possibly because of his childhood, during which he had had so many problems with authority that he had developed a sense of distrust towards it.

We walk a very fine line in Applied PNI, because we rely heavily on the authority of PNI science and the controlled research it produces. At the same time, we recognise the fundamental need when applying this science to promote a sense of healthy scepticism towards any external authority. It is ironic that the people who most exemplify the 'survivors' of serious diseases – those we use as examples of how PNI can work – are also the most likely to be sceptical of any medical or scientific authority on the matter. They tend to be the 'difficult patients', the ones who ask annoying questions and insist on knowing why the doctor wants to do certain things.

When you read this book and do the exercises, don't be afraid to recognise when something does not work for you. Change it to suit your needs. Be a rebel when you feel the need to do so. The ultimate 'authority' in the healing process is you, not PNI, not your family, not your friends, not some medicine, not some herbal remedy, not medical science. It is your right to challenge 'authority' and establish your own.

'Waste no more time talking about great souls and how they should be. Become one yourself!'

— MARCUS AURELIUS

Illness is not a punishment

Lose any sense of guilt you may be feeling for being sick. Guilt is the most useless of feelings – it solves nothing, goes nowhere and only gives you an excuse to do nothing.

Do not blame yourself – or anyone else for that matter – for what you do not know, for what you could have and should have done. We realise it sounds awfully corny, but it is an undeniable truth that the only moment of power to act, to learn, to change, to heal, is now.

We have found that many people who are sick have a deep feeling that they are somehow being punished for some 'sin'. This issue has nothing to do with PNI, but it has a profound effect on its application, because guilt seeks punishment.

So, in your heart of hearts, why do you believe you have your illness? Do you perhaps blame someone, such as your parents (for your genetics), or the person who infected you, or yourself, for doing (or not doing) certain things?

Does this belief give you a sense of wellness? Does it make you feel good? Do you feel, each time you blame someone (or yourself), that some debt is being repaid? We suspect that the answer to all these questions is 'no'.

We would like to introduce you to a fresh perspective on the word 'responsible'. For a moment, forget about your understanding of the word and its association with blame and guilt. The word 'responsible' has two parts: 'response' and 'able'. It is the ability to respond. So when you can say that you are 'responsible' for something, it means that you are able to respond to that thing. Guilt is not a response – it is not a 'doing' – it is an avoidance of 'response-ability'.

With this understanding, we suggest that you take 'response-ability' for your illness.

When you blame someone else for your illness, you lose your power to respond because you are placing this power in the hands of the other person. When you meekly submit to authority, you lose your power to respond, too. When you blame yourself for what you could have and should have done, you place your power in the past and lose the power to respond now. Take your power back and put it where it most benefits you – here and now – so that you can increase your 'response-ability'.

Response-Ability: 'Yes, I can!'

If you do not feel you can stand up to the world and deal with all the various issues by yourself, then perhaps you need to start building that part of you first. This is not difficult, and it helps to do the following exercise several times, until you feel that your sense of 'Yes, I can!' is stronger.

■ ASSIGNMENT I: BUILDING INTERNAL CONFIDENCE

STEP I   **Find a past experience which made you feel confident.**
At some moment in your past you felt confident, even if this was briefly experienced. Write down five such experiences (a minimum of one is required).

1. ....
2. ....
3. ....
4. ....
5. ....

STEP 2   **Select the strongest experience from the list.**
First select the strongest experience – in terms of feeling confident
– from the list in Step 1.

STEP 3   **Recreate the feeling in your body.**
Close your eyes. With your head bent slightly forwards and your
eyes pointed downwards (even although they are closed), remember the experience of feeling confident. Start slowly to focus on
what you were doing physically: walking, standing, sitting. How
was your body positioned?

Then focus on your surroundings. Who was there, were they
behind you, in front of you, to the left or right? Was anyone saying
anything?

Now move your attention to the moment(s) when you had the
strongest feelings of confidence, the 'Yes, I can' moment. Where in
your body are you feeling it? What kind of feeling is it – warm, hot,
electric, calm?

STEP 4   **Make it stronger.**
Imagine that this feeling of '*Yes, I can*' has a shape, size and colour.
Use your imagination to do this. Make the colour brighter and
stronger. Then make the shape of the feeling twice as large.
Increase the size of the shape until your entire body is inside this
shape.

STEP 5   **Tap your chest.**
As you feel this wonderful feeling, take one hand and firmly – but
not too hard – tap the centre of your chest, just below the top of
your breast bone.

STEP 6   **Repeat Steps 3, 4 and 5, with the other experiences you listed in
Step 1.**
For each of the other experiences you listed, repeat the process of
recreating the sense of confidence, feel '*Yes, I can*', magnify the
shape and colour of the feeling, and tap it into your chest.

Probably the most important benefit of this process is that you have learned that inside yourself is a 'part' of you which has confidence. No matter how weak you feel your confidence is right now, there is indeed confidence inside you. It is a matter of finding that 'part' and bringing it into the present situation.

Secondly, this confidence 'part' of you has been strengthened and can be accessed by gently tapping your chest again, which will bring that part of you into the present moment. Try it.

Personality hardiness

A book or workshop can teach you methods and skills. However, personal qualities such as courage and determination cannot be taught – they need to come from inside yourself.

When you look at the practical realities of Applied PNI and the exercises we present, you would be hard-pressed to say they are technically difficult. They are challenging, certainly, and probably uncomfortable much of the time. However, compared to, for example, fixing a car's engine, the exercises are not all that complicated. Most are also quite logical and firmly based in common sense.

The real difficulty lies in persisting – having the stamina to go through the processes despite the discomfort. Many people give up rather quickly, even though their lives may literally depend on persisting. Why? We believe that a major part of the answer – apart from the absence of passion or goals or pleasure, and the presence of fear – lies in the concept of 'hardiness'. The idea of 'personality hardiness' was introduced by Suzanne Kobassa, who is a prominent researcher and theorist in the area of how psychological factors affect health.

Basically, 'hardiness' is a collection of personality characteristics that help you deal more effectively with stressful life events. It consists of three components: commitment, control and challenge *[1]*.

Pretend for a moment that you have been ignored, criticised, rejected and hurt several times in your life, by several important people. There are two ways of looking at these apparent 'facts':

- You can use these 'facts' as evidence that you are not worth attention – that you are not good enough, or life is not worth living;
- Or you could view these same 'facts' as proof that you are strong enough to survive without anyone else's approval!

Which one do you prefer?

The problem with stressful events is not what happened, but rather what you decided they meant.

THE PAINFUL EVENTS OF LIFE:

... and what some people do with such painful events:

Become devastated and victimised by the event   **OR...**   Use the event as part of an ongoing learning (building) process.

When you throw a brick – where a 'brick' is a metaphor for painful experiences of rejection, humiliation or loss – at some people, they get knocked down and become afraid of standing up again, in case another brick gets thrown at them. They see bricks as a source of pain. But other people will catch the brick and build something with it. They see bricks as resources to create something valuable for themselves. They say *'Thank you'* for these bricks, even if they occasionally get knocked down by one!

What have you done with the 'bricks' (difficult experiences in your life) that have been thrown at you?

To quote a famous saying (source unknown): *'When life gives you lemons, do you throw them away or do you make lemonade with them?'* To understand 'hardiness', think of someone who takes the lemons and makes lemonade!

The irony is that the more 'bad' things that have happened to you in your past, the greater your potential to establish hardiness! After all, you have managed to survive quite a bit, haven't you?

This is a new way of looking at the past. The more upset, pain and obstacles you have endured, the more building material you have to create a sturdy and strong future.

'Things turn out best for the people
who make the best out of the way things turn out'
— ART LINKLETTER

Our understanding of hardiness is that it is an acquired – learned, not inborn – quality which reflects some sense of stamina and endurance in the face of adversity, and this is usually the result of difficult experiences in the person's past which the person somehow survived and moved through.

This notion of hardiness coincides with our observations of long-term survivors of life-threatening disease and their sense of 'positive realism', reflected in the thought: *'This situation is painful. However, I know I can get through.'*

Hardiness uses negative experiences to strengthen. Once again, we need to say that it is not your past that is the problem – it is what you have done with it that may be the problem.

Now, we need to make something very clear. In practice, positive realism is not an intellectual concept, it is a gut-level reaction to circumstances. This is the challenge: how do you get yourself to move from *'I believe it's possible'* to *'I know I can!'*

Challenge = I want to

If your life were easy, with no sense of adventure or challenge and no goals to work hard towards, your body would not be very happy. This is because the sense of challenge – taking risks, getting excited about trying to achieve something – causes various hormones to be released, such as human growth hormone.

Therefore, the first quality you need to find inside yourself is this sense of interest in getting somewhere, the determination and excitement to achieve something.

■ **ASSIGNMENT 2: CHALLENGE**

Briefly, write down five periods in your life when you felt this sense of excitement, when you wanted to get out of bed early because you had exciting things to do. These events or periods in your past do not have to be dramatic. They can be simple things such as the excitement of getting up early to learn to ride your brand-new bicycle, or of getting to work for the very first time. It is the feeling of excitement and challenge that is important, not the details of the event itself. The key idea is that these events represent times when you were (a) excited (perhaps nervous too); and (b) you felt a sense of challenge – i.e. you were not quite sure how you were going to achieve your goal, but you were willing to risk trying.

1. ....
2. ....
3. ....
4. ....
5. ....

Commitment = I will

Whereas challenge is focused on the sense or thrill of '*I don't quite know how I'm going to do this, but I'm going to try,*' commitment is more focused on the determination to persevere, and the sense that you really want to do something.

■ **ASSIGNMENT 3: COMMITMENT**

Write down a summary of five events or periods in your life when you felt this sense of commitment, when you were determined to do something even though you did not necessarily know how you were going to achieve it. Again, these events or periods in your life do not have to be very dramatic. They can be as simple as making a decision to do something and doing it – for example, the decision and actions you took to get your driver's licence, even though you were terrified of the tests. Your efforts to study, write the initial test, possibly fail once or twice, write again till you passed and then complete the practical exam demonstrated your determination (or commitment) to achieve what you wanted.

1. ....
2. ....
3. ....
4. ....
5. ....

Control = I can

Control simply means that you have the ability to start or stop something, or change the direction something is taking. You may not know how to do this, but you know you can, if you want to.

■ ASSIGNMENT 4: CONTROL

Write down five specific things you know you can control, or specific events when you felt in control. If you feel very out of control right now, it is useful to focus on small things – the ability to open and close your eyes, the ability to talk, and so forth. What can you control? When last did you feel in control over something quite simple?

1. ....
2. ....
3. ....
4. ....
5. ....

■ ASSIGNMENT 5: BUILDING HARDINESS

In Assignment 1 you learned how to take a small feeling and make it much stronger. You are now going to use exactly the same method to strengthen the three parts of hardiness – challenge, commitment and control.

STEP 1   Select the strongest experiences from each list.
From the lists you made of the events and experiences in Assignments 2, 3 and 4, select one experience from each of the three lists. Select those that will be easiest for you to remember.

STEP 2   Recreate the feeling in your body.
Start with the experience that is the easiest to remember of the three. Close your eyes. With your head bent slightly forwards and your eyes pointed downwards (even though they are closed), remember the feeling you had (of being challenged/committed/in control, whichever is applicable).

Slowly, start to focus on what you were doing physically: walking, standing, sitting. How was your body positioned?

Then focus on your surroundings: who was there, were they behind you, in front of you, to the left or right? Was anyone saying anything?

Now move your attention to the moment(s) when you experienced the strongest feelings of being challenged/committed/in control. Where in your body are you feeling it? What kind of feeling is it – warm, hot, electric, calm?

STEP 3   Make it stronger.
Imagine that this feeling has a shape, size and colour. Use your imagination to do this. Make the colour brighter and stronger. Then make the shape of the feeling twice as large. Increase the size of the shape until your entire body is inside this shape.

STEP 4   Tap your chest.
As you feel this wonderful feeling, take one hand and firmly – but not too hard – tap the centre of your chest, just below the top of your breast bone.

STEP 6   Repeat Steps 3, 4 and 5 with the other two strongest experiences that you listed in Step 2.
In other words, repeat the process for the strongest experiences of the other two categories of challenge, commitment and control.

For each of the other two experiences you listed, repeat the process of recreating the experience, feeling the challenge, commitment or control, magnify the shape and colour of the feeling, and tap it into your chest.

STEP 7 **Select another three experiences from your lists.**
Select another experience from each of the three lists.

STEP 8 **Repeat steps 2 to 7 for the next three experiences.**
In groups of three – one from each list – repeat these steps until you have strengthened all 15 experiences.

LIFE: WHY BOTHER?

One of the major objections to mind–body interventions concerns the fact that, for most such programmes, only about 50 percent of participants benefit from the programme. The criticism is that the techniques are unreliable, working for some, but not for others.

There are probably many reasons why someone responds well to a specific technique. However, we've observed two major reasons for people not benefiting:

a. The person does not have a compelling future to move towards;
b. The person has feelings of low self-worth.

We consider these two factors to be fundamental obstacles to PNI effectiveness. This chapter addresses the first factor, and the next chapter concerns the second. Thereafter, we commence the research-based PNI intervention methods.

Good and bad motivation

There are two main reasons for having some kind of a desirable future to work towards. First, challenge, pleasure and interest have a specific range of hormonal consequences, including the release of adrenaline and growth hormone. Challenge, pleasure and interest also result in the release of various neuropeptides, all of which have the ability to assist in the normalisation of a suppressed or overactive immune system, among other effects. Second, a person with no future-related goals has very little reason to engage in health-enhancing activities.

Let us illustrate. We have observed that when a group of people with the same type of physical condition start a health programme – diet, exercise, yoga, meditation, whatever – the group soon splits into two sections. The first group thrives and gets healthier, and this continues over time. The second group gets healthier for a while, then the effects fade and they get sick again. Why on earth would the same method have such different effects?

A simple reason is that some people want to get healthier because they have a future they want to get to, whereas other people want to get healthier because they are afraid of pain and illness. In other words, some people are motivated away from something they fear (pain, illness, death), and others are motivated by the desire to move towards something. These two groups are doing exactly the same things, but for completely different reasons.

Running away from pain and death is not the same thing as running towards health and feeling alive. The difference is simple: when you are motivated by avoiding pain or death, your mind is firmly fixed on what you fear – pain, illness and death.

Therefore, as these things are your central focus, health or happiness doesn't feature in your mental–emotional state. In addition, when the pain subsides, your motivation decreases and disappears until the pain resurfaces. Therefore, this 'away from' motivation is not constant, but comes and goes.

When running towards health and happiness, you keep your mind firmly on where you are going and, obviously, these things are the central focus. Because you are motivated by what you are moving towards, the motivational force is constant, until you reach your goal. More importantly, this motivation stays constant regardless of pain, absence of pain, health or disease.

It is really important that you understand the difference between these two kinds of motivation. Two people can do exactly the same treatment, technique or exercise, with totally different reasons and with totally different results. When you consider that the internal thoughts and feelings each person has, on an ongoing basis, make a major difference to what happens to the immune system, it makes perfect sense that the first person's immune system will not benefit – in fact it may even be damaged further – by his or her motivation, whereas the opposite will occur with the second person.

This is a major reason why the same medical treatment or other method of healing can work for some people and not for others.

TWO KINDS OF MOTIVATION IN HEALING

1. AWAY FROM PAIN: *'I don't want to die because …'*

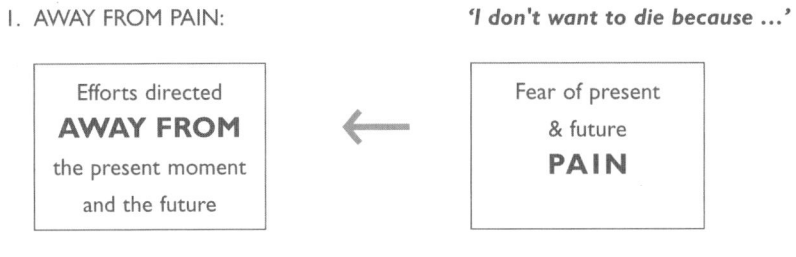

(Motivation strength depends on fear and pain/no pain)

2. TOWARDS PLEASURE: *'I want to live because …'*

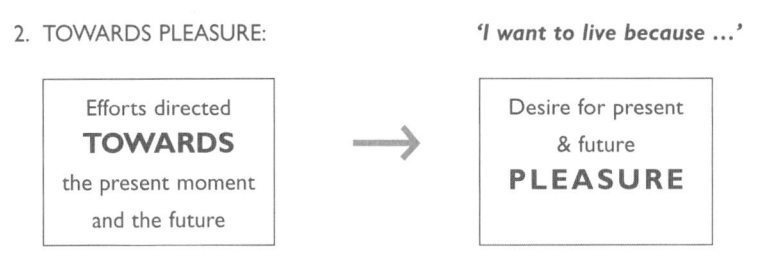

(Motivation depends on achieving goals of health)

In real terms this means that, when you say: *'I am sick and I want to get better'*, you are saying nothing more than *'I want to move from where I am.'* However, if we were to ask you why you wanted to move, you'd say one of the following: *'I want to move because I prefer to be somewhere more pleasurable'* (in other words, you want to move towards something better), or *'I want to move because I don't like it here'* (in other words, you have no specific direction in which you want to move, as long as it's away from the present situation).

Most people who are ill are clear on the fact that they do not want to be ill. However, how many people know what they want to move towards? What kind of future do you want? This is not the same as asking what you do not want!

A simple analogy is that of playing a game of soccer. If there were no goalposts, what would the players do? There they are, running with the ball, knowing that they have to move from one side of the soccer pitch to the other, but with no idea of what to do when they get there! They can't score because there are no goalposts. After a while, they realise that the game is silly, so their choices are to sit down, kick the ball around to anyone, or walk off the pitch.

Life is much the same – you need goalposts, otherwise the game has no real meaning or purpose. Also, like soccer, after you score the first goal there's nothing to stop you from scoring another – it's not a one-off success.

One of the first medical practitioners to acknowledge the mind–body connection publicly, Dr Bernie Siegel [1], asked people who were dying from cancer why they didn't want to die. Most cited the need to live due to obligations – kids, husband, wife and family. So, he tricked them. He asked the families to gather around their dying relatives and proceeded to delegate the dying person's obligations to the family members and friends. Once all the obligations had been dispersed and the patients had nothing left to live for, a very strange thing happened. The patients began requesting his cancer intervention model. Simply put, once their obligation to live had been removed, their passion to live returned. This is a case of 'want-to' versus 'have-to' motivation.

Let us pretend that a woman who has been a mother and a housewife since she got married, develops breast cancer. Let us further pretend that, before she got married, she dreamed of being an architect and designing beautiful buildings. Although she loves her husband and children dearly, her life has been focused strictly on ensuring that their dreams, desires and ambitions are supported and fulfilled. Sound familiar? After surgery, radiation therapy and chemotherapy, which have failed to stop the cancer from spreading, she lies in the hospital with rather limited options for survival.

Now, as she lies in the hospital bed, a doctor tells her there is this wonderful method called PNI which can reverse the cancer so that she can go home. She is tired, hurting and has had enough. What will she do? Will she try the PNI or not? Based on Bernie Siegel's research, and supported by our own observations, she is quite likely to say 'No thanks', even if the PNI programme were offered free of charge. In fact, about 80 percent of people with little or no other healing options left are not willing to try something different, even when they are shown all the remarkable results that have already been achieved with the new method. Why?

We automatically assume that everyone who is ill wants to get better. Even more to the point – we mistakenly assume that everyone who is terminally ill actually wants to live. The evidence suggests that this is not necessarily the case. Think about this carefully. If the woman with the breast cancer looked back at her life, what reason – apart from obligations to her children and husband – would she have to want to resume that life? What, if any, new and exciting challenges could she look forward to?

It is important to realise that, no matter how much you love your children or spouse, taking care of them is not a sufficiently powerful reason to want to live. This is particularly true when you know they will be cared for by someone else if you die. The rather shocking truth is that life will go on after you are gone – the children will be taken care of and your spouse may even find someone else to share his or her life with. No, it will not be the same for them as it was with you, but they will survive without you. And you know this, even if you do not want to admit it. The same can be said about your job – someone will fill your position in very little time. After all, life carries on.

Therefore, if you have given up your own dreams, what really powerful reason is there for you to heal? There are few things more guaranteed than a boring life to drain away the motivation to live. It is crucial that you find a reason to live, which does not depend on children, husband, wife, friends or family.

A compelling future

You need a reason for *you* to live. Perhaps it is your turn to be happy and fulfilled.

We are not questioning your love for your family or your dedication to colleagues and friends. What we are saying is that, at a deep level, these are not sufficient reasons to create a compelling future. In a PNI context, you need something to which you want to move towards – an exciting and powerful reason to get out of bed in the morning. It's called passion or a compelling future.

To understand how this works we need to look deeper into how people are motivated. In the following table, list 20 things you don't want in your life. Now reverse the process and find 20 things you really want. Try it!

	Things I don't want	**Things I do want**
1	....	....
2	....	....
3	....	....
4	....	....
5	....	....
6	....	....
7	....	....
8	....	....
9	....	....
10	....	....
11	....	....
12	....	....
13	....	....
14	....	....
15	....	....
16	....	....
17	....	....
18	....	....
19	....	....
20	....	....

Remember, in the 'Things I do want' column, you write down only things that you want, that give you pleasure. Cross off any items which relate to your children or family.

Notice the ease with which you wrote down your 'Things I don't want' list. Now what about the 'Things I do want' list? Did you notice that by the time you reached point 6 or 7, you started to struggle? For the most part, we are motivated by what we don't want and we are very clear on this. However, we are nowhere near as specific about what we do want. We are clear on what we want to move away from, and are vague and wishy-washy about what we want to move towards. Also note the detail involved in what you don't want and the complete lack of detail in what you do want. We are all very clear on what we don't want in our lives, down to the finest detail. However, we usually lack the same intense details in what we *do* want from life.

The key to moving towards what you do want is to create a very clear picture of what you really want the possible outcome to be. If you don't know where you are going, then any road will get you there!

What exactly is a 'compelling future'? First of all, it usually contains a range of goals (short-term and long-term) that are exciting, interesting, fulfilling and pleasurable for you. These goals may be silly, irrational, meaningless or the opposite – it does not matter. What matters is that you experience excitement and interest in reaching for them, and pleasure and fulfilment in achieving them.

'But,' you may say, 'isn't that shallow and superficial – what about meaningful fulfilment? I understand that my sense of obligation is not "exciting" but at least it's meaningful – I can make a difference in other people's lives.'

If that kind of thought has gone through your mind, you are partially correct. For most people who are ill (and those who are not), life is a mixture of work and family obligations which may or may not bring a sense of fulfilment. For many people the only redeeming quality about 'life' is found in relationships, especially raising children and in an intimate relationship. Another area of potential pleasure is work. What else is there? It is not surprising that, for most people, happiness is locked into a rather small group of people. When you combine this scenario with the fact that, if you died, these people would carry on and get happiness from someone else, you realise that there has to be 'more' to life.

Most people have given up on trying to find that 'more', and have settled for a reasonably 'OK' existence, all dependent on a small group of other people. Deep inside, each one of us knows there is 'more' – that life has meaning and purpose. However, most people set that dream aside to establish 'normal life'.

When a life-threatening disease comes along, what compelling passion is there to counteract the temptation to escape from a painful, monotonous and unfulfilling existence?

Studies of children in orphanages show that lack of stimulation and interest results in deterioration of the brain, mental faculties and health. The same is found in retirement homes. The human species requires challenge and stimulation to thrive and be truly alive. As we have stated before, boredom is as dangerous as a life-threatening disease.

Fundamentally, you need challenge and stimulation as much as you need food and water to survive.

Research by Dr Marian Diamond [2] at the University of California, Berkeley, clearly supports this need for stimulation as a general condition for health and longevity. When isolated and provided with the mere basics for survival (food, water, warmth) but no interaction with others, rats have a much shorter life span than those that are constantly playing with each other and are provided with new toys which are changed every few days. Clearly, having interesting things to do gives the rats a reason to live longer, up to 50 percent longer than the average rat's life span.

Therefore, to return to the initial question, 'Why bother?', probably the most important step towards healing occurs when a person discovers that life does not just comprise pain, boredom and obligation. Life requires pleasurable sensations and activities – almost anything will do. It is crucial that you be engaged in the possibility that 'life is not all that bad'.

A very dramatic example of this process occurred many years ago, while we were still doing our basic research in PNI. We were making a survey of attitudes and needs at an HIV/AIDS clinic in Cape Town. While we were focused on all this 'serious' work, a young man – tanned, healthy, eyes shining – came bouncing up the stairs to speak to one of the counsellors. We were as ignorant as most other people in those days, and mistakenly thought, 'People with HIV look sick.' We assumed he wasn't HIV-infected because he looked happy and healthy. It turned out that he was HIV-infected and had been for quite a bit longer than most of the other people attending the clinic! Apart from realising the truth that people with HIV look like everyone else until they get ill, we were intrigued by this anomaly and requested an interview with him.

John's story truly illustrates the point we have been making so far.

Along with a group of about eight of his friends, John was diagnosed as HIV-positive in the mid-1980s, just after the first HIV test was released. We asked whether his friends were still healthy as well and he said they were all dead. Naturally, we were intrigued as to why he was so obviously healthy and alive, while all his friends had died. When asked why he was different – the exception – he said that, when they were all diagnosed on that fateful day, most of his friends started withdrawing from life, cancelling college studies, giving up their jobs and similar actions. All this clearly indicated that they expected to die.

He, on the other hand, thought, *'Hell, if I'm going to die, I want to do all the things I've always wanted to do!'* So he resigned from his job (which he did not enjoy), sold his house and got a job on a yacht, because he had always dreamed about sailing around the world. Over time, he learned the basics of running a boat and running a charter service, until he had enough money to buy his own boat. Years went by, and his health remained normal.

It was only when he returned to Cape Town several years later that he discovered that his friends had died. John currently runs programmes for teenagers who have been sent to juvenile detention for petty crimes. He takes them on the yacht for several weeks and teaches them about running a boat in the open sea. The results are amazing, because the teenagers feel free from social constraints for the first time and engage in a routine and discipline that makes sense to them.

Why does John not just continue sailing around the world? *'Well,'* he says, *'the first few years were great – I finally gave myself permission to be happy and to enjoy life the way I wanted it to be. After a while, I started getting the feeling that I needed to share this with other people, and the notion of working with delinquent teenagers just popped into my head. I don't really know why these kids grabbed my imagination – they just did, and I trusted myself to just do what I felt compelled to do. It's such a joy to see the transformation in them. I really feel privileged and blessed to be who I am and doing what I do. It is a gift I have been given. Had I not been told that I was going to die, and had I not just thrown caution to the wind, I probably would be buried right next to all my friends.'*

The problem with focusing on your purpose in life is that, until you have experienced the joy and pleasure of life, you will view your 'calling' as just another obligation and not the gift that it is. So, let's get down to the less 'serious' stuff, and let the 'bigger picture' unfold in time! The truth is that, until such time as you have filled your own cup, what do you have to give to someone else?

■ ASSIGNMENT I

STEP 1   Increase the simple pleasures in your life.
Answer the following questions with as much honesty as possible:
1. What is your favourite taste? When last did you have it?
2. What is your favourite smell? When last did you smell it?
3. How many times have you laughed today?
4. Have you allowed someone to touch you gently today?
5. What is your favourite music? When last did you hear it?
6. How much pleasure have you had today? Be specific about what it was that you enjoyed.

We often get caught up in the 'big important meaning of life' stuff, and forget about the small things that fill our world with joy and pleasure. If you are not ready to examine the 'big issues' of purpose, passion and compelling future, that is OK for now, on one condition: have a good day. Laugh today. Rent a movie you love and watch it. Get some more, and watch them too. Eat something you love. Ask someone to give you a gentle massage. Start to enjoy being here and now. Only then does it make any sense to work towards having more of this thing we call 'life'. Decide to have a good life, even if it doesn't last long. Now is all you have anyway.

STEP 2   Find beauty where you are.
Sometimes we get so caught up in the pain, suffering and seriousness of life that we completely forget about what we actually have, right here and now.

Sit still – anywhere – and just look around you. Find something – anything – that you consider beautiful. It doesn't have to be anything profound or incredible, just something you haven't paid much attention to, such as a flower, the clouds, a picture, your own hands. Don't think about what you are looking at – just look at it and appreciate it. It helps to consider that this is the first, and possibly last, time you will see it. If this makes you sad, that is also OK.

STEP 3 **Let something go, and let something new in.**
This is a simple thing to do. Look around you. How many books, papers, objects, pieces of furniture and pictures have been sitting in exactly the same place for a long time? How many drawers and cupboards have had things piled into them for ages? How many bags and photo albums have been sitting there, unchanged, for a while?

Clean your room. Throw or give away all the things you haven't used or needed for a long time. Give old books and magazines away to someone who could use them. Throw away or burn old bills that have been sitting there for years. Move a picture on the wall. Turn the mattress over.

Now get something new, even if it is just a second-hand book you want to read.

STEP 4 **Get your affairs in order.**
Relax … this is not about anticipating death. This is about freeing yourself up to live. Write down what you want specific people to have if you die. If possible, give it to them now, so that you can enjoy their delight in having it. Sort out your finances, pay your taxes. Write down what you want to happen at your funeral. Yes, this sounds bizarre, but until you get these issues out of the way, they will always be in your mind. Right now, you need to move beyond these issues, so that you can focus on living. Ensure that your will is current. If you haven't got one, make one.

Then … do something fun, something you have wanted to do for a long time and have always put off. After all, once you have put your death behind you, what else is there to do except live?

Let me give you an example. David went to a funeral home and tried out all the coffins. The funeral director was horrified.

However, when David found a coffin he liked, he paid for it, and then gave the funeral director the instructions for his funeral, and paid for that too. The same day, he went to an estate agent and went looking for a new house. He signed the papers the next day.

You don't have to go to those extremes, but it is really important that you get your thoughts and plans sorted out regarding your death, so that you can move along into life.

STEP 5   Now, what do you want?
If you have done the list of 'Things I don't want' and 'Things I do want', you have made a start. Even if you have no more than 10 items, this is an excellent place to begin. Now it's time to put each 'want' item through a quick checklist to determine if it will be compelling and pleasure-creating.

When you read or think about this 'want', do you feel a physical sensation of excitement?

A 'good idea' is not the same as 'exciting'. It must cause some physical sensation – a tingle, smile, a blush – anything that indicates 'Ooh – yes, that would be nice!' If this reaction does not occur, you are probably dealing with someone else's idea of what should make you happy. If they think it so marvellous, why aren't they doing it themselves? The focus on some physical sensation is important. How else are you going to start figuring out what you want? **The body never lies!** No matter what you do or believe, your mother, father, husband, wife, partner, kids or friends cannot be enthusiastic or excited for you. It is your body, your life, no matter how you would like it to be otherwise.

When we ask someone what she or he wants to do with her or his life, we typically hear a whole list of rather good ideas. However, if that person's body does not get excited – hand movements, eyes sparkling, flushed cheeks, smiling, laughing, animated movements – we simply ignore what she or he is saying because … **the body never lies!** Listen to your body – it has no reason to lie to you. However, your mind can, and will, lie to you in order to ensure that people like you, or to ensure that you 'fit' in with other people.

Who is sick? Who feels the pain? Whose life is this? Whose body is this? Yours or theirs? No matter how much someone else loves you, she or he cannot experience your pain for you. This person may understand that you are in pain but cannot step into your body and actually know what it is like, which makes you the one and only authority on what feels good and what doesn't, doesn't it?

Is it what you want or is it what you don't want?

This question has been asked before, but it is sufficiently important to be repeated. Is your goal the removal of something you don't want, such as pain, unhappiness and illness? For a moment, we want you *not* to think of a yellow Volkswagen. *Don't think about a yellow Volkswagen!* What was the first picture to pop into your head? Probably a yellow Volkswagen, right? The mind thinks in terms of pictures. So, the person who says, *'I don't want to die'* sees some picture that represents death, be it a funeral, a wake or some Hollywood death scene. Regardless, some image that represents your notion of death flashes through your mind.

The unconscious mind cannot tell the difference between what appears to be the same and what appears to be similar. The mind cannot tell the difference between the two.

When you say that you 'don't want to die', it implies that you already have a mental filing system loaded with pictures of your death. You can work as hard as you like with them, but nothing will change until such time as you see yourself healthy and motivated towards something. Therefore, any goal that contains the words 'stop' or 'not' needs to be rephrased so that it clearly reflects what you want, not what you don't want, what you want to start, not what you want to stop, and so on. In other words, it needs to be stated in the positive, not the negative.

A simple example is: *'I don't want to die from this disease.'* This means that the picture in your head – your motivation – is one of suffering. The picture has to be pretty scary in order to motivate you to do something.

Now try turning this around. If you do not want to die, then logically you want to live, right? So, instead of saying *'I don't want to die'*, say *'I want to live.'* The picture attached to this new thought is one of aliveness, not suffering. However, if you want to do it properly, you now state why you want to live – some exciting goal, such as *'I want to live so that I can create the most beautiful paintings the world has ever seen, and I want to do lots of them!'* Now the picture is even more powerful, because you are motivated by a picture of yourself passionately involved with something you really love, in a place you really want to be.

When you have turned the negative picture around into an exciting and pleasurable one, you will notice that you will want to start moving towards that exciting future *now* – such as starting to paint even while you are in hospital. Go on! Start! Do it *now*! What do you have to lose? **Have some fun, for as long as you can. When you do that, it does not really matter how long your body lasts – as long as each day is wonderful, exciting and glorious! The world is waiting for you to deliver your gift – give it!**

How specific is your goal?

A person is complaining about the quality of her life, and when we ask her what she wants, she says, *'I want love and money.'* All very well and good, right? Uh … nope! A while later, while walking down the road, she finds a coin on the road and, as she bends over to pick it up, a stray dog comes over and licks her hand. So, in a very literal sense, she's just achieved 'love' and 'money'!

But that's not what she meant! Tough luck – the unconscious mind does not know what you 'really meant'. All you said or thought was 'money' and 'love', and lo and behold, it was delivered. The problem is that you need to treat your unconscious mind for what it is – powerful, but child-like and very literal. You have to be very specific and spell out exactly what you mean – how much, where, who, how big or small, what colour, and so on. Pretend you are telling a five-year-old child what you want, in such a way that she will know exactly what to get for you. Do not assume anything!

The lesson? Be clear and specific about what you're moving towards. As we said earlier, if you don't know where you are going on your journey – where the goalposts are – then any road will get you there. Be specific and incorporate as much detail as you can muster. If you want to buy a home for your family, be clear on where, how big, how much, and the overall floor plan.

How often have you seen a child draw a picture of a house and give it to the mother or father and say: *'There you go! You said you wanted a house, so*

I made one for you!' The child is perfectly correct – the parent probably did not say that he wanted a brick house in a certain neighbourhood, with three bedrooms, a garage, a dining room and lounge, a spacious kitchen, and how much he was willing to pay for it. So he got a paper house!

However, be careful about being overly detailed and rigid about what you want! Also, be very careful to avoid stating that you want something which belongs to someone else, or which depends on someone else giving up something so that you can have what you want. This usually backfires. Also, be a little flexible about time.

Another (true) example is of a woman who said: *'I want to drive a red Mercedes-Benz sports car.'* It was something towards which she was working and about which she constantly talked. One day at the office, her employer arrived with a new red Mercedes sports car and asked her if she would mind driving to town to pick up his dry-cleaning. So, factually speaking, she got exactly what she said she wanted. What she failed to emphasise in her intention was that she wanted to own a red Mercedes sports car. Had she been more specific, she might have realised her dream.

STEP 6   Be prepared for criticism (from yourself and others).
          This doesn't always happen but, generally speaking, the minute you hit on something you really want to do or experience, fears emerge – thoughts of *'What will people say?'* and *'Don't be silly! You can't do that!'* and a wide range of other objections. You may even hear the same things from people who love you. Hmm … makes you wonder what 'love' is and how much of it is conditional on your staying bored and predictable.

          This is probably the scariest stage of the process, because you get slammed from the inside and outside with all sorts of limiting, reasonable objections to being happy. One of the most direct and effective ways of countering these objections is to recognise that what you want is not reasonable or 'meaningful' to anyone else, and that you're not doing it to make anyone else happy – you just want to enjoy something for the sake of the pleasure it brings. After all, what is the worst that could happen? You could die! Oh well, that's about the worst, so you might as well have some fun! The only real risk you run is that of being truly happy!

STEP 7   Action!

Picture this. There is a bird in its nest and its fledglings are hungry. In the distance, the bird sees food on the ground – a nice juicy worm. So it takes off in the direction of the worm, but gets blown off course by a strong wind. It ends up going in the wrong direction and lands on another tree. It then looks at where it is, looks at where it wants to go (towards the worm), and then looks at where it has come from – the nest full of screaming hungry chicks! Does the bird say: *'Oh, what's the point – I tried. The wind is too strong so I guess the chicks will have to eat tomorrow?'* Or does it take off again in the direction of the food, no matter how many times it is blown off course? The answer is that it will persist because it has a strong motivation, namely feeding its kids.

For some strange reason people expect to take just one small step, then arrive at the objective – instant gratification!

Unfortunately, it doesn't work that way. As Carolynn Myss says: *'You have to trade in your wishbone for a backbone!'*

Maxwell Maltz summed it up when he said: *'Often the difference between a successful man and a failure is not one's better abilities or ideas, but the courage that one has to bet on his ideas, to take a calculated risk – and to ACT!'* The universe supports action, not thoughts. The formula is actually quite simple:

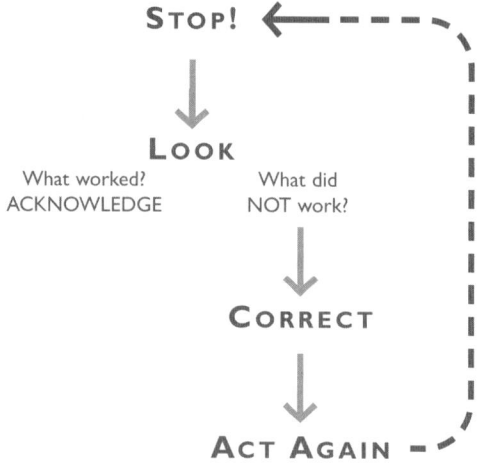

STOP!

↓

LOOK

What worked?   What did
ACKNOWLEDGE   NOT work?

↓

CORRECT

↓

ACT AGAIN

Repeat this process as many times as needed until you reach your desired outcome. Where this process falls apart is when people stop, look and then try to find a reason why it can't work or they get too caught up in looking for blame.

Life is a series of little steps and big steps. The biggest step is the first little step, even if that is a phone call to find out what is available. If the telephone number is engaged, then phone again later, or ask someone else. Just keep on going: STOP–LOOK–CORRECT–ACT…

STEP 8   **Make space in your life for what you want.**
Several years back, during a severe drought in the northern part of South Africa, all the local churches decided to get together and pray for rain. The date was set, all the arrangements were made and a special guest was invited to conduct the service. Several hundred people gathered in a tiny clearing on the outskirts of town, awaiting the guest of honour who finally arrived. The guest of honour stood in front of the group, nodding his head, and, after a period of time, he cleared his throat and began to speak:

'*I see that many of you have come here today to pray to our Father in Heaven to ease the drought affecting our land.*' Exclamations of '*Amen*' and '*Hallelujah*' rumbled from the congregation. '*Well, my brothers and sisters, no matter why you have come here and no matter what you do here today, nothing is going to work.*' Gasps of disbelief could be heard throughout the congregation.

The guest of honour continued. '*You see, I know why it can't work. The reason is simple. Only one person here believes that we can end this awful drought with our prayers – only one person out of all of you.*' At this point the congregation started to become a little uneasy and finally an older lady stood up and demanded that the guest be more specific. '*My sister,*' he said, '*It's really quite simple. There is only one person who believes we can end this drought and believes it so strongly that she is the only person here to have brought an umbrella to protect her from the rain!*'

This is a superb example of something called 'congruency' – when your thoughts and actions are all going in the same direction. In the true story above, everyone except one person was saying one thing but behaving differently. Only one person thought it would rain, and behaved accordingly, by bringing an umbrella.

Remember one simple rule – where your thoughts flow, your energy goes. What is the point of intention when you are not 100 percent committed to it?

In other words, if you want to meet someone special, you actually have to leave the comfort of your room, the safety of the droning television. If you want to travel to Peru, you may want to think twice about blowing every cent you own on a new dress or motorcycle! Orient not only your thoughts towards what you want, but orient your behaviour in the same direction as well.

Even though you may be ill, if your dream is to be an artist, then start art classes! Enrol for that course, start acting on those dreams! Don't wait until you get better or until this round of chemotherapy is over. *Just do it!* Even if you are tired and in bed, this does not stop you from asking someone to make enquiries on your behalf: who teaches art classes in your area? on which evenings are the classes? how much does it cost? what does it involve? and so on.

STEP 9   **Confront your doubts and fears.**
We have devoted an entire chapter to dealing with fears, because this area is of major importance in terms of the immune system. In the interim, simply notice what fears and doubts emerge as you think about your goals. If you aren't honest about them, then you cannot deal with them, and they are the most powerful sabotage mechanisms imaginable. Write them down, and look at them again when you get to the chapter about dealing with fears.

How often have you thought that it would be wonderful to do something special, or you may just want to do the exercises in this book, but you just do not have the time or energy? Have you considered the possibility that laziness and apathy are nothing more than many layers of fear which have become like hard cement? What is it that you fear might happen if you actually took control and started doing something for yourself?

If you are saying and thinking that you want to do something, but you are actually not doing anything about it, then you are like the churchgoers who wanted to pray for rain but did not bring umbrellas. You have a choice. Either act according to your thoughts and words, or stop thinking and saying things that you do not really want or mean. This is all about congruency and integrity – saying, thinking and doing the same thing. Do not say you want to live if you are not willing to do something about it. Rather, say what you really want – either to die, or for someone to rescue you. There is nothing wrong with this – it is simply more honest, which is a pretty good place to start dealing with your issues.

SUMMARY OF STEPS

Just for today ...

STEP 1   Increase the simple pleasures in your life

STEP 2   Find beauty where you are

STEP 3   Let something go, and let something new in

STEP 4   Get your affairs in order
Take care of your death, and do something to embrace life, on the same day.

STEP 5   Now, what do you want?
Make a list.
When you read or think about each 'want', do you feel a physical sensation of excitement?
Is it what you want or is it what you don't want?
How specific is the goal?

STEP 6   Be prepared for criticism (from yourself and others)

STEP 7   Action!

STEP 8   Make space in your life for what you want

STEP 9   Confront your doubts and fears

■ ASSIGNMENT 2: A LETTER FROM THE FUTURE

Write a letter to a close friend, as if you were 10 years into the future and you had not seen your friend for those 10 years.

For example, if today's date is 17 September 2004, then your letter will be dated 10 years from today, 17 September 2014.

Tell your friend what you have been doing, the obstacles you have overcome, the achievements you have made, where you are living and what is happening in your life nowadays. In other words, using the same date (only as an example), write about the 10-year period from 17 September 2004 until 17 September 2014.

Be as specific as possible with as much detail as you can create.

RELEASING STRESS FROM YOUR PAST

The power of the past is very real. It lies in the fact that we have experienced certain (usually painful) events and in those moments of pain have made decisions about ourselves and the world. However, for various complicated reasons, we forget about those decisions. It is in the act of forgetting that we lose power over the event, because decisions affect us until we change them. In other words, the forgetting makes these decisions unconscious.

The 20-second dip

Not every painful event leaves an emotional scar. Specific processes need to occur for this to happen, and these depend on your brain-wave activity during the original event:

Your brain produces a wide range of electrical signals of various frequencies:
1. **Delta brain waves:** These occur when you are in very deep sleep, or unconscious, or in a coma. They are very slow – less than 3.5 cycles per second.
2. **Theta brain waves:** These occur during normal sleep and are a bit faster – between 3.5 and 7 cycles per second. Theta waves are also produced during moments of intense pleasure and pain and correspond to the unconscious mind.
3. **Alpha brain waves:** Just before you go to sleep, and just before you wake up, your brain waves are even faster – between 7 and 14 cycles per second. Meditation, prayer and relaxed waking alertness also produce alpha waves. When you are in the frame of mind of being awake but also not aware of time, this corresponds to the alpha-wave brain state.
4. **Beta brain waves:** When you are aware of time and the world around you (sights, smells, touch and sounds), your brain begins to produce faster brain waves – 14 cycles per second and higher. When you start getting worried, 'stressed', confused or panicked, your brain waves speed up and these are called 'high' beta waves.

A curious event occurs under very stressful situations. Your brain waves first get faster (they become high beta waves), but if the distress is severe enough, at the critical point of the event your brain waves suddenly take a major dip down into theta waves, for about 20 seconds, before returning to the speed of beta waves [1]. This sudden 'dip' in brain waves corresponds to what is commonly understood as 'going into shock'.

During these 20 seconds of theta wave action, you are effectively deep in your unconscious mind, even though you are apparently wide awake. Your mind and brain are operating as if you were dreaming or asleep. People in this state typically have a glazed look in their eyes.

Furthermore, whatever thoughts and feelings you have during this 20-second dip will not be processed through your conscious, logical, realistic and reasonable mind. They are literally planted directly into your unconscious mind. When the crisis is over and your mind has returned to beta and then alpha waves, you will probably not remember what happened during those 20 seconds but it will have a profound effect later.

An excellent example of this 20-second phenomenon is the shock you experience at receiving a serious diagnosis or bad news. What you say, think or feel during those 20 seconds can have a profound effect afterwards and this effect occurs without conscious awareness.

The origin of most unconscious beliefs tends to be located in these 20-second 'dips'.

There are a few important things to note about this process:

- You are more likely to form unconscious beliefs during stressful events.
- These unconscious beliefs are formed during a short space of time in which your normal logic and sense of reality are not fully operating – they can be illogical and based on a weak sense of what is realistically happening at the time.
- Not all thoughts and feelings are as important as others when exploring the major influences in your life today, including beliefs about your disease and those that affect your immune system.

For many people, tracing the trigger events in their past is slow and difficult.

One main reason is that people expect to find such events in obvious places, such as painful times of their lives. Although you will indeed find examples of such 20-second dips in typical painful periods (such as divorce or the death of a loved one), many of these 'dips' occur at unexpected times.

For example, a nine-year-old boy is raised in a large family and his father works many hours overtime to pay the bills. The boy knows this, and appreciates this. However, one Saturday morning while playing soccer he scores his first goal. In his euphoria he looks around to find his father, who is not there. A mixture of profound disappointment and anger leads to a 20-second dip, in which he forms the belief: *'If he really loved me, he would have been here just this one time. Obviously, he doesn't love me.'* With this thought, a deep-seated unconscious sense of abandonment is born, despite the boy being conscious of being loved and supported.

These types of events that do not normally register as important in our investigation of our lives and pasts are often overlooked, but they are just as likely as classic loss events to create opportunities for 20-second dips.

The reticular activating system

It is fairly easy to understand how emotional shocks can lead to deep-seated beliefs forming in the unconscious mind. We have all experienced such events and their effects. However, when we try to be objective about how these past events impact on our present experience, we tend to run into the proverbial brick wall. That 'brick wall' is a comprehensive, undeniable and factual catalogue of personal experiences that prove the belief to be true!

A classic (and stereotypical) example is when a woman or man is emotionally rejected and hurt in a relationship. In the trauma of the rejection, a 20-second dip occurs and a generalised belief forms: *'Men (or women) cannot be trusted.'* This seems like a fair and normal conclusion to make in such a circumstance. However, notice the generalised nature of the belief: 'men' (or 'women') literally means *all* men (or *all* women), as far as the unconscious mind is concerned. This is a key point in such unconscious beliefs – they are rarely specific to a particular situation or person. Instead, they are general – they cover anything or anyone that is similar to the original person or situation.

From that moment onwards, a second brain process kicks into action that affects your experience for the rest of your life, revolving around a portion of the brain called the Reticular Activating System (RAS).

It is the activity of the Reticular Activating System that puts the final piece of the puzzle together in terms of how single events can affect the rest of our lives, lead to chronic stress, and ultimately affect our immune system and health.

Without going into complicated neurological explanations, it is sufficient to know that the RAS is a part of your brain that influences your perception of everything you see, hear, smell, touch and taste. In effect, the RAS screens out awareness of things that are not considered important so that you can focus on what is important. Without the work of the RAS you would be over-whelmed by stimuli every moment of your life. It would be impossible to focus on reading this book, for example, if it were not for the RAS, as you would be equally aware of every other sight, sound, smell and feeling going on right now.

So how does the RAS determine what is important for you to notice, and what is not? The RAS focuses primarily on stimuli regarding your survival. However, it can be equally influenced by any unconscious belief which sits in the same region of the mind as these survival issues. In fact, as far as the RAS is concerned, they are all the same thing.

So, for example, when you get emotionally hurt and form an unconscious belief about men or women, for example, this belief forms part and parcel of what the RAS considers to be essential for your survival. As a result, it will ensure that you mainly focus on anything that concerns these beliefs.

So, if we continue our stereotypical example ('men, or women, cannot be trusted'), the RAS will make sure you notice every word, gesture, sound, smell and action that supports that belief. Also, it will filter out anything that does not seem to fit into this belief. Why? The answer is simple – because the stimulus regarding the belief is considered to be essential to your survival, and a stimulus that doesn't fit into the belief does not affect your survival, as far as the RAS is concerned.

The end result is that you begin to notice only what you believe unconsciously to be true. Obviously, this means that you feel vindicated over and over again, which strengthens the initial belief. The fact that there are as many examples that prove the opposite is simply ignored, because the RAS doesn't consider these stimuli to be important enough for you to notice.

This is how habits of perception and coping develop. This is also why it is so difficult to effect real change in the way you deal with life. It is also the primary reason why logic and reason don't produce much change in Applied PNI. The RAS does not operate at the level of conscious awareness but at the level of the unconscious.

On the upside, this same RAS process can be used to great advantage when trying to change your life. The whole purpose of positive affirmations is to impact on the RAS, which then allows you to notice the 'good stuff', or opportunities that lead you to the 'good stuff'.

In terms of methods, positive affirmations that have no 'oomph' (emotional intensity) also have no impact on the RAS. This is why there are so many different methods to try and get past the conscious mind to make the affirmations work: hypnosis, meditation, relaxation (which slows brain waves), and so forth. However, there is no reason why repetition cannot work, although it is slower than methods with 'oomph'.

Ironically, constant repetition of an affirmation leads to boredom, which is when people typically stop. However, the boredom is an indication that the conscious mind is just about to let the affirmation slip into unconsciousness!

Links with the past

You do not need to go very far to experience the power of the past in affecting you now. Most people have experienced driving in a car, feeling fine and happy, with the radio playing in the background. A little later, for no apparent reason, sadness emerges. Where did it come from? Nothing happened!

On the contrary. The radio was playing, and even though you were not aware of it, some piece of music pulled your emotions into the past. For example, the radio may have been playing the song that was playing in the background as your first boyfriend or girlfriend broke up with you.

Music is a powerful link to the past. So are smells, pictures and sounds. As you will discover when we discuss coping styles in the next chapter, even a person's tone of voice can instantly change your mood because of its association (or link) with past events and people.

Associations: the past is a package deal

Every single event of your life is recorded in your mind. However, it is the way it is recorded that makes it possible to do some useful healing work. Everything is recorded as a 'package' of what you saw, heard, felt, thought, smelled and even tasted. All these aspects of the event are linked, or associated.

This is why, for example, when you walk into a shop and smell a specific perfume, you immediately think of your grandmother, who used to wear that perfume. When you hear a certain piece of music, you automatically think of someone, or a situation, you associate with it.

'What has this to do with my health?' you may ask. How the past influences you has a profound impact on your health and your immune system. In this chapter, we focus mainly on what are referred to as 'trigger' events, and chronic stress. In the next chapter we explore how the past has caused you to cope in a certain way, which may sometimes hurt or harm your immune system.

Chronic stress

Chronic stress is stress you experience over a long time. For example, if a long time ago you were constantly told you were 'wonderful' (or were loved) only when you did something well, but you were ignored or criticised (or not loved) when you failed, you may have some powerful beliefs (decisions) that drive you to succeed today, even when this harms your body. This particular example would lead to health problems associated with 'stressed power syndrome' (see page 51). This is a chronic form of stress because it is always there, just underneath your conscious awareness, driving you to think, feel and behave in a certain way. It is also quite important to realise that you probably think this way of thinking, feeling and behaving is 'normal', particularly if you have been doing this for a very long time.

However, the word 'stress' is a rather useless term, because the experience of emotional and physical distress depends on the individual's perception of what is happening. In other words, the decisions and events of your past have the power to affect how you view (or perceive) events today.

For example, how would you feel about writing an exam or test tomorrow, even on a subject you are pretty good at? Do you get anxious, nervous? Why? What are the thoughts that race through your mind?

One definition of stress is that it is a perception of actual loss, potential loss or imagined loss.

In other words, stress is the emotional and physical process that happens' when you are faced with actual loss of something important (person, object, body or self-image), or you think you might lose these things. Imagining that you could fail can be as stressful as actually failing.

Good stress (eustress) and bad stress (distress)

For some people, a specific situation is challenging and stimulating, while for others, the same situation is frightening, especially if they believe that they don't have any control over it. To distinguish between these kinds of 'stresses', we use the terms 'eustress' and 'distress'.

Eustress: This is a term used to describe situations and challenges that may be considered 'good stress' because they are stimulating and enjoyable. For example, having goals you are working towards, or going for a hike in the mountains.

If you enjoy crossword puzzles, the challenge of struggling to complete them may be called 'eustress' – you feel thrilled and satisfied at having done them. However, for someone who is not good with words and spelling, the same process can simply confirm their sense of unworthiness, and cause 'distress'.

Some people love the thrill of certain activities, and for them, if you removed the 'eustress' from their lives, they would be miserable and depressed. Typically, this kind of stress leads to release of the hormone adrenaline.

Distress: This is what people normally mean by 'stress' because it refers to the situations and feelings that involve anxiety, fear, frustration, pain and anger. This is the classic 'bad stress'. Typically, this kind of stress leads to the release of the hormone cortisol.

The two-year loss-to-symptom syndrome

How does all this information relate to chronic illness? A combination of all these processes –20-second dips, unconscious decisions, the RAS – creates a phenomenon called the 'two-year loss-to-symptom' syndrome.

This syndrome refers to the widespread finding that **in most chronic immune-based diseases, there is a significant event involving loss about 18 months to two years before symptoms begin to develop.**

This has been found in a wide range of chronic diseases, including cancer *[2]*, rheumatoid arthritis *[3]*, lupus *[4]*, diabetes Type I *[5]*, inflammatory bowel disease *[6]* and multiple sclerosis *[7]*.

When you consider that there is usually a 20-second dip in brain waves during such loss events and that, thereafter, the thoughts that occurred during this dip continue to operate as a self-supporting unconscious belief because of the RAS, this phenomenon starts to make sense.

In its most basic form, any event that leads to the formation of an unconscious belief that revolves around a sense of helplessness or woundedness will thereafter create a chronic increase in the activity of the HPAC (hypothalamus–pituitary–adrenal cortex) system, with continual release of hormones such as cortisol. Similarly, the formation of an unconscious belief revolving around fight-or-flight causes a chronic stimulation of the SAM (sympathetic nervous adrenal medulla) system, and continual release of hormones such as adrenaline.

But that is not all. We are highly resourceful creatures – we learn to develop methods of coping and defence to keep our fears and perceived inadequacies contained and manageable. These mental–emotional defences require constant energy and attention, which are also stressful for the body. They are explored in the next chapter.

Low-grade chronic stress

When you add up the effects of unconscious beliefs and coping mechanisms, you arrive at a situation of continual stress referred to as low-grade chronic stress. Over a period of time – typically 18 months to two years – this low-grade chronic stress acts on the mind–brain–hormone HPAC system (or SAM system, or any other system, depending on the belief and how the person unconsciously deals with it), slowly weakening the immune system. There is no sudden effect on the immune system – it is very gradual.

However, at some point the immune system becomes too weak to detect and destroy cancerous or virally infected cells. This does not mean that either the event or the unconscious belief 'caused' the cancer, AIDS, or anything else. The existence of cancerous cells, bacteria and viruses is independent of all these psychological events and processes. However, your psychological processes have a major influence on how your body deals with these disease-causing agents.

A few years ago, we were working with an HIV-infected client who had developed AIDS symptoms in the previous year. For many years he had been healthy, living beyond most of his friends who had died from HIV-related illnesses. Everyone thought he was one of the lucky few who would never develop AIDS. Despite being HIV-infected for more than 12 years, his immune system had remained normal except for the last two and a half years when his T-cell counts began to drop rapidly for no known reason. When we asked him if any significant loss had occurred in the two-year period before his immune system started deteriorating, he said his best friend had died in a car accident. However, he added, he had lost many friends and lovers prior to that time and, therefore, he did not consider this specific loss of any great significance.

We then asked him whether he had lost any other friends or lovers after that specific friend had died, and he replied: *'No – I had no friends left – he was the last friend I had. When he died, I decided to stop making new friends because I knew I would lose them as well and I am tired of losing the people I love.'*

Unwittingly, he had revealed what had occurred during the loss event (in the 20-second 'dip'). His fear was to care and lose again. As a result, he built up mental walls against affection and friendship, and the maintenance of these walls created the low-grade chronic stress that gradually eroded his previously strong immune system.

Incidentally, a key aspect of his subsequent therapy focused on his belief that *'Everyone I love dies'*. Strictly speaking, his belief was correct. However, death does not mean rejection – people do not necessarily die to show you they no longer want to be with you! Also, we focused on his willingness to engage in future relationships. Three years later, his immune system had recovered to just below normal levels and he is now symptom-free with occasional out-breaks of minor infections.

It needs to be clearly understood that, in some cases, the actual loss, in terms of the 20-second dip, RAS and the unconscious, is not obvious to you. This is why it is so useful to have a therapist or friend guide the PNI process for you – you are not conscious of certain aspects of what you are really saying and the therapist can objectively identify critical statements which you may simply gloss over. Also, what appears to one person as terrible may be liberating for another – it all depends on what happens in the 20-second dip into theta brain waves.

For example, Jim had prostate cancer. He told us that his first marriage was a 'disaster'. When it ended, the only thought to go through his head was *'I'm free!'* During the subsequent custody battle for the two children, he and his estranged wife had a major argument during which she told him he was a lousy lover and *'not a real man'*. He was totally unprepared for this criticism and it had a devastating effect. The shock of the statement resulted in a 20-second dip during which he thought about how this was possibly true. Moments later, when his thought processes were again logical and partially rational, he defended himself against his soon-to-be ex-wife.

However, the damage had been done in those 20 seconds. Without realising it, he began to act and feel according to the unconscious belief that he was *'not a real man'*. He started to have many sexual partners (to prove his manli-ness), during which he sometimes experienced impotence. He also had peri-ods of not wanting to be with women who wanted anything more than sex and indulged in many other behaviours reflecting the belief of his inade-quacy. His conscious reason for this behaviour was *'I'm free of this marriage and I want to have fun before settling down again.'*

This period of 'fun' lasted for several years but, because of his anxiety and anger towards women, it was definitely not 'fun'. The continual effort to hide his belief that he was 'not a real man' produced continual stress, which gradually eroded his immune system over several years.

It would have been unthinkable for Jim to discuss his belief as this would have created a tremendous amount of anger and defensiveness. Instead, we discussed the marriage and divorce, and then asked him to give a moment-by-moment account of the argument that occurred outside the custody court. It was only when he became aware of what went through his mind during those 20 seconds that his subsequent behaviour began to make sense to him, and it was possible to change this powerful unconscious belief which was causing low-grade chronic stress.

It is logical to assume that loss (real or perceived) involves pain, rejection, failure and criticism. However, there are also less obvious situations of loss that are usually overlooked, namely events of achievement or completion of some project and success. A typical example is a person who builds a business from scratch, working hard and passionately for several years, until he finally 'makes it' and the money starts flowing in or he sells the business for a substantial sum. Certainly, this is a wonderful achievement. However, unless there is some project in which he can place passion with equal energy, this 'success' is usually accompanied with a profound sense of loss of purpose – *'What do I do now? Who am I without this project?'*

Retirement after many years of work can produce the same sense of emptiness and loss of purpose. In some cases, this loss is devastating and difficult to repair, such as in the case of a woman who sacrificed a personal life for her sport and finally achieved a gold medal at the Olympics. Once she had achieved this height of success, and being 'too old' to repeat the success four years later, what was left for her in terms of passion for life and purpose?

This syndrome, in less extreme forms, is quite common. How often have you heard someone say that she would love to start a specific project about which she is passionate, but she is too old now? These people have effectively lost their dream or, alternatively, lost their belief that life has any further purpose or hope of fulfilment.

Mothers who see their children grow up and leave home to pursue their own lives, often experience a sense of achievement and one of profound loss, called the 'empty-nest syndrome'. During such moments of sadness or confusion, several possible 20-second dips can occur, producing profound effects on psychological and physical health.

A very common phenomenon involves sacrificing personal purpose for others, especially for children and other loved ones. For example, Joanna had been a successful paediatrician in Brazil for many years, and she loved her job. However, her children reached an age when they needed college education and she and her husband decided it would be best for them to live in Europe so that their sons could get the best education available. So Joanna resigned from her job and the family moved to Portugal. Within two years, Joanna had developed liver cancer. In therapy, it emerged that, although she did not regret the sacrifice for her children, a part of her was deeply angry at having to give up her passion for this to happen.

It is alarming how few people know how to find a balance between fulfilling their own needs and supporting the needs of others. Usually, there is a perception of 'you *or* me' in such decisions, instead of 'you *and* me'.

Finally, we must recognise that there are losses involved as a result of the disease itself – a loss of physical functioning (and therefore the ability to do the things you enjoy), loss of self-esteem, perceived loss of future and many other possible or actual losses.

Where to look for trigger events

In practice, when we begin the Applied PNI process we scrutinise the three years prior to diagnosis for trigger events. We extend this period to three years because sometimes symptoms are undetected for some time and are often noticed or diagnosed only when they begin to be painful or obvious.

For certain conditions, such as a cancer which goes into remission and which then returns, we focus on the period preceding the first appearance of symptoms. Subsequent re-occurrences are usually linked to the initial triggering event, in some form or another, and may reflect a temporary overcoming of the initial unconscious belief, which is reactivated by a secondary event.

It is also important to distinguish between continually chronic conditions (such as cancer, multiple sclerosis, diabetes, arthritis and AIDS), and repeated intermittent conditions (herpes or eczema outbreaks) that can be activated and then go dormant.

In the case of recurrent (or repeat) conditions, there is typically some original trigger event to 'set the scene', which is later activated, usually through stressful events or periods of stress [8]. For example, with *Herpes simplex* (chickenpox) or *Herpes zoster* (shingles), the clinical symptoms are preceded by a period of depression [9], typically six months or more beforehand. These viruses reside in the nerve endings and can remain dormant for several years between outbreaks. However, a prolonged period of high activation of the nervous system – stress – can activate these viruses.

David, for example, sometimes gets outbreaks of shingles. This is typically preceded by a period of anger at a situation or person, which he does not express.

The frequency of stressful events also affects the duration of active symptoms [10]. A similar relationship is found with the common cold [11]. Once again, **it is important to distinguish between virus activity – which is linked to psychological factors – and the presence of the virus itself, which is not 'caused' by psychological processes.** Even in such recurrent conditions, it is useful to examine the loss events preceding the initial outbreak of symptoms, because the stress that reactivates these symptoms may be linked to them.

Identifying loss events

In the following Loss Assessment (see page 120), you are asked to identify any major loss event in your life. From this, you will extract the trigger event(s) that preceded your illness symptoms. We will then introduce some basic processes to deal with the decisions and emotions of that trigger event. For the purpose of this process, focus only on events that happened within the three years before you first noticed the symptoms of your illness. For chronic infections, focus on the three years prior to any major changes in your health (e.g. development of AIDS-related symptoms).

■ LOSS ASSESSMENT

THE MAJOR STRESSFUL EVENTS OF YOUR LIFE

The following list contains many kinds of stressful events. It is not comprehensive, so you should feel free to add to it.

Read through the list, item by item. If such an event, or anything similar, happened to you within the three years before your symptoms developed, then tick it off and write down the approximate date or year in which it happened.

Please keep in mind that the 20-second dip is an unconscious phenomenon. Therefore, even though you feel some event has no significance, or is 'positive', tick it off anyway. It's not necessary to think about the contents or significance of the event.

Please realise that it is often difficult to determine whether something actually (factually) happened, or whether it was something you think (believe/imagine/perceive) happened. In truth, there is little difference in the effects. This is particularly relevant in childhood events and stresses. For example, you may have felt rejected or abandoned regardless of whether this was factually true or not. A parent may have spent a great deal of time at work because she or he needed to ensure food and shelter for the family, but you noticed the parent's absence and concluded that the parent did not want to be with you, hence your feelings of rejection.

Tick it off, regardless of whether the specific event occurred in 'fact' or you simply perceived it to have happened.

YOUR PREGNANCIES AND FERTILITY, BIRTHS OF YOUR CHILDREN

EVENT	WHEN?
☐ Unwanted pregnancy (too young or forced sex).	....
☐ Difficult or complicated pregnancy and/or labour.	....
☐ Baby very ill after birth.	....
☐ Baby born with physical or mental problems or defects.	....
☐ Death of baby at birth or soon thereafter.	....
☐ Giving up career or ambitions due to pregnancy.	....
☐ Failed attempt at abortion during pregnancy.	....
☐ Successful abortion during pregnancy.	....
☐ Miscarriage(s) during pregnancy.	....
☐ Inability to fall pregnant when you wanted to / infertility.	....
☐ Artificial insemination required.	....
☐ Giving baby away for adoption or foster care.	....

YOUR CHILDHOOD

EVENT	WHEN?
☐ Physical abandonment by parent (one or both) – perceived or actual.	....
☐ Emotional abandonment (or rejection) by parent – perceived or actual (for various reasons, including birth of brother or sister; parents ill; parents constantly working; parents taking care of someone else who required a great deal of attention; parents alcohol or drug-dependent, etc.).	....
☐ Divorce of parents.	....
☐ Adoption / foster care.	....
☐ Being sent to boarding school.	....
☐ Rejection by peers (e.g. for being different in some way).	....
☐ Criticism or abuse by teacher(s).	....
☐ Criticism or abuse by minister or priest or any other authority figure.	....
☐ Physical abuse, assault, violence, torture, deprivation.	....
☐ Sexual abuse / rape / attempted rape.	....
☐ Incest (sexual molestation / rape by family member).	....
☐ Physical neglect.	....
☐ Forced to live with people other than your parents.	....
☐ Alcohol or drug-addicted parent(s).	....
☐ Humiliation – perceived or actual.	....
☐ Severe criticism by adults or parents.	....
☐ Being forced to take on adult responsibilities too soon.	....

DEATH OF LOVED ONES AND OTHERS

Event	When?
☐ Death of mother.	....
☐ Death of father.	....
☐ Death of grandmother.	....
☐ Death of grandfather.	....
☐ Death of brother or sister.	....
☐ Death of an aunt or uncle.	....
☐ Death of a child.	....
☐ Death of a spouse (husband, wife, lover).	....
☐ Death of a friend.	....
☐ Death of a beloved pet.	....
☐ Death of a client or patient.	....
☐ Death of affiliate groups or community members (during catastrophic events, such as war, floods, fire, bomb, terrorism).	....

PAIN CAUSED TO YOUR LOVED ONES

Event	When?
☐ Assault.	....
☐ Rape.	....
☐ Attempted rape.	....
☐ Mugging.	....
☐ Robbery.	....
☐ Life threatened by violent means (e.g. gun, knife, bomb, etc.)	....
☐ Life threatened by disaster (e.g. fire, flood, war, etc.)	....
☐ Physical persecution or torture.	....
☐ Hijacking (car or other vehicle).	....
☐ Kidnapping.	....
☐ Destruction of personal property (e.g. house burned down or through violence).	....
☐ Witnessing or participating in death of or acts of aggression towards others during war or acts of war.	....
☐ Physical pain or disfigurement due to aggression or violence.	....
☐ Physical pain or disfigurement due to accident or disease.	....
☐ Invasive or complicated surgical procedures.	....
☐ Witnessing abuse or bad treatment of a loved one (e.g. your father abused your mother).	....

VIOLENCE TOWARDS, AND VIOLATION OF, YOUR BODY

EVENT	WHEN?
☐ Assault.	....
☐ Rape.	....
☐ Attempted rape.	....
☐ Mugging.	....
☐ Robbery.	....
☐ Life threatened by violent means (e.g. gun, knife, bomb, etc.).	....
☐ Life threatened by disaster (e.g. fire, flood, war, etc.).	....
☐ Witnessing a natural disaster first-hand.	....
☐ Physical persecution or torture.	....
☐ Being hijacked (car or other vehicle).	....
☐ Theft of possessions.	....
☐ Being kidnapped.	....
☐ Destruction of personal property (e.g. house is deliberately burned down, or through violence).	....
☐ Witnessing or participating in war, acts of war or acts of aggression.	....
☐ Physical pain or disfigurement due to aggression or violence.	....
☐ Being bullied by others.	....
☐ Invasive surgery (e.g. hysterectomy, vasectomy, mastectomy, amputation, removal of ovaries, prostate, spleen, any other organ).	....

PAIN THROUGH SOCIAL AGENTS

EVENT	WHEN?
☐ Discrimination or persecution (e.g. racial, political, religious)	....
☐ Being sued for civil or criminal reasons, justifiable or not.	....
☐ Criminal charges, justifiable or not.	....
☐ Prison or jail service.	....
☐ Deportation.	....
☐ Refusal of access to institutions or facilities (e.g. clubs, voting rights, societies, education, medical, employment), i.e. you are deemed socially undesirable or unacceptable.	....
☐ Forced removal from home or community.	....

WORK – CAREER – AMBITIONS

EVENT	WHEN?
☐ Starting a new job.	....
☐ Starting your own business.	....
☐ Spouse/lover starting his/her own business.	....
☐ Being fired from your job.	....
☐ Being retrenched from your job.	....
☐ Being sexually, emotionally or physically harassed at work.	....
☐ Firing of spouse/lover from his/her job.	....
☐ Retrenchment of spouse/lover from his/her job.	....
☐ Harassment of spouse/lover at work, sexually, emotionally or physically.	....
☐ Retirement due to age.	....
☐ Retirement due to age of spouse/lover.	....
☐ Retirement due to illness or other non-age reasons.	....
☐ Retirement due to illness (or other non-age reasons) of spouse/lover.	....
☐ Losing your own business.	....
☐ Being forced out of your own business.	....
☐ Being forced out of someone else's company.	....
☐ Loss of your spouse/lover's business.	....
☐ Selling your own business.	....
☐ Own (or spouse/lover's) business facing bankruptcy or other serious threats.	....
☐ Periods of involuntary unemployment (self).	....
☐ Periods of involuntary unemployment (spouse/lover).	....
☐ Demotions.	....
☐ Own career progress blocked for some reason.	....
☐ Giving up career and dreams for family.	....
☐ Promotions.	....
☐ Doing a job you did not feel competent to do.	....
☐ Giving up a job or career you loved (for whatever reason).	....
☐ Doing a job or career that bores/bored you.	....
☐ Being forced to do a job (e.g. because you are the sole breadwinner, parental insistence, need the money, etc.).	....
☐ Persistent conflict with superiors, partners or colleagues.	....
☐ Compromising yourself to keep or get a job.	....
☐ Threats of dismissal when you really needed the job.	....

FINANCES

Event	When?
☐ Loss of income.	....
☐ Serious decline in value of investments.	....
☐ Serious decline of financial status.	....
☐ Insolvency.	....
☐ Bankruptcy.	....
☐ Liquidation.	....
☐ Repossession of household goods due to inability to pay.	....
☐ Heavy debt load.	....
☐ Bond.	....
☐ Being overinsured.	....
☐ Being underinsured.	....
☐ No insurance.	....
☐ Inadequate medical scheme benefits.	....
☐ High medical costs to pay.	....
☐ Bad credit rating.	....
☐ Overextended credit.	
☐ No, or little, savings to get you through bad times.	....
☐ Pension inadequate or absent.	....
☐ Theft, defrauding, or robbery of your money, savings, etc.	....
☐ Irregular income.	....
☐ Not having enough money to ensure basic survival.	....

FRIENDSHIPS

Event	When?
☐ Losing a friend due to relocation (moving away).	....
☐ Losing a friend due to betrayal of trust.	....
☐ Losing a friend due to an argument or misunderstanding.	....
☐ Watching a friend suffer pain or disease.	....
☐ Betraying a friend, due to necessity or other reasons.	....
☐ Being rejected by a friend for someone else.	....
☐ Refusal of friendship by someone you wanted as a friend.	....

INTIMATE RELATIONSHIPS AND SEXUALITY

Event	When?
☐ Divorce.	....
☐ Separation.	....
☐ Being told by your partner that you are not sexually attractive.	....
☐ Being told you are not a good lover.	....
☐ Discovering you are no longer sexually attracted to your partner.	....
☐ Continual emotional abuse towards you by partner.	....
☐ Continual physical abuse towards you by partner.	....
☐ Continual mental abuse towards you by partner.	....
☐ Hurting someone you love and feeling unable to stop it.	....
☐ Breaking off a relationship and realising that this was a mistake.	....
☐ Being stood up by your partner (e.g. at the altar).	....
☐ Discovering your partner is in love with someone else.	....
☐ Discovering your partner is having a long-term affair with someone else.	....
☐ Loving someone who will not (or cannot) commit to you.	....
☐ Forced separation due to distance.	....
☐ Serious cultural or religious differences between you and your partner.	....
☐ Interfering family members.	....
☐ Betrayal of trust by partner.	....
☐ Betraying your partner's trust.	....
☐ Living with an alcoholic partner or drug addict.	....
☐ Living with a partner who is a compulsive gambler.	....
☐ Living with a partner who has a serious psychological problem.	....
☐ Living with a partner with a terminal or serious disease.	....
☐ Discovering your partner is attracted to people of a different gender to you.	....
☐ Knowing you are gay, and trying to maintain a heterosexual relationship.	....
☐ Living together for the sake of the children when the relationship is over.	....
☐ Suppressing a secret fetish (e.g. cross-dressing) in a relationship.	....
☐ Being forced to marry someone you do not love.	....
☐ Being forced to break off a relationship with someone you love (e.g. through family pressure).	....
☐ Losing the one you love to someone else.	....
☐ Your partner discovering you are having an affair with someone else.	....
☐ Having a secret affair with someone else.	....
☐ Loving and living with someone in a relationship that is rejected by family or friends.	....

☐ Sexual impotency or frigidity of yourself. ....

☐ Sexual impotency or frigidity of partner. ....

☐ Discovering you have a sexually transmitted disease. ....

☐ Discovering your partner has a sexually transmitted disease. ....

☐ Inability to find someone to love or who will love you. ....

☐ Disputes with or harassment by ex-partner. ....

EDUCATION AND AMBITIONS

EVENT WHEN?

☐ Wanting to study further and being prevented from doing so. ....

☐ Being rejected when applying for entrance to a career you want. ....

☐ Being forced to study something in which you're not interested. ....

☐ Failing an important test or exam. ....

☐ Realising you are not capable of doing something you want to do. ....

☐ Being told you're stupid or incapable. ....

☐ Achieving something and realising that you cannot achieve any higher. ....

☐ Stating your ambitions and being criticised or ridiculed for it. ....

☐ Sacrificing your ambitions for the family. ....

☐ Not having enough money to pursue your chosen ambitions. ....

☐ Following a specific career when you really want to do something else. ....

☐ Being rejected by family or friends for choosing a specific career or field of study. ....

☐ Losing friends or family due to promotion or advancement in your career or studies. ....

☐ Being punished for failing. ....

☐ Being punished for succeeding. ....

☐ Negative comparison of abilities with brother, sister or someone else. ....

☐ Being told you will never amount to anything. ....

☐ Being told you will be loved only if you succeed. ....

☐ Witnessing the humiliation, rejection or pain of someone for failing. ....

☐ Witnessing the humiliation, rejection or pain of someone for succeeding. ....

☐ Promising someone you love that you will follow a specific career to please or win his or her approval. ....

HEALTH AND ACCIDENTS

EVENT	WHEN?
☐ Receiving a diagnosis of a life-threatening disease.	....
☐ Being told by a doctor you're probably going to die.	....
☐ Being told by a doctor that the illness you have cannot be cured or reversed.	....
☐ Seeing a loved one suffer and die from a serious disease.	....
☐ Losing the function of some part of your body (e.g. through paralysis, blindness or deafness).	....
☐ Injury during an accident.	....
☐ Hospitalisation.	....
☐ Pain – on-and-off (intermittent) and recurrent.	....
☐ Pain – chronic (almost all the time).	....
☐ Failure of treatment or surgery.	....
☐ Recurrence of disease symptoms you thought had gone.	....
☐ Getting old.	....

■ ASSIGNMENT

The sole purpose of the following assignment is to reveal the decision(s) you made following the loss event(s) in the three-year period before your symptoms developed.

We are presenting two different approaches to access these decisions. The first is an emotionally intensive process, which can take several hours to complete per event. Not only will you uncover the decisions you made, but you will also release many of the emotions associated with the event.

The second method is less intensive, and the chances of discovering the decision(s) made during these loss events are fairly good, but not so good as in the first method. Also, there is not as much emotional release as with the first method.

The third method is used to complete methods one and two. It can be done either immediately after methods one or two, or you can do it in another session.

Please do all the exercises for each loss event you identified as having happened within the three-year period before your illness symptoms developed.

GENERAL GUIDELINES

1. Choose the method you are most comfortable with. If you have any doubt about your ability to deal with the loss events, please do not hesitate to consult a counsellor or mental health professional for assistance.

2. There are essentially three 'levels' of an event: the physical details (what happened, in time sequence), how you felt at different moments in the event, and the thoughts you had and decisions you made in moments of great emotion or stress. Generally speaking, the unconscious decisions and thoughts emerge only after the emotions are released. Therefore, it is necessary to release emotions in order to access unconscious decisions. The act of writing (or speaking) about the exact details will help to release many of the trapped emotions, which will be of great benefit to your immune system.

3. We strongly recommend that you drink plenty of water during this process, which seems to assist in releasing some of the physical stress chemicals.

4. Do not do these processes if you are not sure that you have enough time to complete them, which may take a few hours. Ensure that you have privacy, and that you do not have other commitments for a few hours. Switch off the phone.

METHOD 1: FULL RELEASE

Intensity level: High

Duration: Can take a few hours per event investigated.

Alternative approaches: Talking out loud with someone who will record what you say.

Materials: Pens, plenty of writing paper, tissues.

Cautions: Impatience – you will need to write and rewrite the sequence of events several times. Pay attention to details.

Tip: When writing down the sequence of events, leave enough space between each line of writing so that you can insert more information later. This will cut down on the amount of times you have to rewrite it completely.

STEP 1   **The physical facts of the event.**
Write down the physical description of the event in this stage of
the process, step by step, factually.

1. Where were you, and what were you doing, before anything
   happened?
   e.g. *'I was sitting in my living room, watching television. I was wear-
   ing my pyjamas, eating popcorn out of a red box.'*

2. What happened to let you know something was about to happen?
   e.g. *'I heard the dog barking outside, and it didn't sound like a normal bark – it was a stronger, deeper bark than normal.'*

3. What happened next? i.e., what did you do, see, hear, smell, etc.?
   Describe it step by step.
   e.g. *'I put the popcorn down next to the couch and stood up. I opened
   the curtain to see what the dog was barking at. I couldn't see anything
   because it was dark.'*

4. Then what happened? Step by step, remember all the details, even
   small details, until the moment of shock, pain, or loss.

5. Describe exactly what happened – physically – in terms of what
   you saw, smelled, heard, did, what was done or said to you, to
   cause the pain, loss or shock.

6. Then what happened? Describe what happened physically, in
   detail, until you knew it was 'over'. How did you know it was 'over'?

   You may need to repeat this several times until you have all the
   physical details, in time sequence. Include body movements,
   sounds, sights, heat and cold, the direction from which these came,
   and so forth. This step creates the platform to investigate the emotional and mental processes during the event.

STEP 2   **Write down your feelings before, during and after the event.**
With your detailed physical description of the event in hand,
rewrite it, and this time add how you were feeling – emotions and
physical sensations – during each step of the event. This includes

describing how you were feeling before the event started, and also after you knew it was over.

Be very careful to write down exactly how you felt. If you felt conflicting emotions, write this down too, and what all the conflicting emotions were. This step can be very emotional. Remember to drink water.

STEP 3   **Write down your thoughts before, during and after the event.** Rewrite the entire sequence of events again, but this time add exactly what you were thinking – use the exact words that were going through your mind – at each stage of the event, including before and afterwards. Pay particular and careful attention to those moments of greatest pain, shock or sense of loss.

Sometimes, we do not think a thought, but rather accept something that someone else says. This is just as important as actual self-generated thoughts.

For example: If someone tells you you are useless, there are two types of thought you can have in response:

- *Active thought response:* You can think (and say) something about it, either to confirm or oppose the statement;
- *Passive thought response:* You can think nothing, and just accept the statement as true, at that moment.

When writing about your thoughts during each part of the event, please include both types of thought responses – the active and passive thought responses.

The purpose of this intensive exercise is to bring into your conscious mind what had been placed into your unconscious during the loss event. Oddly enough, an indication that you have brought the entire event into consciousness is boredom with the process and the event itself. Irritation and frustration indicate that there is more to reveal. Keep writing until you get bored.

STEP 4   **Turn the decision around.**

Write down the decisions you made during the most intense parts of the loss event. There may be only one, or several. Repeat the following process with each decision or thought:

Each decision or thought presents itself as being 'true', even if it is objectively illogical. For example, a wonderful mother – according to her children and everyone else – may insist that she is a bad mother; a very creative and successful businessman may insist that he is useless and a failure. Why?

After the event, you may have begun to find evidence to support the thought or decision made during the 20-second dip, which then became a belief. In other words, the thoughts or decisions entered the RAS and began to direct your attention to only those things that supported their 'truth'. All evidence that opposed this belief was ignored.

Now it is time to reverse this process, not by denying or ignoring it, but by expanding it with evidence that it is not always true, or even hardly ever true, if at all.

1. Write down each thought or decision as clearly and exactly as it was when it was formed. Use one page of paper per thought or decision.
2. Now ask yourself, 'Is this really true?'
3. Divide the page into two columns, with the following two headings: 'Evidence that it is sometimes true', 'Evidence that it is sometimes not true'.
4. Under the first heading, list all the evidence that supports the belief. Number each item on the list. For example:
   - 'I am useless at fixing the car'
   - 'I don't spend enough time with the children.'
   You can list as many examples as you like.
5. Under the second heading, list any and all evidence that proves that the belief is not true. However, you need to find evidence for this in exactly the same area of your life that you wrote about in the first column. This may be difficult at first, as your RAS has not been providing you with awareness of items for this list!

Example 1:

THOUGHT – DECISION

e.g. *'I am useless'*

Is this really true?

Evidence that it is sometimes true	Evidence that it is sometimes not true
1. I am useless at fixing the car.	1. I am clever enough to get someone else to fix it.
2. I don't spend enough time with my children.	2. When I spend time with my children, I give them all my attention. This is more important to them than lots of time.

Example 2:

THOUGHT – DECISION

e.g. *'I am going to die'*

Is this really true?

Evidence that it is sometimes true	Evidence that it is sometimes not true
1. I have heard and read of other people dying from this illness.	1. I have now read and heard of several people who have stayed healthy with this illness.
2. When I went for my last blood analysis, it showed that my T-cells are getting low.	2. David also had low T-cells, but his T-cells increased afterwards.

Get the idea?

6. Write down the conclusions you come to about yourself and the world when you look at all the evidence.

We are not trying to encourage 'positive thinking', which can be a form of denying all the factual evidence. Instead, we are encouraging you to examine all the evidence and come to your own conclusions. We refer to this as being 'realistically positive'.

STEP 5   **Release blame and regain your power.**
This is the final stage of releasing attachments to the loss event. It does not need to occur immediately after steps 1 to 4, but does need to occur soon afterwards. The full instructions are contained under Method 3: *Release blame and regain your power* (page 135), which follows Method 2, below.

METHOD 2: PARTIAL RELEASE

Sometimes, a loss event can be so traumatic that you feel you cannot face it, at least not now. However, the decisions made in that event somehow need to be accessed. For this purpose, we use a 'dissociated' approach in this method.

As stated in the introduction to the assignment for this chapter, this method is not as reliable as the first method, nor will you experience as much of the immune benefits that come from releasing all the emotions attached to the event. However, for some people it is more important at this stage to simply uncover the decision(s) they made following the event, to get their personal journey started.

STEP 1   **Write down a brief description of the event.**
Include basic information such as the date place, and time. Give it a descriptive title, such as 'Diagnosis of cancer'.

STEP 2   **Imagine what someone else would feel if that happened to him/her.**
We are referring to the emotion as the event is happening, not afterwards, particularly focusing on the most intense moments.

Examples: Terror
Anger
Helplessness
Rejection
Humiliation
Paralysis
Abandonment

STEP 3   Write down what someone else probably would have decided
          about themselves as a result of an event like this.
          Always put the thought or decision in the first person
          ('I', 'Me', 'My').

Examples: 'I am not good enough'
          'I am not wanted/I don't belong'
          'I am helpless'
          'I'm going to die'
          'My life is over'
          'I am bad'
          'I am not loved/lovable'
          'He/she will never love me'
          'I am useless/a failure'
          'I am never going to make it'
          'I'm not a real man/woman'
          'Nothing I do is good enough'

STEP 4   Follow the same instructions for Step 4, as in Method 1.

STEP 5   Release blame and regain your power.
          This step does not need to occur immediately after Steps 1 to 4,
          but does need to occur soon afterwards. The full instructions are
          contained under Method 3, below.

          You may find that the completion of Method 3 allows you to face
          the intensity of Method 1, because it may reduce the sense of being
          overwhelmed by the loss event.

METHOD 3: RELEASE, BLAME AND REGAIN YOUR POWER

There are two sensations caused by stressful past events that may get you
stuck and cause ongoing stress:

- **Emptiness:** When you lost something you valued – a person, career,
  dream, dignity, identity, sense of purpose, ability – and this has left a
  'hole' inside that you have seemed unable to fill since;
- **Being overwhelmed:** When something happened to you – an assault, too
  many demands on you, rape, war, an accident, devastation – that caused
  you to feel powerless to respond. The event still seems too much to bear.

Past events cannot be changed. However, you can change the feelings of emptiness or of being overwhelmed.

In some events, both sensations are present, such as losing someone you loved, and then having to take care of a business you had no idea how to handle. However, in such cases, each feeling – emptiness and being overwhelmed – needs to be dealt with separately.

STEP 1   **Name the 'part of me' from the past.**
The part of you that experienced the specific loss event is a memory. To distinguish between the 'me' that is here and now – the 'real me' – and the memory itself, it is necessary to give the 'past me' a name or description. Write this down.

Examples: The sad 23-year-old me.
The part of me that is terrified.
The rape victim me.
The retrenched me.
The utterly empty me.

STEP 2   **Who caused this loss or sense of being overwhelmed?**
In this step, it is OK to blame someone for your loss or being overwhelmed. It is essential that you are honest about this. Don't say *'Well, I guess it was really my fault for not doing ...'* when in your heart you blame someone, rightly or wrongly. If you blame someone, then name him or her. Yes, you can blame yourself, but you need to be very sure that you are being honest when you are doing this.

Please note that if your loss or being overwhelmed was caused by an organisation or institution – e.g. government, committee, company – then identify a person who represents this organisation in your mind. Write this down.

Examples: Mr Green (the manager who retrenched me).
The man who raped me.
God (who took my baby away).
Bob (my husband who divorced me).

My mother (who abandoned me by dying).
Mrs Brown (who drove the car).
The President (who ordered my son to go to war).
Myself (for smoking too many cigarettes).

STEP 3   **Why did they do it? Speculate on their inner motives.**
It is important to allow yourself to speculate freely, and not block this speculation by being overly 'reasonable'. In effect, you are being asked to step inside the head of the people you blame, to identify the fears, insecurities and weaknesses that caused them to do what they did. This doesn't have to be 'true' – all it needs to be is under-standable (not the same as acceptable) to you. Write this down.

Examples: He fired me because he was told to cut down staff, and he was afraid of standing up to the Board, in case he lost his job too.
He raped me because he wanted to prove that he was powerful. Obviously, he felt weak inside, and needed to prove to himself and others that he wasn't.
God took my baby because He doesn't care.
Bob left me because he was too afraid of his real feelings, and he didn't want to face up to the fact that he wasn't young anymore.
Mother died because she was tired of life and didn't love life enough to stay.
Mrs Brown didn't look where she was driving because she was drunk, and she didn't care about other people – only her own needs.
The President ordered my son to go to die in war because he was afraid he would lose the next election if he didn't give in to the demands of those crazy right-wing voters who voted him in the last time. He just wanted to hold on to power, no matter what the cost.
I smoked too many cigarettes because I was stupid enough to think that the dangers didn't apply to me.

STEP 4   **What did they need – inside – to have acted differently?**
Identify – in your mind and heart – what resource (belief, attitude, feeling) they would have needed to act differently. Write this down.

Examples: Courage.
Feeling loved for being who they were.
Self-confidence.
Joy.
Caring.
Trusting.
Awareness of the consequences.

STEP 5   **Find that resource inside yourself.**
In this step you are asked to look inside yourself for a time when you felt the courage, being loved for who you were, confidence, joy, caring, trusting, awareness, etc. In other words, find inside *yourself* the very thing that the people you are blaming needed in order to have acted differently. Awareness of what was 'missing' in them means that you know or have experienced that same 'thing'. Write this down.

STEP 6   **Relive this feeling, now.**
Close your eyes. Try to remember – as best you can – that experience when you felt the resource, e.g. the time when you felt the self-confidence, courage or caring. It helps if you lean slightly forwards as you sit, with your eyes pointed downwards, even though they are closed.

Spend a few minutes recalling the place – what you saw, heard, smelled – how you were standing or sitting or walking, and then focus on how you were feeling in your body as you felt this resource feeling.

The feeling does not have to be strong or vivid.

STEP 7   **Give the resource feeling a form.**
With your eyes still closed, describe this feeling as follows:
- **Where in your body do you feel it?** Be specific: eg. chest, stomach, hands, running down my spine.
- **Colour:** Pretend that the feeling has a colour.
- **Size and shape:** Describe it, e.g. round ball, about the size of a football.

Open your eyes and write down this description of the feeling. The shape, size and colour of the resource feeling are your 'anchor' (reminder) of that feeling. This means you can simply close your eyes at any time and recall that feeling.

STEP 8: **Recreate and expand this feeling.**
Close your eyes once again, and – using your description of the shape, size and colour of the resource feeling – allow yourself to experience that feeling once again.

- Now, imagine that the colour gets a little brighter. Then, imagine that the shape of the feeling is twice as large. This does not require effort, only imagination.
- Make the colour even brighter and the shape twice as large again. This will intensify the feeling.

STEP 9 **Give some of the feeling away.**
1. With your eyes still closed, imagine the people you blame standing near you. If you are afraid of those people, imagine that they are standing a safe distance away.
2. Imagine that you can take half of the feeling you have created and give it to those people. Remember, this is the resource feeling that they would have needed to act differently.
3. Double the size of the feeling inside you again. Give them half again. Double the size of the feeling inside you again.
4. Repeat this process of giving half and replenishing it within yourself, until you sense (feel, suspect, know) that the other people have received enough of this resource feeling to have acted differently were the painful situation to arise again right now.
5. When you are satisfied, let the image of those people fade away, and open your eyes.

STEP 10: **Assess how you feel.**
You have essentially 'given' something to someone 'for' what they did to you, i.e. 'for-given'. Write down how you feel to have the power to give back to the person who hurt you, in a way that serves both you and them.

Step 11: Extract the gift from the loss or overwhelming experience.
Write down what have you learned or gained from the past experience. This may seem to be a difficult question, but it is essential that you can identify one valuable lesson from the experience that will benefit you from now on.

Example: I learned how much I can care about someone.
If that hadn't happened, I wouldn't have met John.
I have learned to ask questions, instead of just trusting authorities.

During the next few chapters, consider the connection between these potential trigger events and your illness. This may not be immediately apparent. Furthermore, become aware of how often you think similar thoughts, on a day-to-day basis, and how this relates to the SAM or HPAC mind–body system. Please note that the list of stressful events has further uses, especially in Chapter 10. So, don't throw the list away yet!

EFFECTIVE AND INEFFECTIVE COPING METHODS

Human beings tend to be creatures of habit (refer to our friend, the RAS, on page 109). One of the keys to successful Applied PNI therapy is identifying your coping skills, ie, why you cope the way you do and whether your habitual method of coping is beneficial or detrimental to your health.

However, one of the main findings of PNI research is that there is no such thing as a generic 'perfect' or ideal coping style for all situations. In fact, **certain ways of coping may be ideal in one situation and detrimental in another. Effective coping is thus contextual – it all depends on the situation itself.**

For example, during the 1970s, a nuclear reactor near Three Mile Island (USA) had serious malfunction problems and there was a real likelihood that the surrounding communities would be exposed to radiation. PNI researchers utilised this situation to examine how people cope with such a chronic real threat. They found that people who used emotion-focused coping – focusing on how they felt and talking about how they felt – experienced much less stress than those people who used either denial coping (pretending that everything was fine and ignoring the problem) or problem-focused coping (i.e. looking for solutions and being action-oriented) *[1]*.

Therefore, in chronic (or long-term) stressful situations, it is more effective to deal with how you feel instead of trying to deny what is happening, or trying to fix situations that cannot be fixed, or to control them.

However, when we examine short-term stressful situations, PNI research indicates something quite different. **Under conditions where the stress is of short duration – such as going to hospital for an operation – denial coping and problem-focused coping are more effective in terms of how much stress is experienced.** Furthermore, under such short-term conditions, emotion-focused coping simply worsens the stress *[2]*.

It is important to realise that rigid coping styles do not serve you in dealing with disease. There are situations in which it's appropriate to talk about how you feel and there are other situations that require practical action and solutions with little emotional involvement [3].

How should people support you?

What does this mean in terms of social support? If, for example, you went to hospital for minor surgery, how would you want your friends and family to support you to make the event less stressful?

According to Robert Costanza and colleagues [4], if your friends were to chat to you about how you were feeling (emotion-focused coping), this would increase your stress. However, if they were to talk to you about the weather or about practical problem-focused issues, such as the actual and factual sequence of events involved in the operation, this would decrease your stress. In essence, short-term situations require problem-focused or denial coping to keep stress levels low.

When dealing with chronically stressful situations, the reverse is true. Denial coping and problem-focused support are detrimental whereas emotion-focused support is beneficial. Therefore, it is important for friends and family to understand that they need to offer different kinds of support in different situations.

Your coping habits

How do you cope in general? Most people would like to believe that they cope effectively, but in reality we all tend to have habits of coping that sometimes work and sometimes do not. More importantly, we all tend to have coping habits that do not change according to the situation. It is this inflexibility (or habit) that is the problem.

In the following questionnaire (Shadows, [5]) you are going to assess your coping habits. Please do not confuse this with a 'personality assessment'! Your personality is basically your expression of identity, which is unchanging. However, your coping habits were all learned and developed over time, and can change again.

The purpose of this coping assessment is to discover your unconscious habits of coping, and then to examine whether they help your body to heal or help it to be sick.

In the assessment you are required to rate how accurately each statement applies to you, particularly in the last year or so. Please be honest – there is no point in deceiving yourself. As you will discover in the analysis of this Shadows assessment, there are literally no right or wrong answers and comparisons are not made with someone else. There is no 'normal' or 'average' for any of the questions. It is simply an assessment of your thoughts, feelings and behaviour, and provides an important foundation for further exploration.

How to answer each question:

Indicate how accurately each statement describes you. Each person experiences certain feelings or acts in certain ways, depending on the circumstances or the people involved. When deciding how accurate each specific statement is for you, try to include your thoughts, feelings and actions in most circumstances, such as at work, with friends, and at home. Circle 0, 1, 2, 3 or 4, whichever is true for each specific question.

**PLEASE ANSWER ALL THE QUESTIONS.
DO NOT SKIP ANY QUESTIONS.**

Does not describe me at all (almost never) = **0**
Describes me a little (not often, but it does happen sometimes) = **1**
Describes me sometimes (about half the time) = **2**
Describes me quite well (often, but not always) = **3**
Describes me very well (very often, almost always) = **4**

O-I:　　　　　　　　　　　　　　　　.............................

1. Few people can stop me from doing something
   I have planned.　　　　　　　　　　0　1　2　3　4
2. I can be quite stubborn when I want to be.　　0　1　2　3　4
3. When I have made up my mind about
   something, no one can change my mind.　　0　1　2　3　4
4. I don't mind doing things. I just don't like
   being told that I must do them.　　　　0　1　2　3　4
5. When someone gets pushy and demanding
   with me, I stand firm and will not budge.　　0　1　2　3　4

C-D:　　　　　　　　　　　　　　　　.............................

1. When I'm with people I don't know, I become quiet
   and withdrawn and just observe.　　　0　1　2　3　4
2. To be embarrassed in front of other people is one
   of the worst things I can imagine.　　0　1　2　3　4
3. I like to look good – when I walk past a mirror or
   window, I quickly check to see that I look alright.　　0　1　2　3　4
4. I feel that no one really knows who I really am
   deep inside.　　　　　　　　　　　0　1　2　3　4
5. I struggle to talk about my feelings. I prefer to be
   objective and think about things.　　0　1　2　3　4

A-F:　　　　　　　　　　　　　　　　.............................

1. When things go wrong around me, I feel I am
   somehow responsible.　　　　　　0　1　2　3　4
2. My feelings of self-doubt stop me from doing many
   of the things I want to do.　　　　0　1　2　3　4
3. The people who know me well often tell me I need
   to gain more self-confidence.　　　0　1　2　3　4
4. Even when things are going well, I feel anxious,
   and I don't know why.　　　　　　0　1　2　3　4
5. I find myself repeatedly checking the things I do
   because I know I could make a mistake.　　0　1　2　3　4

I-R:

....

1. I have much to do, and there is no time to waste.   0   I   2   3   4
2. I get frustrated with people around me because they move too slowly.   0   I   2   3   4
3. I feel a sense of urgency, because there is just not enough time to get everything done.   0   I   2   3   4
4. I feel tired and stressed.   0   I   2   3   4
5. When I get bored, I tap my fingers or feet.   0   I   2   3   4

B-S:

....

1. People don't know how much I have done for them. They take me for granted.   0   I   2   3   4
2. It's hard to find someone who understands my special circumstances and who can help me.   0   I   2   3   4
3. Things have been done to me that can never be made right by anyone.   0   I   2   3   4
4. I think I have bad luck because things just go wrong in my life – more so than for the average person.   0   I   2   3   4
5. I feel my choices are limited because of circumstances.   0   I   2   3   4

N-E:

....

1. The thought that I might end up with nothing worries me.   0   I   2   3   4
2. Shopping makes me feel much better when things are going wrong in my life.   0   I   2   3   4
3. When I have indulged and spoilt myself, I feel guilty afterwards.   0   I   2   3   4
4. It worries me that I may never find the satisfaction that I'm seeking.   0   I   2   3   4
5. I think about how happy I will be if I had everything.   0   I   2   3   4

F-D: ....

1. I have feelings of desperation.   **0   I   2   3   4**
2. Even though I try to be in control of myself and situations,
   I find that I somehow lose control.   **0   I   2   3   4**
3. I have emotional or physical outbursts which are
   destructive, and which scare other people and me.   **0   I   2   3   4**
4. I have thoughts that I will not live very long.   **0   I   2   3   4**
5. I do risky things, such as driving fast or trusting people
   I know I shouldn't, and similar risky activities.   **0   I   2   3   4**

Scoring your Shadows

The Shadows questionnaire contains seven groups of questions, each with five questions.

STEP I   **Add the scores for each section**
           Write each total in the top right-hand open box.

Example:

O-I: **Total = 13** ....

1. Question   0   I   2   ③   4
2. Question   0   ①   2   3   4
3. Question   0   I   2   3   ④
4. Question   0   I   ②   3   4
5. Question   0   I   2   ③   4

The maximum score per group of questions is 20.
The minimum score per group is 0.

STEP 2   **Calculate the eighth Shadow**
           You now have the total scores for 7 of the 8 Shadows.
           But there is one more Shadow (P-R), which is calculated by subtracting the total of O-I from 20:
           20 minus (O-I total:)....................=....................(P-R total).

Example: If O-I = 13, then **P-R** = (20 minus 13) = **7**

STEP 3   Transfer the totals to the Score Summary below
          To avoid confusion, please follow the instructions:
          1. First transfer the O-I score.
          2. Then transfer the P-R score that you calculated in step 2.
          3. Finally, transfer the remaining 6 total scores, checking to see that
             you transfer them to the correct category box.

SCORE SUMMARY

Code	Your Score	Shadow Name
O-I	....	Obstinate – Inflexible
P-R	...................(Calculated)	Passionless – Reasonable
C-D	....	Controlling – Distant
A-F	....	Apologising – Failure
I-R	....	Impatient – Restless
B-S	....	Blaming – Suffering
N-E	....	Never Enough
F-D	....	Frantic – Destructive

What is a 'normal' score?

There is no 'normal' score to compare your scores to. Each person's scores are relative to their own life, not to anyone else's. The ranking – which Shadow is strongest or weakest for you – tends to stay the same regardless of the presence or absence of current stress. The scores will change when you work with the Shadows. In other words, forget about comparing your scores to some 'normal' score. It doesn't exist. If your highest score is 8 or 26, this makes no difference to the impact the Shadows have on your life.

Why are all my scores so high?

If you are going through a stressful time, all your Shadow scores will tend to be higher than those of someone who is not stressed. When you are less stressed, the scores may be lower. However, the ranking (order of highest to lowest) tends to stay the same, regardless of stress levels. Simply focus on the ranking – highest to lowest – regardless of the high scores.

What if all my scores are very low?

People with high levels of *Controlling–Distant* (C-D) tend to have lower scores on all Shadows, simply because their dominant coping style causes them to be less aware of their emotions per se. If your scores are all low, then you will probably find that one of the highest – even if the score is 2 or 3 – is C-D. By its very nature, the C-D Shadow suppresses emotional awareness, leading to low awareness of or sensitivity to emotions. In this case, simply rank the Shadows from highest to lowest, regardless of the low levels of the scores.

Important precautions before you read further

There are a few things we need to set straight before you read any further about your Shadows.

- **Everyone has all eight Shadows, to some extent or the other.**
  Some Shadows dominate all areas of your life, whereas others are strong in some areas and weak in other areas. However, for the moment, we are interested only in those Shadows that are your strongest ones, as they are most likely to have a major influence on your health.

- **Shadows can change over time.** Once you begin to understand and work with your Shadows, they weaken, and other Shadows may emerge.

- **Your Shadows are not your personality!** People are accustomed to being assessed as a specific 'type of person'. The Shadows are not that kind of assessment, nor are they an indication of who you really are. Quite the opposite is true: your Shadows are learned methods of coping. They are not inborn or genetic, nor are they any indication of your 'true self' or potential. To reinforce this thought, it is useful to refer to each Shadow as a 'part' of you.

- **Various factors influence how high the scores will be at any given period of time.** Your scores reflect how strong that specific Shadow is at this moment, and how strong it has been for a while. During very stressful periods, you will find that you feel more sensitive and more aware of how you think and feel, and this will automatically push your scores higher. During less stressful periods, the same Shadows will have lower scores but the ranking will tend to be the same.

- **Yes, there are 'good' and 'bad' aspects of each Shadow.** Also, specific Shadows may be helpful in certain illnesses and detrimental in others. It all depends on the specific condition. Therefore, before you get upset and disturbed by your Shadows, remember that the only important question is: 'Does this Shadow help or hinder my health?'

  We believe that there is no such thing as 'normal', except in textbooks and theory. Nor are you expected to change those Shadows you do not want to change and which work for you. For example, the O-I (Obstinate–Inflexible) Shadow and the I-R (Impatient–Restless) Shadow in combination may be beneficial in keeping viral infections, such as HIV, at bay, but could prove destructive when dealing with a heart condition.

- **In a specific individual, specific Shadows tend to remain higher than others for long periods of time, even for many years.** The reason is simple. Owing to events in your past, you have developed ways of coping. If these learned methods of coping are effective, you will hold onto them. Over time, they become a habit – you probably do not even remember that you did not always behave or feel that way. As a result, you tend to believe that this is the way you are. This is simply not true. Your Shadows are simply who you believe you are.

The difference between saying *'I am my Shadows'* and *'I have certain Shadows'* may seem unimportant, or just a game with words. However, the difference between what you believe you are, and what you actually are, is probably the most important principle of this entire book. When you say or believe that you are a certain way, you automatically lock yourself into a specific identity. This limits your possibilities for change.

It also implies that you are a helpless victim in terms of the forces and factors that led to the forming of that Shadow in your past. Once again, this is untrue and deeply disempowering. When you feel that you can do nothing to change who you are, you are forced to find some way of making that specific problematic characteristic 'right'.

For example, if you score high on the *Obstinate–Inflexible* Shadow, you will probably defend that Shadow, simply because you believe it is the way you are, and not merely a habit you have. It is fascinating to observe how people justify their Shadow habits and develop rational reasons for why their Shadows are 'good' or 'right' or 'reasonable'. This is a defence mechanism.

What is more important: to be 'right' or happy and healthy?

Not everything applies to you, as each person's development is different. However, in our experience, the descriptions offered are generally accurate to a fair degree. In the following pages are stereotypical descriptions of each Shadow, how they typically develop and how they usually affect your thoughts, feelings and behaviour. Some of the information you will not like. But before you dismiss it, take some time to consider whether it is true for you or not.

Which Shadow to focus on

STEP 1   **O-I (Obstinate–Inflexible) or P-R (Passionless–Reasonable)**
The scores of O-I and P-R are dependent on each other: the higher the one, the lower the other. There are only two possible score situations:

- **O-I score higher than P-R:** Regardless of what the scores are of the other Shadows, include O-I in your personal analysis and work.
- **P-R score higher that O-I:** Regardless of what the scores are of the other Shadows, you must include P-R in your personal analysis and work.

STEP 2   **The remaining six Shadows (C-D, A-F, I-R, B-S, N-E and F-D)**
Select the two highest scoring Shadows.
If you can't distinguish between two Shadows with the same score, then include them both in your assessment.

☐ SHADOW 1: OBSTINATE–INFLEXIBLE (O-I)
'No! You can't make me!'

KEY ISSUE: *Inflexibility; a rigid, often inappropriate, coping style; rebelliousness against perceived authority.*

CAUSE: *Based on the core fear that other people are trying to remove your choices. Therefore, you believe that you must defend your choices, even when they harm you, at all costs.*

You are plain stubborn! You think your stubbornness is a good thing, because it's the source of your determination, right? Well, perhaps not. It all depends on the issue or problem at hand. Certainly, being determined and inflexible can be a valuable quality when people are trying to push you around or when you have an important goal to achieve. However, there is a 'dark side' to this quality, namely being inflexible and obstinate to your detriment. For example, if you have a high score for the *Obstinate–Inflexible* Shadow, it makes your other Shadows stronger and more rigid.

But what is the cause of this inflexibility and obstinacy? Generally, there are three patterns of development, any one of which can result in its formation.

- **The stalling tactic:** As a child, you may not have been informed of changes, such as being dumped with the baby-sitter without warning, or there may have been sudden changes in your environment, so you became anxious and felt out of control. Maybe you also felt betrayed by your parents (or guardians) and became mistrusting of change and new experiences. One way of trying to regain choice and control over such situations would have been to throw tantrums and be 'difficult'. The reason was simple. By delaying the event, you would have had time to think about things, which would have allowed you some sense of control and choice. In this scenario, the actions or statements such as 'No – I won't! You can't make me!' served to buy time and became a stalling tactic.

- **The protection of personal integrity:** This is quite a common scenario. As a child, you may have displayed a talent or ability – music, sport, etc. – and a parent or teacher tried to 'hijack' your talent and to control the direction of this talent.

  For example, you may have had an unusual talent for playing the piano and loved music. A parent, owing to his or her own unfulfilled abilities, may have become demanding and insistent that you practised five hours a day, playing only the music that the parent or teacher thought 'right'. This parent or teacher may have drained all the joy and pleasure out of the talent and, in an attempt to regain some sense of control and personal integrity, you may have put your foot down and refused to play the piano ever again. Once again, you were saying: 'No! You can't make me!'

- **The silent resistant fighter:** This may have occurred when you, as a child, were over-controlled by parents or teachers or by an institution, such as boarding school or military training. You may have been robbed of all choices and possibly bullied. You may have felt threatened and frustrated, and that your competence was being destroyed. Your only defence may have been silent resistance, such as simply refusing to do what you were told, no matter what the other person said or did.

In all these development scenarios, obstinacy and inflexibility were an important defence mechanism against other people robbing you of choices, personal integrity and against bullying or lack of consultation. Naturally, you retained this defence mechanism because the world is full of people who try to control and bully others, even in adulthood.

The problem is that you eventually forgot why you do what you do and, therefore, you respond to all situations in the same inflexible and obstinate way, even when it is completely inappropriate. You automatically distrust authority, which can cause problems at work, and you automatically reject any suggestion because you perceive it as some kind of order or attempt to control you. This can lead to major problems in relationships.

One of the amusing aspects of people with a high score for this Shadow is that you believe you can't be manipulated by anyone. But it's really easy to manipulate you, for the following reason. If I confront you or tell you what to do, you'll shut me out and dig in your heels, right? However, when I speak quietly to you, making subtle suggestions, always carefully using words such as 'I was wondering' or 'What do you think about ...', you are defenceless! Why? Because your defences are focused on hearing certain phrases, such as 'You must' and 'You have to' and 'You had better', as an attempt to control you. When someone uses some other method of manipulating you, such as kindness, you have no defence against it! This Shadow is defenceless against kindness and subtle manipulation.

Another flaw in this Shadow's defences is that it results in what are referred to as 'polarity responses', especially when you have high scores for this Shadow. Because you are so focused on blocking attempts to control your behaviour, you have a tendency to react by doing exactly the opposite of what you are told to do. Again, if someone else knows this about you, you are easy to manipulate. If I tell you to do the opposite of what I want you to do, you will do the opposite of what I've instructed – to prove that I cannot make you do anything – which is what I wanted in the first place!

The real difficulty with this defence strategy is that it inclines you to make decisions you feel you cannot change, even though you are aware that the original decision was unwise or that the situation has changed. Just to prove a point, you dig in your heels and doggedly stick to your decision. And, in this way, you lose flexibility and the ability to adapt to changing situations. This can have major consequences, and can be very destructive in many areas, including relationships.

You are probably already justifying your inflexibility and obstinacy as a good trait. There is a degree of truth in this statement. However, it's important not to confuse inflexibility–obstinacy with determination. Determination is based on a future vision or goal that you want to achieve, where your desire compels you to stay on course, persisting despite obstacles.

However, inflexibility and obstinacy are based strictly on fear, fear of being forced to do things you don't want to do, fear of losing your freedom, fear of sudden change, fear of losing control and choice in your life. This Shadow is fear-based, and these fears were created by past events.

The power game played by this Shadow is based on the belief that by resisting authority and change, you are powerful because you can slow down or stop the game when you want. However, this strategy often leads to the loss of goodwill from other people, who eventually turn away because they do not want to deal with such a 'difficult' person.

In exceptional circumstances, such as being told you are going to die, this strategy may be a saving grace – the automatic rejection of authority can prevent accepting the inevitability of death from this illness. It is not uncommon to hear that it is the 'difficult patient' who seems to survive and thrive. It is for this reason that we do not attempt to moderate this Shadow in PNI interventions, unless it is extremely inflexible. However, we strongly suggest that those with very high scores examine the appropriateness of this Shadow in areas such as personal relationships, which are important sources of support.

The physical posture of the high-scoring *Obstinate–Inflexible* Shadow is quite distinctive: arms folded across the chest, tense jaw, stiff movements, and sometimes redness in the face. In some cases, it can result in chronic muscle tension that in turn can lead to hearing loss and tension in the pelvis and lower back. The body may say *'No!'* even if the words say something else. Your eyes are often focused, with a direct gaze, checking the other person out – friend or foe? You may also have what might be described as a no-nonsense expression. You enter into competitive discussions without holding back, which is a nice way of saying that you can be quite argumentative and won't back down, even when you are wrong!

Dealing with people dominated by this Shadow

It has been mentioned that confrontation is the last thing to do with someone with a high score in this Shadow, as it results in immediate stiffening of attitude. However, the person with the *Obstinate–Inflexible* Shadow loses respect for those with meek and mild approaches. People dominated by the *Obstinate–Inflexible* Shadow respond best to clear, calm and confident approaches. It is advisable to appeal to their sense of discipline and determination. Therefore, be assertive without being aggressive. It is also crucial for the health practitioner to keep people led by this Shadow informed and to consult them on all matters concerning their health, as opposed to just telling them what to do. Give them as much information as you can, give your opinion, and then give them time to make up their own mind. If you rush these people into agreeing, they will instinctively respond by disagreeing. Be very careful to respect their choice in all matters.

■ ASSIGNMENTS FOR THE OBSTINATE–INFLEXIBLE (O-I) SHADOW

STEP 1   Immediate tasks
   a. After reading the three main ways in which this Shadow develops, write a page on how this Shadow developed in your own life. Focus on childhood events and circumstances, and boarding school or military circumstances, if applicable.
   b. Identify at least three recent events in which you made a decision, discovered it was not the best one, but refused to change it.
   c. Regarding your present health condition, identify three occasions when your obstinacy helped you to deal with medical authorities. Then identify three occasions when your obstinacy caused a problem in this area.
   d. Practise saying the following choice-protecting statements:
      ■ *'I don't know. Give me five minutes (or a day) to think about it before I decide.'*
      ■ *'Are you asking me, or telling me?'*
      ■ *'Next time, I'd appreciate it if you would ask me first.'*
   e. Write a paragraph regarding the difference between a suggestion and an order.

STEP 2: Issues to start thinking about and to be addressed in subsequent sessions:

a. Identify five fears you have in terms of losing choice over your life and being forced to do things you do not want to do. Just identify these fears and be specific. A subsequent chapter will show you how to deal with these fears.

b. When you are upset by someone telling you what to do, who (from your past) do they remind you of? Make a list of the authority figures in your childhood who you believe tried to remove your choices or who bullied you. Process your feelings towards these people in Chapter 10, *Get it out of your body*, page 244, specifically in the anger section.

c. What future goals and desires do you have that will provide you with a sense of determination, and also allow you to be sufficiently flexible to adapt as the situation changes? These future-related goals will be addressed in greater depth at a later point.

d. What do you perceive to be the lesson of this Shadow? In other words, what has your experience of this Shadow (and your new knowledge of it) taught you? What do you perceive to be the gift of this Shadow. In other words, what does it give to you, what power does it bestow?

☐ SHADOW 2: PASSIONLESS–REASONABLE (P-R)
'Be reasonable' … 'I am OK'

KEY ISSUE: *Excessive flexibility and reasonableness; not standing firm on issues; an absence of determination due to the belief that (a) the most important choices that would bring happiness and fulfilment have been lost already, and (b) the best that can be accomplished is to attain an 'OK' state with minimal pain and risk.*

CAUSE: *Based on the core fear of potential risk and pain.*

'But I haven't given up on goals and dreams!' you splutter. Oh yes you have, but not in the way you think. The *Passionless–Reasonable* Shadow is very reasonable, rational, functional and efficient. However, at the level of deep-seated desires and passion, the light has been switched off. If you score high in this Shadow you will typically state that you are *'OK'*. You are totally cor-

rect. You are 'OK' – nothing terrible, nothing wonderful, basically nothing at all except a general emotional numbness and sense of being comfortable. Reasonableness can deaden any sense of being alive.

It is typical for people dominated by this Shadow to justify it as a good quality, by saying: *'If everyone did what they wanted to do, there would be chaos! There have to be level-headed people who are reasonable and objective.'* For you, reason is king, and risk is a no-no. Emotion is set aside for reason, resulting in a flat line of emotion. We describe people led by this Shadow as having had a local anaesthetic to the heart!

However, you probably focus all your joy and sense of happiness on one or two people, typically a child or spouse. You live through them, doing your utmost to ensure that their life is happy and fulfilled. This may be described – rather harshly, admittedly – as self-imposed emotional slavery. Imagine what it must be like to be the child or person on whom you are so focused – the sense of responsibility and obligation must be enormous for him or her. What would happen if she or he wanted to leave you? What reason would you have to wake up in the morning? Do you think she or he does not know this?

Whereas other Shadows typically develop in early childhood, this Shadow develops from a more recent event in which you experienced profound loss – of a loved one, a dream or ambition, or any hope that you will ever fulfil your dream. You have lost your passion. From that moment onwards, you became compromising and compromised at a deep level.

When you experienced this loss event, it is almost as if you said to yourself: *'I can't bear to go through this pain again. I will never be able to risk that again. I'll play it safe, do a good job with my life, but I'll do nothing that will expose me to that level of pain again.'* As a result, you've become highly effective and efficient in whatever you do. There is no passion – you are just efficient and highly functional. It is extraordinary how many people score high with this Shadow – the Shadow of the lost dream and the compromised soul. It is most noticeable in the lack of sparkle in the eyes.

Often, people dominated by this Shadow will argue strongly that they have not given up on their passion – they are working towards it, and have a plan of how to get there eventually. However, the bottom line is that they are nowhere near doing the thing that excites them – it's all in their head, all in the so-called 'plan'. It's nothing more than a dream, with thousands of reasonable excuses for why it is not happening now. But thoughts and dreams mean nothing – action is what counts.

A person led by this Shadow can be the ultimate politician, diplomat and conciliator – always willing to compromise. You say things such as *'I don't know – what do you want to do?'* instead of making a choice and risking opposition. Whereas the *Obstinate–Inflexible* Shadow drives people away with sheer bull-headedness, the *Passionless–Reasonable* Shadow drives people away because they don't know where you stand. The *Passionless-Reasonable* Shadow often puts a damper on any exciting idea. The best excuse is, of course, *'Well, let's think this one through carefully, plan it properly, and then wait for the "right" time.'* This is, on the surface, a wise strategy. However, you will notice that you never get to the point of the 'right time'. There is always a reason why it is not the 'right time'. And so life goes on …

When dealing with an immunological problem, challenge and excitement are essential for the secretion of important hormones, such as human growth hormone. Thus, people with a high score in this Shadow cannot deal with immunological problems until challenge and excitement are reintroduced. Also, when faced with the possibility of dying, this Shadow undermines the willingness to take risks and explore new options. There is a large degree of resignation in this Shadow. After all, if you believe that you will never get what you really want from life, what is the point of going through all the effort and struggle to prolong it?

We want to be quite clear here – the operative word is resignation, not acceptance. In our experience, most people confuse the two. Resignation is about giving up, acceptance is about dealing with reality. When your doctor suggests a treatment, you tend to comply, thinking *'OK, whatever you think is best,'* rather than considering, researching and working with your practitioner as an equal partner, thinking *'That's an option. But what do I want to do?'*

People with a predominant *Passionless–Reasonable* Shadow tend to find themselves in supportive roles, typically supporting the dreams and goals of others who have vision and passion. As parents these people often focus all their joy on their children. It is almost as if they live their dreams through other people, because they don't believe they can fulfil their own dreams. However, it should be clearly stated that you are not a whining, miserable, dejected and waiting-to-die kind of person! On the contrary – you are very efficient and successful in what you do, largely because you focus on doing the 'right thing', and doing things 'properly', complying with whoever you believe is in charge.

You also tend to be very rational and plan everything meticulously. You often have five-year plans, which you have discussed with the family: *'For the next five years, I am going to work very hard and for long hours, so you won't see much of me. I'm doing this to make sure you have money for your college education.'* Very reasonable. The problem is that your family would probably rather spend more time with you! You are a great asset in the work environment. However, this does not serve you on a personal level.

Think about this carefully. What excites you and gives you joy? Your own potential and desire to create, or someone else's potential, vision and ability to create? Are you focused on your own desire to make a difference in the world, or is your focus on ensuring that someone else makes a difference in the world? Are you living through someone else, or are you living with someone else?

This Shadow is based on the fear of pain – of re-experiencing the pain you felt when you lost what you loved. There is a fundamental fear of caring too much (again), as this could result in losing it again. The defence is this: *'I will never have what I really want. Therefore, I will simply do the best I can from now on to have a decent life – a life with a minimum of pain. I can't make the difference I want to make in this world. Therefore, I will dedicate myself to ensuring that someone else makes their contribution to the world instead. Their joy will be my joy. I cannot create my own joy anymore.'*

If you are led by this Shadow, it is useful to think back in time to when you were really excited and full of passion. At some point this stopped, and you went into 'reasonable' mode. When did this switch occur? What happened? Here are some possibilities that can activate this Shadow:

- The death of a loved one.
- You tried to do something about which you really were passionate, and failed.
- There were situations in which you may have achieved something remarkable, and realised you would probably never reach that height of success again.

- Your passion was knocked out of you through criticism or even abuse and, as a result, you retreated from that dream because it resulted in pain.
- This Shadow can develop as a result of sympathy for someone you loved very much but who died, for example. You are so distraught by this loss that you psychologically try to hold onto that person by absorbing that dead person's unfulfilled dreams and goals in life. Essentially, you trade in your own passion out of sympathy for someone else's unfulfilled passion.

No matter how it occurred, somewhere along the line you lost your true passion. It is essential that the lost passion is located and restored or a new one found. That is the subject of another chapter.

This Shadow manifests itself as an absence of expression – or through inaction – regarding what is felt inside. For example, if this Shadow is combined with the *Impatient–Restless* Shadow, we have found hypertension to be prevalent, probably because these people keep their urgency and haste inside, thereby activating the SAM cardiovascular system. People with this Shadow often have a flat look in their eyes with no sparkle. Their facial expressions are often serious and kind, with a tendency to appear concerned and burdened by something. Their bodies are often out of shape, with a slow and determined walk. These physical aspects can be different if these people also have strong elements of the *Impatient–Restless* or the *Never Enough* Shadows, which add an element of haste to their movement.

The style of communication of those led by the *Passionless–Reasonable* Shadow is similar to that of the *Control–Distance* Shadow. You rarely refer to yourself as 'I'. Instead, you talk about yourself in the third person: '*When one …*' or '*A person might think …*' or '*You would think that …*' When are you going to reintroduce the words '*I think*' and '*I feel*' into your vocabulary?

The ultimate irony of the *Passionless–Reasonable* Shadow is that it's based on the belief that, by avoiding risk and choice, you will avoid pain. However, by doing this, you become emotionally numb, and if you can't feel pain, you can't feel pleasure either. Any true sense of being alive and joy is lost in the process, thus removing any real passion and fighting spirit. Unfortunately, that day never seems to arrive because happiness is the starting point, not the destination.

Spontaneity is a rare thing with this Shadow. Consequently, lovers and partners can become bored with someone dominated by this Shadow and seek stimulation elsewhere. This simply reinforces the person's original belief that, if you care too much about something, you lose it. Alternatively, you become dependent on your partner for excitement and don't create your own. Your partner may thus begin to perceive you as heavy, depressing or boring. This results in a rather one-sided situation in the relationship.

People led by this Shadow detest confrontation, avoiding it like the plague. As far as you're concerned, there is no reason to get upset about anything – everything can be sorted out reasonably. As a result, you have a tendency to get headaches when you're in situations you don't want to be. You also tend to smile a lot, but rarely laugh out loud from your heart or stomach. Whereas the *Obstinate–Inflexible* Shadow is based on the fear of losing choice, the *Passionless–Reasonable* Shadow is based on the consequences of dealing with that feared lost choice, coupled with the belief that the loss cannot be reversed.

Dealing with people dominated by this Shadow

When dealing with people led by this Shadow, ensure that you acknowledge them for their hard work and efforts. It is useful to appeal to their sense of reasonableness and loyalty, sensibility and responsibility. You need to be relatively confrontational with this Shadow. Therefore, be direct and focused in your approach. Unlike the *Obstinate–Inflexible* Shadow, this Shadow requires a sense of safety (or authority) in someone else. Keep these people informed and consult them on all matters concerning their health, by appealing to their sense of responsibility.

■ ASSIGNMENTS FOR THE PASSIONLESS–REASONABLE (P-R) SHADOW

STEP I   Immediate tasks
    a. After reading the five main ways in which this Shadow develops, write a page on how this Shadow developed in your own life. Think carefully about when your life changed, when you shifted from an excited, enthusiastic person to a more serious, reasonable way of seeing the world. What event occurred to cause that change?

b.   Identify at least three recent events in which you made a decision, and backed down from that decision because it was not worth the effort to fight for it.

c.   Regarding your present health condition:

■   Identify three occasions when your reasonableness and level-headedness helped you to deal with medical authorities.

■   Identify three occasions when this same reasonableness caused a problem in this area (e.g. when it resulted in your being inconvenienced or compromised because you did not want to push the issue into a confrontation).

d.   List three unreasonable activities you would like to do, for no reason other than you want to do them.

e.   Write a paragraph regarding the difference between being flexible and lacking determination.

STEP 2   **Issues to start thinking about (to be addressed in subsequent sessions)**

a.   Identify three fears you have in terms of taking risks in your life. Just identify these fears and be specific. A subsequent chapter will show you how to deal with them.

b.   What decisions did you make about yourself and life at the time of the loss when you gave up on your own personal dream and passion? Why did you decide it wasn't worth risking that kind of pain again?

c.   What future goals and desires do you have – unrelated to anyone else in your life – to provide you with a sense of determination, and also allow you to be flexible enough to adapt as the situation changes? These future-related goals will be addressed in greater depth at a later point.

d.   What do you perceive to be the lesson of this Shadow? In other words, what has your experience of this Shadow, and your new knowledge of it, taught you? What do you perceive to be the gift of this Shadow? In other words, what does it give to you, what power does it bestow?

☐ SHADOW 3: CONTROL–DISTANCE (C-D)
'I am special' (everyone is looking at me)

KEY ISSUE: *A strong need to be perfect; image is everything; a marked need for control over self and environment; aloofness and emotional suppression due to fear of criticism and humiliation; will not allow anyone 'inside'; terrified of intimacy; feels isolated, misunderstood and alone.*

CAUSE: *Based on the core fear of criticism (for not being perfect).*

One way to describe people scoring highly with the *Control–Distance* Shadow is to compare them with someone living in the quintessential Ivory Tower. They lock themselves away from others, spending their days peering through a telescope, closely watching everything done by others and sending messages to them about what they are doing right or wrong. These people are also very aware of the fact that everyone is watching them from a distance, but feel safe because they can never be reached in the locked tower. These people communicate with others, but always from the safety of the tower. Naturally, being locked in a tower is a very lonely experience and they cannot understand why no one seems to understand them.

If you are dominated by this Shadow, you live with an inauthentic (i.e. not your own) standard of perfection which you measure everything against, including yourself. No matter what the situation, you will strive to be 'perfect'. This is why your image is so important to you and why you have a high need for control – so that you can ensure that it all turns out 'perfectly'. There are two fundamental problems with this need for perfection. First, the standards you set may not be your own, and you end up trying to be someone you are not. Second, you will automatically avoid anything – including emotions or taking risks – that may be criticised as being 'imperfect'. You are literally trapped within some abstract, dream-like, 'perfect' world that has little to do with who you really are. Is it any surprise you feel disconnected from other people and the 'real' world of emotions? Have you also noticed how, the harder you try to be 'perfect', the more other people enjoy pointing out your 'imperfections'?

If you have a high score in the *Control–Distance* Shadow you will often fantasise about being special and respected one day. You often believe that other people know or suspect you'll be famous one day. Obviously, when people ignore you or do not treat you in a respectful and 'special' manner, you're devastated. People led by this Shadow tend to get highly upset when they are ignored.

You work hard and you are usually very systematic and efficient. You also fully expect that other people will notice all this effort and achievement. You find it rather degrading to have to point out how 'special' you are – after all, they are watching, aren't they?

You strongly identify with your achievements (especially intellectual achievements), about which you feel justifiably somewhat smug and arrogant. You tend to pay attention to details – being the consummate perfectionist. When someone else does something, you will notice every single mistake. Therefore, when something is important to you, you insist on having full control of the process. Quite frankly, you do not believe that anyone can do it quite as well as you and, often, you're right.

You're often overlooked for advancement because others are more outspoken and actually 'degrade themselves' by 'marketing' themselves! It is not surprising that you tend to become cynical and judgmental if you're not treated and recognised as being 'special'.

You often get caught in a vicious cycle regarding intimacy. Your manner and posture indicate aloofness and a 'holier-than-thou' attitude that drives people away or silently indicates to people to stay away. This is due to your fear of being vulnerable – which you equate with a high risk of criticism.

The problem with this 'stay away from me' attitude is that there are specific people you would love to be close to, but they are also driven away by your attitude. You are probably not aware of this. One part of this attitude is communicated to other people through your body language, such as tilting your head up so that you seem to look down your nose at other people.

The other part of this impression of aloofness and arrogance concerns your wariness and quietness when meeting someone for the first time. You first want to have an idea of who the other person is before you decide whether or not to have anything to do with him or her. An important aspect of this perceived attitude is the fact that you want the other person to approach you, because you are 'special'. Heaven forbid that you should actually make the first move!

One of your favourite games is: *'If people really knew me, they would love me more than anyone else. However, I'm not going to let them get close enough to know me – I am in control! They can come and find me.'* The strategy for this Shadow – in group interactions – is to stand alone to one side until someone asks you to join in the activities. After all, you are 'special', aren't you? Once you are in the group you want to control it. If the other people do not listen to you, then you try the 'standing alone in the corner' routine again. Are you surprised that people find you difficult to get close to?

You often meet up with similar people who are intent on avoiding intimacy but who are also looking for someone to hold them in high regard (or notice them). In such situations, appearances are everything. Although you are in each other's company, each of you feels undervalued and unnoticed by the other. In reality, this is nothing more than being alone in a crowd! However, it is at least safe due to the lack of intimacy.

It is ironic that, although you have a high need to be perfect and 'the best', you have tremendous anxiety regarding tests of performance, in case you make a mistake. You have some pretty clever justifications for avoiding such tests, such as: *'If I did the exam, I would probably do better than anyone else. But I'm too busy … I can't be bothered … I'll let someone else have the chance.'* Where most people are content to pass a test, you get frantic over the one percent you lost out of a hundred!

People with high *Control–Distance* scores make excellent accountants, analysts and therapists (oops … did we say 'therapists'?) Their Shadow compels them to be highly observant of details and nuances in the world around them, in the effort to mask their own flaws and to find the flaws of others.

In a sophisticated form, the *Control–Distance* Shadow can mask itself as a 'people's person' – humble, open and vulnerable. You have analysed people well enough to know what you need to say and do in order for them to feel that you are 'human', vulnerable and 'one of us'. For example, if someone makes a mistake, you may tell him or her about the time you made a similar mistake. This reassures the other person, who may feel that you really under-stand that everyone makes mistakes. However, without this person knowing, you will gradually remove any control she or he has over the project until you are in control. But this does not always happen – it depends on whether you believe the project is important to you or not.

Even when you have perfected the strategy of appearing to be 'human', closer inspection reveals a part of you that is totally walled off and out-of-bounds to anyone else. If you believe judging people is a flaw, you'll hide this part of yourself as well and rather be secretly critical, never revealing any such flaw to anyone else. In this situation, one half of you criticises the other half: '*Why don't you say hello to her? Even if she is an idiot, do you think that you are better than her?*' This is the sophisticated form of this Shadow, the internal critic. At this stage of the Shadow, you believe you are completely safe from external criticism, largely because you are doing a superb job of criticising yourself in your quest to be perfect.

Why do you feel such a strong need to protect yourself from criticism, keep people at a distance and strive so hard to control yourself and your environment? Why do you feel as if everyone is always watching and judging you?

The cause of this Shadow invariably contains two parts:
- **The special child:** As a child, you were the 'special one', for your father or mother. This may (or may not) have been stated out loud. Something about you set you apart – being the first born, the last born, being clever, pretty, the 'good' child, or a much-longed-for child. The phrases 'Daddy's little girl' and 'Mommy's blue-eyed boy' are phrases often used to describe this 'special' status. It is not unusual for people with this Shadow to report that, as a child, they looked for adoption papers because they felt so 'different' from their family.
- **I must be perfect – fear of criticism:** The very second you became aware that someone important to you – mother or father, for example – regarded you as 'special', you automatically realised that you had to be, do and have certain things to ensure that you remained 'special'. The alternative was to lose that love and attention. This is where the need to be perfect emerged. Basically, you realised that the love and attention you received was conditional on whatever made you 'special'.

One of two things happened at this point in the development of the Shadow:
- One parent was critical of you, causing you to close off those aspects of yourself that made you vulnerable to criticism;

- You simply started to strive for the values, behaviour and beliefs you believed your parents considered 'good' (i.e. you started to create the model of perfection you needed to strive for).

Whichever strategy you used, you began to live according to an image of perfection, and you began to fear imperfection, hence the fear of criticism. Being so high on a pedestal, you were highly susceptible to criticism from others. You had to maintain those high expectations and, therefore, criticism was deeply painful. The most painful criticism came from authority figures, such as parents and teachers.

The combination of factors given above produces a special kind of tension: '*I am special*' (thus expected to be perfect), but '*I am not OK*' (according to the criticism, as well as according to the imaginary system of perfection). The paradox is that you want to be noticed but you fear being judged or ignored. Therefore, the only solution is to build a high wall around yourself so that no one else can see the flaws – including your emotions and vulnerability – and they will, therefore, have nothing to criticise you for.

You begin to become hyper-alert and observant regarding what other people consider acceptable and desirable, and you begin to become what it is they want you to be, keeping the 'secret self' inside the wall. It is not surprising that you become overly self-conscious, and driven to be one step ahead of the rest! Also, you secretly become very critical of yourself, to fix or hide any imperfections before anyone else notices. In the process of keeping others out, you lock yourself inside, a prisoner trapped in the solitary tower of your own making.

Once the tower walls are firmly in place and you have mastered the act of appearing to be perfect, you turn the tables by becoming critical of others: '*I have succeeded in becoming pretty good, so good in fact that I'm better than they are. I can criticise them and find their flaws. One day I will be respected and they will be nothing – they'll be sorry they ever criticised me.*'

It is useful to remember that all this developed as a result of wanting to hold on to the love and attention you received from being 'special'. It is ironic that the love and attention you so desire – the feeling of belonging and feeling connected to others – becomes harder and harder to achieve because of the walls you have built around you.

Make no mistake – this Shadow is superb for specific things, such as analysis and observation. It promotes awareness of details and detachment, all of which are essential skills in specific situations, such as psychotherapy, accountancy, medicine and such fields. However, there is a tremendous personal price for such benefits: lack of true intimacy, suppressed spontaneity, little freedom of expression, and a host of other disadvantages. One of the major disadvantages of this specific Shadow is that you're 'trapped inside your head'. In practice, when the situation requires examination and expression of feelings, you are lost – you 'know' what you are talking about and you 'understand' why and how it is necessary, but you find it very difficult to actually feel anything in your body. Because you don't have a very good sense of what is happening inside your body, you may have an inflated sense of toughness, and overestimate your abilities. You physically push yourself beyond what is healthy, which is detrimental to healing.

In relationships, intimacy is difficult due to the distance and isolation you bring with you. You are more concerned with competence than honesty, and thus truly intimate and vulnerable communication is difficult. Seduction is easy, but intimacy very challenging. Your partner begins to feel like an object.

Creativity is often blocked because of the obsession for detail and perfection. The fear of taking a risk, even a mistake, is huge. You're usually scanning the near future, checking for potentially embarrassing situations, chattering away to yourself, rehearsing what you'll say, and how you will deflect criticism.

You usually justify (make 'right') your emotional detachment by saying that someone needs to be level-headed – naturally, referring to yourself – and it is not uncommon for you to believe that emotions, and people who get emotional, are a sign of 'weakness' and mental inadequacy. While you secretly recognise the power of being free enough to feel alive, you cannot overcome your personal prison walls to reach that state. After all, you are terrified of being made a fool of. The same applies to religion. You know exactly what is 'right', 'wrong', and 'the way to do it', but you cannot seem to feel the forgiveness, the bliss or the divine presence that the 'idiots' seem to feel!

Unfortunately, from striving to appear perfect and competent, other people begin to resent your superiority, increasing the criticism. People have a deep mistrust of 'holier-than-thou' people, and a strong need to 'bring them down a peg or two'. Therefore, this Shadow contains its own inevitable downfall.

When you are criticised and feel humiliated, you slide into the *Apologising–Failure* Shadow. It is not uncommon to score high on both these Shadows, particularly when one of the two interactive major areas in your life (e.g. work and home) contains criticism. For example, you may be highly competent and efficient at work, receiving reinforcement for your *Control–Distance* Shadow. However, when you get home, your partner is very critical of you and you slide into the *Apologising–Failure* Shadow. The reverse can also be true, such as a hypercritical and dictatorial boss at work and a supportive partner at home. Either way, fluctuation between the two Shadows can occur.

Many arrogant politicians and other leaders have this *Control–Distance* Shadow. However, notice what happens when they get too arrogant – people begin to attack their reputation, try to uncover secrets they are hiding, and then strive to humiliate them publicly. Then you witness the *Apologising–Failure* Shadow emerge. Often, this lasts for a while, especially if sympathy and forgiveness are received, following which they resume the *Control–Distance* Shadow.

You can detect the *Control–Distance* Shadow fairly easily due to a distinctive physical posture. The head is typically held high, with a slight tilt backwards. Also, the shoulders and back are tight and fairly rigid. These people tend to sit with the upper back touching the chair, but the lower back forward from the chair.

Dealing with people dominated by this Shadow

It is important to recognise that the primary fear is one of criticism that is considered humiliating, especially public criticism. Therefore, do not criticise such a person in front of other people.

People with this Shadow also do not tolerate stupidity or weak logic very well. They love to find fault with your logic or competence, as a form of establishing their own power (control) in the situation. Therefore, answer their questions completely, without apology for what you do or do not know. Let them have control of their own process, but ensure that you check that they have done what they are supposed to do.

Such people tend to be visual (think in pictures) in their understanding. Therefore, include verbal imagery in your explanations, explain the so-called 'big picture', and use diagrams to assist in your explanations. These people need pictures and images to understand.

When dealing with feelings and emotions, it is important that they feel you will not criticise what they tell you. It has to be safe and confidential. They will not access emotions for no apparent reason. They need a logical and legitimate reason to, for example, express their anger.

It also helps to suggest that these people experience some form of physical therapy – massage or aromatherapy, for example – so that they can begin to get a better sense of what their body is about, and what does and does not hurt. It is very difficult to process emotions such as anger or guilt when you have closed off awareness of your body and feelings. Try to steer such people away from an intellectual 'understanding' of emotions, towards awareness of their bodies.

■ ASSIGNMENTS FOR THE CONTROL–DISTANCE (C-D) SHADOW

STEP I **Immediate tasks**
   a. After reading about how this Shadow develops, write a page on how this Shadow developed in your own life. Think carefully about who indicated that you were 'special', and who criticised you. What occurred to cause you to close off your spontaneity and hide your emotions?
   b. Identify at least three recent events in which you felt angry or vulnerable, and then decided to say nothing because you rationalised your feelings as 'silly' or you first wanted time to think of a 'clever' response.
   c. Regarding your present health condition:
   ■ Identify three occasions when your understanding, analytical ability and level-headedness helped you to deal with medical authorities and situations.
   ■ Identify three occasions when this same sense of the detached intellectual caused a problem in this area, perhaps because it resulted in your not saying what you felt or thought, because you did not want to appear like an incompetent idiot.
   ■ List three mental–emotional–spiritual states you would love to experience (not understand – but actually feel and experience).

d. Write a paragraph regarding the difference between criticism and feedback, and another paragraph regarding the difference between being special and being unique.

STEP 2 **Issues to start thinking about (to be addressed in subsequent sessions)**

a. Identify five fears you have in terms of being vulnerable – fear of being criticised for expressing your feelings of being afraid, inadequate, failing, telling someone you love him or her. Just identify these fears and be specific. A subsequent chapter will show you how to deal with these fears.

b. Can you remember the time when it felt OK to cry and express your vulnerability? When did that change? This is similar to question 1(a). However, focus more deeply on what decisions you made about yourself and life at that time, and ask yourself whether that decision is still valid today. What are you going to do to reconnect with your body?

c. What future goals and desires do you have that will provide you with a sense of determination, and also allow you to be flexible enough to adapt as the situation changes? Also, ensure that these goals do not exclude dreams and desires that have the risk of making you vulnerable or exposing you to possible criticism. Imagine life outside the tower walls around you. These future-related goals will be addressed in greater depth at a later point.

d. What do you perceive to be the lesson of this Shadow? In other words, what has your experience of this Shadow (and your new knowledge of it) taught you? What do you perceive to be the gift of this Shadow? In other words, what does it give to you, what power does it bestow?

☐ SHADOW 4: APOLOGISING–FAILURE (A-F)
'I'm sorry'

KEY ISSUE: *Believes failure is inevitable; apologises before and after doing anything, as a means of destroying other people's expectations of them, a strategy that attempts to reduce the criticism (or rejection) that comes from the 'inevitable' failure.*

CAUSE: *Based on the core fear that nothing you do will ever be good enough, and the consequent belief that you will fail, somehow.*

This Shadow presents itself as the classic low self-esteem Shadow. However, this is not strictly true, as all the Shadows are based on a core fear and sense that *'Who I truly am is not good enough.'* However, this sense of not being good enough is most obvious and easy to see in the behaviour and words of people dominated by the *Apologising–Failure* Shadow, simply because their central strategy is to remove other people's expectations by purposely putting themselves down and appearing incompetent.

For example, when someone gives you a compliment, you are likely to ignore it or tell the person that she or he is mistaken. You present yourself as humble and modest, but in fact you are systematically destroying other people's expectations of you for the sole purpose of relieving yourself of the pressure to succeed.

The 'secret' of this Shadow is that you honestly and deeply believe that, no matter what you do, you will fail. Furthermore, when that failure occurs, you want to ensure that other people do not reject you. How do you do this? Easy – just tell people you probably will fail and that they shouldn't expect too much from you! Therefore, if people do get disappointed in you, it is quite clearly their own fault – you warned them, didn't you? Very clever strategy.

One of the consequences of this Shadow is an automatic impulse to apologise. However, it is such a habit that you end up apologising for everything and anything, even events which have nothing to do with you.

There is a difference between saying *'I'm sorry'* out of sympathy or empathy, and saying *'I'm sorry'* out of some weird sense of responsibility for something in which you had no involvement! The *Apologising–Failure* Shadow falls into the second category.

Probably the most definitive 'test' for the presence of the *Apologising–Failure* Shadow concerns situations and periods when things are going well. When this happens, you begin to feel uneasy, even panicky, experiencing what may be referred to as 'free-floating anxiety', which is anxiety for no apparent reason. You'd describe this feeling as 'waiting for the other shoe to drop' – waiting for the fall, the 'catch', the inevitable hidden failure or lurking disaster.

You have a fundamental belief that you will fail, no matter what you do. This belief is so pervasive and fundamental that you've arranged your entire life – actions, ambitions, hopes and expectations – around this 'inevitable failure'. You do this to such an extent that you feel safe and comfortable only when things are not going well. When things go well, you feel as if something is 'wrong', and that there has to be some hidden agenda or failure or criticism hiding somewhere. When the failure happens, you feel a sense of relief.

How did this Shadow develop? The development of this Shadow is similar to that of the *Control–Distance* Shadow (page 162) and contains three aspects.

- **The special child:** As a child, you were the 'special one', for your father or mother. This may or may not have been stated out loud.
- **I must be perfect – fear of criticism:** The very second you became aware that someone important to you – mother or father, for example – regarded you as 'special', you automatically realised that you had to be, do and have certain things to ensure that you remained 'special'. The alternative was to lose that love and attention. This is where the need to be perfect emerged. You realised that the love and attention you received was conditional on whatever made you 'special'.
- **I can't be perfect:** This is where this Shadow differs from the *Control–Distance* Shadow. Somewhere along the way you discovered that either this image of perfection you wanted to strive for was impossible to achieve or you honestly did not know what the criteria were – no one told you exactly what the requirements were. As a direct result, you accepted the fact that you could not achieve this image of perfection. For example, your father or mother may have frowned on your behaviour without telling you what they really wanted or expected from you. This parental behaviour is often caused when your parents themselves are led by either the *Control–Distance* or *Blaming–Shaming* Shadows, which result in the inability to state what they want or feel. As a direct result, you are left with the feeling that you will never know what it will take to succeed (in terms of getting love and approval), and that failure (in terms of meeting other people's expectations) is logically inevitable. This is when the apologising strategy emerges, as a method to keep getting love and approval by ensuring that no one expects too much from you. After all, if you ensure that someone does not expect much from you, there is not much reason for them to criticise you, is there?

To someone without high levels of this Shadow, this behaviour and way of thinking appears extremely odd. However, to the person with high scores in this Shadow, it makes perfect sense. Furthermore, there is ample evidence in the real world to illustrate that nothing ever goes right and that failure is unavoidable. Your most compelling justification is: *'I'm just being realistic about things – nothing good lasts.'*

It is important to understand the impact of being treated as 'special' by one or both parents while, at the same time, being told that you are not perfect, and then not knowing what to do to be perfect! The pressure on the child to live up to these expectations is enormous.

In the *Control–Distance* and *Apologising–Failure* Shadows, children learn that love is conditional, and a great deal is expected from them because they're 'special'. Both these Shadows are based on the belief that *'I am not loved for who I am'* and feelings of inadequacy.

However, what happens if the expectations are too high, and you cannot possibly live up to them? The *Control–Distance* Shadow is the method of coping when you believe you can still try to attain the illusion or appearance of perfection, whereas the *Apologising–Failure* Shadow is the result of your conclusion that you can't possibly maintain the illusion. That is why *Control–Distance* slips into *Apologising–Failure* when the façade of perfection and control is ripped apart by criticism and failure, and why the *Apologising–Failure* Shadow slides into *Control–Distance* when things go well, and there is the illusion of 'holding it together'.

Logic dictates that, to prevent 'real' failure, all you have to do is destroy other people's expectations of you. In this Shadow, the pre-emptive strategy develops, along the lines of: *'I'll get me before you get me – I will hurt myself before you can because then I can control the pain, not you.'* Consequently, there is a powerful sense of self-righteousness about being a failure, and great insecurity about leadership, success and raising expectations of yourself and others regarding your abilities. The unspoken communication to other people is: *'Be nice to me – I am just a useless loser who is no threat to you, with little to offer except that I really don't expect much from you.'* This is a subtle and powerful manipulation of the sympathy of other people. Do not forget the hidden *'I am special'* part of this Shadow, which will utilise sympathy to get the attention you feel you deserve!

Your presentation of being a humble, helpless victim of inadequacies invariably attracts people into your immediate circle who want to protect you, abuse you or blame you, or all three. You often set yourself up for failure in this regard.

Other people, who recognise your real abilities and potential, eventually give up encouraging you to feel good about yourself. If someone doesn't put you down or ridicule you, you oblige by making degrading jokes or comments about your appearance and inadequacies.

You may wonder whether this description is a little harsh. It is intended to be. This Shadow results in passivity, unlike the *Control–Distance* Shadow, which, at least, is active and attempts to establish control. If the *Apologising–Failure* Shadow is strong, you accept abuse, you accept statements made by perceived authorities, you even accept unfair treatment at work, home and in your medical treatment. You accept all without question or resistance, because you think you don't deserve any better.

Eliciting sympathy is part of the *modus operandi* of this Shadow, hence the absence of such sympathy in our description of it. With this Shadow, you may present yourself in a specific manner – slouched, drooped shoulders, almost as though you're retreating into your own body, speaking quietly or in a manner that is difficult to hear. (This may be modified by other Shadows.) Your eyes are often downcast, with a rather distressed, disappointed and wistful expression. The use of the phrase '*I'm sorry*' spews out at every opportunity. Even when you're defensive in the face of criticism, you quickly crumble, apologising constantly afterwards. Nervous behaviour, such as nail-biting, playing with the hair, or picking at the skin, is not unusual for this Shadow. In projects, you become obsessive regarding details, and will check and recheck every detail over and over, because you know you've forgotten something or that you've made a mistake somewhere.

Dealing with people dominated by this Shadow

First, sympathy is not helpful. Nor is criticism! The key to dealing with this Shadow is to realise that people dominated by it are suppressing a great deal of passion and intensity, which is locked away deep inside. Appeal to that passion. Appeal to their hearts, not their heads.

Direct their conscious attention to the number of times they apologise or put themselves down. Do not allow statements such as *'I don't know,' 'I'm not sure,' 'This may sound stupid, but …'* Or any variations on the *'I'm sorry'* theme. Make it clear that you will not tolerate such statements. Do this in a firm but non-abrasive manner. Insist that these people distinguish between the things they are responsible for, and those things they are not responsible for. When they say *'I can't'*, immediately confront them with *'You can't, or you won't?'*

Focus on their abilities. Sometimes they need a little push to get going in this regard. Be straightforward and respectful. Above all, do not fall into the sympathy trap, which is the power game on which this Shadow is based. Avoid terms that refer to blame – instead, refer to responsibility and facts. At all times, keep the objectives of the process clear and visible, and proceed with small, manageable steps to avoid or reduce failure.

Reinforce and acknowledge every success along the way, no matter how small, to erode the belief that failure is inevitable. Encourage these people to 'applaud' each success (they will try to dismiss success, rather than to acknowledge and feel good about it). Get them to become very aware of what they say (i.e. unconscious beliefs) and to 'edit' these in terms of now, as against then.

Clearly and consistently bear in mind how this Shadow formed in the first place, namely as a reaction to unrealistically high expectations from parents or teachers. Also keep in mind that these people are likely to have entered relationships that reinforce this pattern of criticism. Therefore, make it clear that you do indeed have specific expectations from them, but that these expectations are clear and attainable, and that you will not withdraw your attention simply because they may take a little longer than expected.

■ ASSIGNMENTS FOR THE APOLOGISING–FAILURE (A-F) SHADOW:

Step 1   **Immediate tasks**
       a. After reading how this Shadow develops, write a page on how it developed in your own life. Think carefully about who indicated that you were 'special', and who criticised you. Was there a moment or event in which you decided there was no way you could ever meet their expectations?

b. Identify at least three recent events in which you felt responsible for something that went wrong, even though it had nothing to do with you.

c. Regarding your present health condition:

- Identify three occasions when your humility helped you to deal with medical authorities and situations.

- Then identify three occasions when this same sense of 'It's all my fault' caused a problem in this area.

d. List three specific areas in which you are competent. Do not edit or censor them.

e. Write a paragraph regarding the difference between failure and incomplete success, and how you delete all your accomplishments – small and big – from your awareness. Name at least three areas in which you unfairly put yourself down.

f. Write a page on your belief patterns, regarding your own sense of deservingness, and how you can change them.

STEP 2 **Issues to start thinking about (to be addressed in subsequent sessions)**

a. Identify five fears that you have in terms of trying and failing. Just identify these fears and be specific. A subsequent chapter will show you how to deal with these fears.

b. Can you remember the time when you felt you were loved for exactly who you were? When did that change? Focus on the expectations made of you as a child which, when you think about it, were unrealistic for a child of that age. Would you expect the same from a child of that age?

c. What future goals and desires do you have that will provide you with a sense of determination, and also allow you to be flexible enough to adapt as the situation changes? Ensure that these goals do not exclude dreams and desires that involve several attempts and possible mistakes. For what would you strive, if you truly believed you deserved what you wanted? These future-related goals will be addressed in greater depth at a later point.

d. What do you perceive to be the lesson of this Shadow, i.e. what has your experience of this Shadow (and your new knowledge of it) taught you? What do you perceive to be the gift of this Shadow, i.e. what does it give to you, what power does it bestow?

☐ SHADOW 5: IMPATIENT–RESTLESS (I-R)
'Hurry – we don't have time to waste!'

KEY ISSUE: *Self-worth is understood as what you can do, not who you are; excessively goal-oriented; focuses on the future, neglects the present.*

CAUSE: *Based on the core fear of running out of time, of not making it because there's not enough time. Believes that time is something you can save or waste.*

It is surprising that you have actually read this far before getting bored! Well done! People dominated by the *Impatient–Restless* Shadow are distinctive in many ways, including speech, attitude and behaviour. You are impatient and locked into the whole tick-tock 'time' thing. There may be times and situations where you escape tick-tock but, for the most part, you're constantly 'missioning' to get things done, running around, hurrying people along, and generally trying to cram 25 hours into 24! In fact, when you die, we'll engrave *'Got Everything Done – Died Anyway!'* on your tombstone.

You will rarely stand in queues in banks or post offices at the end of the month, unless someone sent you there as punishment. Shopping with you is a nightmare – you're quickly bored and frustrated and end up rushing home with only half your shopping done!

You tend to be short-tempered, abrupt and sometimes reckless in your haste. You rant and rave about how slow and incompetent other people are, and you have to force yourself not to finish other people's sentences for them. You're a dream colleague for those who don't want to do something – they just have to do something slowly and you automatically take over, shoving them aside because you cannot tolerate their slowness! You find it very difficult to sleep without a watch, your compass in life.

This Shadow is an interesting one, especially for specific health conditions. Combined with the *Passionless–Reasonable* Shadow, the restlessness is suppressed, creating inner tension, and hypertension is common. However, when combined with the *Obstinate–Inflexible* Shadow and, especially if this combination is high for more than a year or two, it produces constant activation of the SAM system, which can lead to heart conditions.

However, for people with suppressed immune system conditions, such as AIDS or cancer, the combination of the *Impatient–Restless* and *Obstinate–Inflexible* Shadows is actually beneficial, because it counteracts the lethargy of the immune system's activity. It is not uncommon for a remission in such conditions to occur, due partially to the 'wake-up call' – and subsequent impatient urge to do many things – that a terminal diagnosis sometimes causes.

The fundamental fear behind this Shadow is one of running out of time before completing whatever it is that you want to complete. What is 'wrong' or incorrect about that? More basic beliefs cause this fear, namely that:

■ 'Doing' is more important than 'being'. In other words, your self-worth and need for attention and approval are hinged on what you do, not who you are; and

■ 'Time' is some tangible commodity that can be saved or wasted, and is in limited supply.

When we look at the competitive world in which we all live, these notions are supported in many ways by business and social systems and values. The emphasis is on accomplishment, schedules and deadlines. Success or failure is usually defined in these terms. Often overlooked is the basic misconception that intrinsic value depends on behaviour – if you behave and achieve, then you are 'good', but if you do not behave or perform well, you are 'bad'. The person behind all these behaviours is not valued simply for who he or she is.

This Shadow develops in various ways, some of which are not obvious:

■ **Pressure to achieve:** Often, this Shadow stems from an over-achieving parent – someone who has accomplished a great deal despite limited education or financial background. This person – often your father – instilled in you the urge to achieve, and approval (or love) was conditional on performing well. It is not unusual for this pattern to be passed on from generation to generation. If you failed, or moved too slowly, love and approval were withdrawn.

■ **You were rushed around:** Another way in which this Shadow may develop includes being rushed by parents or guardians, accompanied by statements such as *'Hurry – don't waste time!'* or *'If you don't get a move on, we'll never make it!'* Time becomes associated with fear and urgency, often panic. The consequences of 'running out of time' are never discussed, but you formed vivid images of something horrible happening if you 'ran out of time'. A very common breeding ground for this Shadow is boarding school and military training, which instil a strict, regimented timetable on every activity, with unpleasant consequences for being late or slow.

- **You were slowed down:** One further possible circumstance to cause this Shadow's development is when your parents or guardians were slow, middle-aged (or older) and constantly suppressed your need to run around, make noise, and generally be an active, curious child. You may have felt frustrated, as if you were missing out on so much and couldn't wait to get out into the world and do so many things. Alternatively, you were forbidden to take part in certain activities because you were 'too young' or 'too much trouble'. When you saw other children doing all these things, you felt as if you were missing out on life, and began to fear that you would never do everything you wanted in life. In this way, 'running out of time' becomes associated with 'death'.

Make no mistake – people with this Shadow get things done and get them done quickly. However, there is a serious price to pay. In your rush to do as much as you can, you miss out on the pleasure of the present moment, because you're always solely focused on future goals and 'what's next'. You are so busy doing things that you rarely take time to enjoy what you do. You gloss over details in your rush, which can cause problems, and you have a strong tendency to over-commit and burn out. Ironically, although you detest people being late for appointments, you're often late because you have an unrealistic idea of how much you can do in a certain period of time. So, you run from one appointment to the next, and the delays cut into your timetable.

Creativity is stifled because the creative process sometimes requires periods of silent incubation of a thought, in which nothing is 'done' at the physical level. You try to short-circuit this crucial aspect of creativity, and consequently feel 'creatively blocked'.

When sitting, you often tap your feet, tweak at your moustache or hair, tap your fingers, and generally appear agitated and restless. You stride along, usually with your body leaning forwards slightly, almost as if you're trying to 'get ahead of yourself'. It should be apparent that you're highly goal-oriented, and need a project – if not several at once – to feel happy. Holidays – just doing nothing – are a severe strain, and can easily cause increased anxiety and tension! Not surprisingly, passive relaxation techniques, such as meditation, have been shown to increase your blood pressure. Sitting still results in your mind racing even faster, thinking about all the things you need to do, how much time you're wasting doing nothing, and generally getting very frustrated and more impatient.

People with high levels of the *Impatient–Restless* Shadow appear to be very self-focused and confident, preferring to take the lead and drag everyone behind. However, your fundamental dependence on activity and achievement, as a measure of self-worth, becomes very apparent when you run out of time, such as when you're late or have completely over-committed yourself. When this occurs, you blame time: *'If only there were 25 hours in the day!'* In other words, you slide into the *Blaming–Shaming* Shadow, which is defined in terms of placing all responsibility for unhappiness on some outside source.

The bottom line for people with this Shadow is that, yes, it is marvellous how much you do. However, when are you actually going to *enjoy* what you are doing, *now*?

Dealing with people dominated by this Shadow

Good luck! People led by this Shadow will want to rush in and do everything you suggest, right now! Make sure you work through the details very carefully, as they will be strongly inclined to overlook some pretty important details in their haste to get finished.

If you slow down the pace too much, they will get very impatient and dismiss what you have to say. However, if you present them with an Action List, they will be delighted! However, you need to consider the focus of the intervention carefully. If you are dealing with people who have cancer or AIDS, then it might be inadvisable to even try and moderate this Shadow, as it may serve them well.

If, on the other hand, you are dealing with people who have a heart-related condition, such as hypertension, then this Shadow needs to be moderated, especially if it is combined with the *Passionless–Reasonable* Shadow. Don't waste your time trying to get this person to sit down and meditate – it will drive them up the wall with frustration. Rather focus on active relaxation methods, such as walking, yoga or other physical activities. Sometimes, listening to music will work in achieving the required relaxation.

One method of moderating this Shadow is to point out the following paradox. If you do not slow down, you will run out of time, and then you will have no more time to do any of the things you wanted to do in the first place! Literally, 'haste makes waste'.

People who score high with this Shadow invariably require someone to fill in the details for them, and to slow them down long enough to notice how much they have achieved. Also, it is essential to point out that their self-worth is not dependent on their activities, but instead on their internal value.

Finally, ensure that you keep your agreements regarding time with these people!

■ ASSIGNMENTS FOR THE IMPATIENT–RESTLESS (I-R) SHADOW:

STEP 1   Immediate tasks
   a. After reading how this Shadow develops, write a page on how this Shadow developed in your own life. Who told you your value depended on what you do? Where and when did you get fixated on time?
   b. Identify at least three recent events in which you noticed your impatience in terms of dealing with other people you care about.
   c. Regarding your present health condition:
   ■ Identify three occasions when your sense of urgency helped you to deal with medical authorities and situations.
   ■ Then identify three occasions when this same impatience and failure to check details caused a problem in this area.
   d. List three specific areas or situations in which you have patience, and can relax without worrying about time.
   e. Write a paragraph regarding the difference between doing something effectively and doing something efficiently.

STEP 2   Issues to start thinking about (to be addressed in subsequent sessions)
   a. Identify five fears you have of not completing or accomplishing something before you die. Just identify these fears and be specific. A subsequent chapter will show you how to deal with them.
   b. Can you think of a time when you were 'in the moment', not overly

worried about time? When did that change? Focus on the expectations that were made of you as a child which, when you think about it, were unrealistic for a child of that age. Would you expect the same from a child of that age?

c. What future goals and desires would provide you with a sense of determination, and also allow you to be flexible enough to adapt as the situation changes? Also, ensure that these goals are not quickly completed projects. Find one or two goals on which it's worthwhile spending a great deal of time, effort and attention, such as developing some talent you have never had the time to develop. Examples are art or music, which will require years of practice, and in which you can get 'lost' and oblivious of time. These future-related goals will be addressed in greater depth at a later point.

d. What do you perceive to be the lesson of this Shadow, i.e. what has your experience of this Shadow (and your new knowledge of it) taught you? What do you perceive to be the gift of this Shadow, ie what does it give to you, what power does it bestow?

☐ SHADOW 6: BLAMING–SHAMING (B-S)
'You don't understand my circumstances!'

KEY ISSUE: *Places power and/or responsibility for personal happiness on some external agent – another person, government, God, and situations; holds and protects a wound from the past, and refuses to let it go; will not forgive; uses 'suffering' as a weapon to demand attention and also to hold people hostage with guilt; will not tell people what she or he wants and needs, then says she or he doesn't care.*

CAUSE: *Based on the core fear of ending up unloved and trapped.*

The person led by this Shadow gets rather angry when you say things such as 'You create your own happiness,' or 'You are the master of your own destiny.' This Shadow rears its head and starts listing all the reasons why it is not possible to be happy, and will tell you how someone or something took that choice away.

Now, let us get very clear about this blame and fault stuff. Unless you make some major group effort (such as starting a new political party), you are not individually responsible for a whole range of things, including other people's behaviour, government or the economy.

We are not talking about blame or whose fault all this is. What we are talking about is your personal and internal state of happiness, fear, anxiety, joy, anger or sadness, which you *are* responsible for. There is a huge difference between the words 'fault' and 'responsibility', and no, this is not just playing with words!

The words 'blame' and 'fault' directly imply that something is 'bad'. These words also imply that guilt and punishment are appropriate, and that someone should 'pay' for what has happened. Usually, very little attention or effort is directed at actually 'fixing' or repairing the damage or pain. It is assumed that, when someone is guilty, they should be punished, and that this will miraculously erase the pain or damage. But look around you. Punishment does not lead to the easing of pain – it does not undo the trauma of a rape, nor does it bring back a lost child, for example.

However, the word 'responsibility', which is often (and incorrectly) used to indicate blame, means something quite different. It has two components: 'Response' and 'Ability'. In other words, who or what caused the situation in the first place, and who or what is accountable for rectifying the situation.

Why are we telling you this? The reason is simple, and goes to the heart of this Shadow. Somewhere, a long time ago, someone hurt you and caused pain. You may claim that you have dealt with it, and you may claim that you have 'forgiven' that person, and put it behind you. The fact that you have a high score on this Shadow indicates that you have not dealt with that pain, and you have certainly not forgiven that person. It is not 'behind' you, it is firmly influencing your life today.

Take the case of a woman who is attacked and raped. Should she try to 'forget' it? Of course not! The event should be reported to the police and the rapist sent to jail. That is justice. However, let us go forward in time, to about 15 years later. The rapist may have been released from jail. The woman, however, has serious problems in relationships with men, is still afraid to venture outside her home alone, and has serious issues about her self-worth. If you were to ask her why she had all these problems, she would say that the rapist is to blame for her present state of affairs. Is this true?

The person who hurt you so long ago probably does not give it another thought today. She or he may not even remember it. Yet you still give this person the power today to determine your emotional state. Every day, you hand this person your power. Forgiveness has nothing to do with making what happened 'right' or 'OK', because what happened was not 'right' or 'good'. Forgiveness is about taking your power back, and saying, *'Enough! I refuse to let you control my life anymore.'*

In the example of the woman who was raped, she can view herself as a 'rape victim', with all the consequences that come from that label, or a 'rape survivor', with all its consequences. The 'rape victim' remains stuck in the event, leaving her power in the hands of the rapist, whereas the 'rape survivor' takes her power back, gets on with her life, and does not allow him to determine her future happiness.

With this Shadow comes an enormous opportunity for personal growth. Keep this in mind while you read the rest of the description of this Shadow.

It is useful to know how this Shadow typically develops:

- **The unjust infliction of pain:** There is no doubt that, somewhere in the past, usually in childhood, some unjust pain was inflicted on you. This could range from one of your parents leaving you, or your being hurt and abused, or it could be more recent, such as losing an unborn child. The circumstances can vary enormously. However, if you look closely at your life, you will find one or more events in which pain was caused for you, and this pain seemed unfair and uncalled for. Try to find the earliest event.
- **Unfair conditions for obtaining love and attention from parents:** Alternatively, a parent may have insisted that you earned love through being 'good' or 'nice'. Love could have been withheld if you didn't comply, and being 'not nice' could include being sick, not being hungry, and various normal things. Obviously, you felt trapped, unwanted, and could not fulfil these requirements for love.
- **Overpowering parents:** As a child you may have been unable to respond to the adult's anger, temper or physical power. Consequently, you gave in to ensure your survival. You became obedient but resentful, and found ways of getting revenge in covert ways.
- **Modelling:** Watching someone (such as your mother) act out this Shadow. You may have copied it and continued to carry her pain into

your own life. For example, as a child, you may have watched your mother passively submit to your father. When he wasn't present, she complained about the way she was treated, but did nothing about it. You saw that your mother was abused when she asserted herself. However, you also noticed that your mother's strategy was more powerful than your father's, because her methods of revenge were quiet, continual, and relentless.

The development of this Shadow appears, at the superficial level, to be wide and varied. Rejection, abuse, oppression, inflicted pain and suffering, miscarriages, accidents, or a whole range of possible wounds were inflicted on you at some point in your life.

Please note that it is important not to be side-tracked by more recent wounds, as these are simply repetitions of much earlier wounds. In almost every single case, the actual or perceived 'cause' of the pain (wound) would have been external – mother, father, teacher, husband, wife, government or God. In a few cases, the 'wound' may have been self-inflicted, but this is not common. There is no disputing these facts, as they are a matter of record.

One aspect of this Shadow is that all the possible formative events associated with it contain situations in which you felt powerless and trapped. This is your greatest fear – to be trapped and unloved.

The second aspect of this Shadow is the component of revenge. Why? When someone else hurts you, it is natural to try and inflict the same amount of pain on the other person, to 'make it fair and equal'. The belief is that, if you can hurt this person in the same way, she or he would understand that what happened was not OK, and would be sorry about it. The only problem with this belief is that it is not based in reality or experience – you can never inflict the same pain you feel on someone else. It will always be different because pain is subjective. There is no such thing as 'getting even' and you will not succeed, ever, in erasing the pain through revenge. That is a fact.

Second, every time you think about the pain that has been caused to you, you do not re-experience exactly the same pain again – every remembering is a slightly different, 'new' pain. So, there is the original pain, which is then compounded and increased over time. Do you want to continue giving that person so much power over your life?

However, when you cannot inflict the same amount of pain, then you find other ways of revenge. The most subtle and powerful method is to ensure that the person who hurt you sees your pain and suffering. Usually, however, the actual person disappears from the scene, and you use this strategy on anyone who represents that original person.

For example, if a father hurts his daughter, she will transfer her need for revenge to other men, or a man who was hurt by his father may transfer this to authority figures, governments or even God ('our *Father* who art in Heaven'). The very nature of this Shadow lies in the statement *'Look at how I suffer! See what you've done!'*

This is why, when you ask for help from someone and that person offers some solution, you may resist the solution. Underlying your request for help is the fact that you are merely asking someone to witness your suffering. You are not interested in finding a solution. You want revenge. Typically, this explanation is followed by: *'Yes, but … if you understood my special circumstances (i.e. my wound from the past), you would understand why I cannot be happy.'*

The bottom line is that you hold your wound up to the world as a beacon for attention. You do not want to let it go, because then how will you get your revenge? How will you get attention? How else will you justify your suffering today? How else can you control other people with guilt?

As previously stated, your greatest fears are of being trapped and of being unlovable. You feel that, if someone really loved you, that person would find out how to make you happy. But you will not tell him or her what will make you happy! Wonderful way of getting revenge, isn't it? Consequently, everyone fails to make you happy, and you make sure that other people know how they have failed in this. Evidence to this effect can be seen in the fact that you rarely complain to someone who can change the situation. Instead, you complain to someone who cannot fix the problem.

The very moment you think or say something like *'If she/he loved me, then she/he would say/do/be something,'* you know that you are operating from this Shadow and handing your power to someone else. You are also abusing the love of someone, in order to suit your own agenda. The tables could be easily turned by saying to yourself: *'If you really loved him/her, you would tell him/her what you want and need, so that s/he can love you in the way you want to be loved.'*

When you 'test' your loved ones, and set them up to see if they really love you, you are abusing their love, and setting yourself up for being rejected and attacked for being so manipulative. If you want or need something, say so! Do not assume that anyone else can read your mind. People are different, and therefore you cannot assume that someone will know what you need.

People who score high with this Shadow are in a difficult situation. They are intensely needy for sympathy and attention to compensate for the pain they have suffered. But, at the same time, they believe that if they admit to this neediness, people would reject them. It is therefore very difficult for them to tell the truth about their needs and wants.

For example, a friend invites you to a picnic, but you refuse, saying you have too much work to do. If she persists in asking, you will eventually give in, saying *'Oh, if you insist. I'll come just so you won't be angry with me.'* Meanwhile, what you really wanted to say was, *'Thank you! I really wanted you to ask me! Thank you!'*

Notice that the statement *'I will come so that you won't be angry with me'* immediately places responsibility for your enjoyment of the picnic on the other person. Nice manipulation of guilt, isn't it?

When you land up in a situation in which you feel trapped, you switch to the *Impatient–Restless* Shadow, and the pent-up anger explodes into a tirade and then you dissolve into tears. This frustration of feeling trapped can result in your making rushed and rash decisions, leading to an even more trapped situation.

It can be argued that everyone has had some pain in their lives – so what makes this Shadow different? Several things. First, you use your pain as a weapon to control other people and keep them locked into a relationship with feelings of guilt and sympathy. You will not – you refuse to – let go of the pain of the past.

Second, as previously described, you use various strategies to manipulate people into 'proving' how much they care or love you. Furthermore, if the other person gives up in frustration, you silently say to yourself: *'If s/he cared for me, s/he would have tried one more time, asked one more time …'*

Naturally, the therapist, partner or friend feels a sense of failure, and feels tremendous guilt. Your justification for this is: *'It's not my fault – it's his fault that I am not happy,'* and it is powerful and convincing, because you use logic, justice and facts as your armour.

The only problem with this brilliant manipulation is that you say you want to be happy today, but you claim that you can't be because of what has happened in the past. This is simply not true. This Shadow knows full well that, to be happy today, the past has to be released. But this is not the same as forgetting what happened.

No one is suggesting that what happened didn't happen. Furthermore, we are not suggesting that what happened was not unfair and unjust, or that it shouldn't be viewed as such.

What we are suggesting is forgiveness, but our interpretation of the word is important. Forgiveness is not reconciliation. Forgiveness is not restitution. Forgiveness is not 'making it right'. Forgiveness does not mean that you stop seeking legal justice. Forgiveness does not necessarily involve both parties. To forgive the person who hurt you, for example a family member, does not mean you now have to go to family dinners and pretend that everything is OK, and that the slate is wiped clean. In fact, if you wish to pursue legal action, that course of action is perfectly compatible with forgiveness. Understand that we are not approving of the offender's behaviour. We are not defending him or her and we are certainly not interested in how he or she feels. Furthermore, you do not have to confront the people who hurt you, or say anything to them at all, nor do they have to return the gesture, or even be aware of what you have done.

Forgiveness is a personal, one-sided process. It involves only you and releasing your own pain, so that you can move on in your life.

Forgiveness simply means that you take back your power from whoever hurt you, and that you give (for-give) the pain of the past back to the past. Forgiveness means ceasing to blame and giving up the emotional need for revenge. It does not mean that you let the other person 'off the hook' in terms of his or her responsibility and accountability for his or her actions. All it means is that you let yourself off the hook in terms of the effects of that person's actions.

Most importantly, there is a way of viewing forgiveness that makes it the most sane and logical thing to do, from your personal perspective. Do you think the person who hurt you thinks about what she or he did to you as often as you do? Who is hurting, you or the person who hurt you? Do you realise that this person is blissfully unaware of your pain, still continues to dominate your life and still manages to live inside you, simply because you will not let the matter go? To put it in a more radical perspective: You say that the pain you hold on to is important to you – which it must be, seeing that you will not let it go. So why do you not write a letter of thanks to that person for giving this pain to you? After all, you insist on holding it close to you, don't you?

Forgiveness is the only healthy option and, by this, we mean healthy for you.

How do you forgive? Forgiveness is the act of 'giving back' what you do not want, namely the pain. The exact process is explained in another chapter. Suffice to say, it involves taking back your power from that person.

Isn't there anything 'nice' about this Shadow? Oh, indeed! The above descriptions are rather ruthless, because people with this Shadow are tough survivors. Yes, you whine and complain a lot, and can be quite spiteful. However, you tend to stay when others flee the battlefield. The 'gift' of this Shadow is hardiness – knowing you can survive pain and difficulty. This 'gift' is hidden under layers of other things, including perceived powerlessness, but it is there.

Make no mistake, you are a tough cookie! Your ability to endure difficulties will stand you in good stead in difficult times. What we are suggesting is that you do not need to hold on to past difficulties and pain to prove the point! It is time to start enjoying your power to create pleasure and happiness in your life. You can do it, if you let yourself.

Dealing with people dominated by this Shadow

One of the keys to dealing with people scoring high with this Shadow is to insist that they say what they mean, and to not use 'Yes, but' phrases or variations on this statement. Second, make sure that your boundaries are very explicit and clear: *'This is what I do, and what I am responsible for. You are responsible for …'* Also, make it clear that you do not 'do guilt trips'. When these people start complaining about how unhappy they are, do not be seduced by the reason, and avoid blame at all costs. Point to what they are willing and capable of *doing* to rectify the matter.

Often, people with *Blaming–Shaming* are unaware of how their whining and complaining, and especially their vagueness to state what they want, alienates others. Without being derogatory or critical, it may be useful to point this out to them. Make it clear that you do not 'read minds', particularly when it comes to support. This is particularly important in restoring their sense of power over their lives, which was damaged by past injustices, and the (past) inability to counter that injustice.

We have made some interesting observations regarding the link between this specific Shadow and autoimmune disease – allergies, multiple sclerosis, arthritis, and also certain kinds of diabetes. There is no comprehensive research on this at present, but we are gathering information. When dealing with such issues, we suggest careful attention is given to this Shadow, especially in relation to issues of guilt, 'mistakes that can't be rectified', issues that the person refuses to deal with, and similar related subjects. We reiterate that these suggestions are based on a range of observations and cannot be regarded as definitive.

This is a very rewarding Shadow to work with, regardless of how high the scoring. To some extent, we all hand over our power to a past event, person or circumstances, and this will always affect the body.

■ ASSIGNMENTS FOR THE BLAMING–SHAMING (B-S) SHADOW:

STEP 1   Immediate tasks
    a. After reading about how this Shadow develops, write a page on how this Shadow developed in your own life. Who did what to you

to instil a sense of powerlessness and a feeling of being trapped? Who do you blame for your unhappiness? Who do you need to forgive, in order to reclaim your power?

b. Identify at least three recent events in which you failed to tell someone what you wanted or needed, and then you got hurt because they could not figure it out, and you interpreted this as a sign that they did not care enough about you?

c. List three situations in which you feel trapped by circumstances.

d. List five things which 'someone should do something about', and about which you have failed to do anything.

e. Regarding your present health condition, identify three occasions when your insistence that the doctor or nurse was responsible for some aspect of your state of health helped you to deal with medical authorities and situations. Then identify three occasions where this same sense of 'it's your fault' and your failure to tell someone what you needed caused a problem in this area.

f. List three areas of your life in which you have power.

g. Write a paragraph regarding the difference between excusing (or condoning) wrongdoing and forgiving.

STEP 2   **Issues to start thinking about (to be addressed in subsequent sessions)**

a. Identify five fears you have in terms of being trapped in circumstances or being rejected for being perceived as needy. Just identify these fears and be specific. A subsequent chapter will show you how to deal with them.

b. Can you think of a time when you knew that, no matter what anyone said or did to you, you were in control of your life? What about the times when you knew exactly what was expected, and you could proceed with confidence? Who, in your childhood, did not tell you exactly what they wanted from you, and you had to struggle to 'read their minds'? Finally, who in your life do you also 'keep in the dark' about what you want and need, expecting them to figure it out?

c. What future goals and desires do you have that will provide you with a sense of determination, and also allow you to be sufficiently flexible to adapt as the situation changes? Ensure these goals are not dependent on any other person, destiny, luck or any external force – only you are responsible for whether it's achieved or not.

d. What do you perceive to be the lesson of this Shadow? In other words, what has your experience of this Shadow (and your new knowledge of it) taught you? What do you perceive to be the gift of this Shadow? In other words, what does it give to you, and what power does it bestow?

☐ SHADOW 7: NEVER ENOUGH (N-E)
'Just one more, then I'll be happy.'

KEY ISSUE: *Constant craving for 'something' that will bring final fulfilment and happiness. You fear the 'something' will never be found, and that you'll die unhappy and unfulfilled. No matter how much you have, you are focused only on what you do not have. Nothing is ever 'enough' – there must be 'more out there'. The 'something' is a substitute for the real love that you believe is unattainable.*

CAUSE: *Based on the core fear that you will die unloved and unfulfilled – i.e. the 'thing' you lack will never be found.*

What is wrong with wanting things, and wanting more of what you already have? Absolutely nothing! However, this Shadow has nothing to do with 'normal' wanting and desiring things. Rather, it is about wanting – even craving – things out of a deep sense of emptiness inside. For example, when you feel upset, you may go shopping to buy things you do not need, just so that you can feel better. Also, no matter how much you get, or how well things are going, you tend to think only about the things that you do not have. In other words, it is very difficult for you to feel satisfied about anything – there is always the need for more.

Even when you are talking to someone, your eyes and ears are roaming around the room, 'in case' there is someone more interesting. Even when you have an excellent relationship, you will notice only the small things that are not 'enough', and you may even destroy a good relationship 'in case' there is someone better for you somewhere else.

No matter how much money you accumulate, it is never enough. There is a fundamental belief that there is not enough to go round, and so you either tend to hold on to what you have, which can result in your being a bit of a miser, or you can focus all your attention on getting as much as you can. All this comes from a sense of emptiness, anxiety and fear. We need to repeat that this desire for 'more' does not come from a simple desire to experience and have things whick you want, and which will give you pleasure. Not at all.

This Shadow can manifest itself in many ways. When you get upset, what do you do to feel better? Shop? Eat? Gamble? Have sex? Do a course? Make more money? What is it you crave when you feel upset? You will notice that when you are doing this 'thing' (e.g. eating, shopping, gambling) you feel better for a short while, but the feeling of satisfaction disappears quickly, until the next time. It is almost as if there is a hole you are trying to fill, but it never seems to be full.

This feeling of trying to fill a hole inside yourself is what this Shadow is all about. In fact, it is the 'hole' that creates this Shadow.

At the outset, it needs to be very clearly stated that the single focus of dealing with this Shadow lies in addressing issues of abandonment – real, perceived, physical or emotional.

However, before we even discuss this abandonment issue, we need to make something very clear. The abandonment does not necessarily make sense from an adult, logical, reasonable perspective. An excellent example would be the situation of being sent to boarding school as a child. Let us imagine that there is a family living in a rural area, who really want to ensure that their child gets the best possible education. Furthermore, the local schools are quite a distance away, and it would be difficult to get the child to school and back every day. So, after much discussion between the parents and the child, it is decided that the child will go to an excellent boarding school. All this makes perfect sense from an adult perspective, and when the child grows up, she would say that it was a really positive stage in her development, and would probably recommend the school to other parents. However, those are simply the facts of the situation, and facts do not always include all the other unseen truths. For example, the parents drove for hours with the child until they finally reached the boarding school. The child was excited, a bit nervous, but otherwise quite happy. After putting her bags in her dormitory, meeting the teachers, and ensuring that everything was in order, the parents returned to their car to drive home. Still, everything was fine. However, as the child stood there, watching her parents drive away, it finally dawned on her that they were going away, and that she was being left behind. Although she knew this intellectually, she was unprepared for the emotional aspect of this reality.

Within the period of a minute or two, the child would have gone through an entire range of irrational thoughts and emotional feelings, including the thought and feeling *'If they really loved me, they wouldn't leave me here'.* This thought doesn't have to last for more than a few seconds in order to create a powerful emotional feeling of being abandoned, despite the 'logical' facts of the situation.

Everyone has been a child at some point in his or her life, and so everyone can understand feelings that are not based on logic or facts. Therefore, when we say that the central issue of this Shadow is 'abandonment', do not dismiss this if you were not literally and physically abandoned – it could have been a brief feeling similar to the example described, seen from a child's perspective.

There are also the more obvious examples of physical abandonment, such as being given up for adoption, or one of your parents leaving the home. The father of the family may have had to leave home for extended periods of time in order to obtain work in another part of the country or even in another country altogether. He may have had no choice in this, as the company he worked for or the work he did may have prohibited him from taking his family with him. The father's child may have 'understood' why this was happening but nevertheless may have felt abandoned, because a child tends to see things in very simple terms: *'If he loved me, he would be here with me. He is not here, therefore he does not love me.'* The logical facts of the situation do not make any difference to the feelings that were felt at that time: the child felt abandoned, and that is enough to create this Shadow.

An even subtler form of abandonment concerns emotional abandonment. In this kind, the parent may have been physically present all the time, but the child may not have felt as if the parent was emotionally present for him or her. For example, the child comes running to her mother, saying: *'Look at the picture I drew!'* And the mother, without even looking at the picture for more than a second or two, says, *'That's nice dear,'* and then carries on with her other activities. The child is not stupid – it knows the mother was not interested! This form of emotional abandonment occurs often when one or both parents are always busy with something, and, apart from ensuring that the child is fed, clean and has a warm bed to sleep in, do not pay much attention to the child. This can also happen when parents are alcoholics, addicts or depressives and are simply incapable of providing emotional attention and interest in the child.

The impact of the death of a loved one must not be underestimated in terms of creating this Shadow. Although people are reluctant to admit to the feelings of anger that follow the death of someone they love, these feelings are very real. Again, there is the overwhelming feeling of abandonment. A great deal of unresolved grief centres around such feelings of anger and abandonment, which the person will not discuss because she or he may feel terribly guilty about these 'bad' feelings.

So basically, this Shadow develops as follows:
- **The abandonment:** There are various types of abandonment:
a. *Physical abandonment:* Adoption, desertion, one or both parents leaving the child with someone else, or a loved one dies.
b. *Emotional abandonment:* The parents were not emotionally present for the child.
c. *Perceived abandonment:* A feeling of abandonment which was not necessarily based in fact, but the child simply saw it that way, even for a brief period of time.
- **The child's decision that she or he will never get the loved one's love.** This is the crucial part of the formation of this Shadow. Regardless of the situation that led to this, the belief that *'I will never get his or her love'* is the foundation for the creation of that 'hole' inside. From that moment onwards, methods will be found to try and fill the 'hole inside'.

As an adult, you may struggle to understand when this sense of abandonment developed, largely because you're trying to analyse the past in adult terms and concepts. For example, you intellectually understand why you were sent to boarding school, or that your parent had to work hard to put food on the table. However, when you place yourself back in your 'child' experience, where your thought processes were not logical, it becomes easier to comprehend. Children are very ego-centred and literal.

The sense of abandonment can also occur when a parent is preoccupied with the needs of a chronically ill spouse or family member. The bottom line regarding abandonment is that the child wanted love, protection and attention from someone, typically a parent. For whatever reason, that love, protection and attention was not there at the time the need arose. All the hindsight and adult understanding in the world cannot erase the feeling of unfulfilled need for the parent. It is not, we repeat, necessarily logical or rational. The consequence is a feeling of 'emptiness' deep inside, and a driving need to fill that 'empty space' where love is absent.

However, before you panic about the effects that your odd lapse of attention is having on your own children, it is important to remember that this Shadow comes about only as a result of repeated and consistent experiences of actual or perceived abandonment. Occasionally, a single traumatic event can produce the same result, such as physical abandonment or being sent to boarding school. Usually though, it is the result of a consistent pattern of less obvious and perceived emotional abandonment. The clincher for this Shadow is when, as a child, you made the decision that, no matter what, you would never get the love you wanted from the person you wanted love from. Clearly, the core issue is '*I am not lovable*', and the core fear is of dying alone and unloved.

To deal with this 'empty hole inside', the child sought a substitute for the missing love. The substitute manifests differently from one individual to another and is dependent on the developmental stage of the child at that time and the substitute offered by the parent. For some it is food, while for others it is buying things or accumulating specific objects. A less obvious form is the accumulation of knowledge, or constantly doing courses to find the answer, as 'guru hoppers' or 'workshop junkies' do. The substitute itself is unimportant in the greater scheme of things – there is usually nothing inherently 'wrong' with the substitute itself. However, the important aspect of the substitute is that you tend to crave it when you feel insecure, upset or stressed, you indulge in it and feel better for a brief period, and then you crave more, hence 'Never Enough'.

The reality is that there is no lasting external substitute for what is missing – the love from the person whom you perceive as having abandoned you.

One of the more profound effects of this Shadow, directly emerging from its development, is that you don't believe you will ever get the 'real thing'. This even applies to times when you have obtained the 'real thing'. This deep-seated suspicion can cause fundamental problems in relationships and career, where you turn down a good job out of suspicion, or end a perfectly good relationship, or ignore loyal friends for the possibility that *'There must be something better out there.'*

Whatever is available is simply not good enough. The phrase *'The grass is greener on the other side'* is a classic *Never Enough* Shadow statement. For this reason, this Shadow tends to create its own worst nightmare, namely ending up alone, unloved and unfulfilled. You criticise and reject whatever is available and consequently end up with very little or nothing at all.

An outsider would consider that you have gathered a great deal of 'stuff'. However, it is important to realise that, from your point of view, you're aware only of what is not there – what is missing. In other words, your primary focus is on what you don't have – money, sex, relationships, career and possessions – regardless of how much you already do have. The old saying that money brings misery and loneliness is an accurate statement for people dominated by this Shadow. However, we need to make it quite clear that the connection between wealth and unhappiness is restricted to this Shadow, and is not true in and of itself. Certainly, money cannot buy happiness. However, poverty provides even fewer choices! Indeed, it is the greed for 'having stuff' – including money – that is associated with misery in this Shadow, simply because the Shadow has a constant craving which never completely subsides.

Naturally, jealousy and envy can be powerful elements in the life of a person led by this Shadow, as these emotional forces are based on the desire to have something that someone else has, or the fear that someone else will take away what is yours.

Another manifestation of this Shadow is the opposite of greed, namely self-imposed deprivation. When the fear of never having what you want is strong, you retreat from reaching for that object or person, because you instinctively know that it will never satisfy you, cutting off any avenue of fulfilment. Therefore, this Shadow's somewhat distorted logic may try to hold onto the hope of eventual fulfilment by purposely depriving you of what you want.

The fluctuation between the two extremes – 'must have' and 'must not have' – is at the basis of binging and purging problems, including eating disorders and drug and alchohol abuse. For example, in bulimia, the thought patterns may be as follows: *'I hate being deprived – I am going to have as much as I want of everything.'* Then, after the bingeing period, there are feelings of remorse, self-rejection, and lack of total fulfilment, no matter how much you consume. The pendulum shifts to the extreme, and the purging (self-deprivation) stage enacts itself.

In many cases, this Shadow is quite destructive within relationships. After the 'conquest' – getting what you want – you become a classic 'taker', demanding a lot from your partner, giving little in return. You resent any error or slip by the partner, in terms of attentiveness, understanding and sympathy. The irony is that you desperately want and need a partner, but resent your partner for not being exactly what you want! Inevitably, you push your partner away, either because of high and strict demands, or because you are unfaithful, which you view as some form of punishment for the 'imperfect' partner, or as a strategy to get more attention from the other.

At an intellectual and spiritual level, this Shadow can result in a 'greed' for knowledge. This manifests in the feeling that, no matter how many teachers, gurus or professors you consult, no one has the 'right' answer, neither do any of these people have the means or methods to fulfil all your needs. Ironically, some forms of this Shadow view deprivation – of money, sex, material goods or happiness – as being the means to eventually 'have more' salvation.

Dealing with people dominated by this Shadow

A distinctive physical characteristic of people who score high with this Shadow is intense, 'hungry' and roving eyes – always seeking something. Because they're constantly focused on what they may be missing, their attention is easily distracted. Other physical characteristics can include extreme weight loss or gain.

When dealing with people with this Shadow, don't expect them to be team players – they are in the game for themselves. If they believe you have the knowledge or power they want or need, they are easily persuaded to do as you ask. However, if they believe you have nothing to offer, they will ignore you. Motivation is fairly easy. Use the 'carrot approach' – tell them what they will 'have' as a result of the process, and point out what it is that is 'missing' in their lives. Although this sounds like manipulation, and it is, keep in mind that these tactics are measures to engage the Shadow in supporting the process. If this is not done, these people will be blocked by the Shadow. Once they have a grip on this Shadow, such tactics are no longer necessary.

Regardless of the various other issues that arise in the PNI process, the key to resolving this Shadow – and the healing process itself – is dealing with the issues of abandonment and feeling unloved. Attention needs to be paid to what these people believe they will never have and what they desperately want – the feeling that they are lovable. In the chapter dealing with creating resources, this issue is addressed.

Read the *Frantic–Destructive* Shadow to understand what happens when these people fail to get what they want.

■ ASSIGNMENTS FOR THE NEVER ENOUGH (N-E) SHADOW:

STEP 1   Immediate tasks

   a. After reading about how this Shadow develops, write a page on how this Shadow developed in your own life. Who did you believe abandoned you, either physically or emotionally? Remember to view this in terms of the child's mentality, and not in terms of the adult you are today. Carefully re-read the various possible scenarios presented earlier to understand this sense of abandonment.

   b. Identify at least three recent events in which you felt unhappy, unfulfilled or stressed. What did you do to feel better? Shopping, eating, drugs, alcohol, reading – what is your substitute, your comfort-producing activity?

   c. List three important things you believe to be missing in your life.

   d. Regarding your present health condition:

   ■ Identify three occasions when your sense of '*This is not good enough – I want better and more*' and the drive to have what you want has helped you to deal with medical authorities and situations.

   ■ Identify three occasions when this same sense has caused a problem in this area, such as cutting off help and support, or failing to recognise that people were doing the best they can for you.

   e. List three specific people who, without question or doubt, love you and consider you lovable. If this is difficult for you to answer, spend some time carefully thinking about it – these people do exist.

   f. Write a paragraph regarding the difference between wanting something because it brings you satisfaction and pleasure, and wanting something because you feel incomplete until you have it. In other words, the difference between '*I am OK, and I want XYZ*' (your happiness is not dependent on having it – you simply want it) and '*I will feel OK when I have XYZ*' (your happiness is dependent on having it – you feel you need it).

STEP 2   **Issues to start thinking about (to be addressed in subsequent sessions)**

a.   Identify five fears you have in terms of never attaining happiness, never being loved and never reaching total fulfilment. Just identify these fears and be specific. A subsequent chapter will show you how to deal with these fears.

b.   Can you think of a time when you felt completely satisfied and fulfilled about something? How long did that feeling last?

c.   What future goals and desires do you have that will provide you with a sense of determination and also allow you to be sufficiently flexible to adapt as the situation changes? Also, ensure that these goals are not necessarily linked to some final point where you can say '*I have done it*'. Include some goals that provide pleasure in the striving itself, which will make you feel OK about yourself no matter how long it takes to achieve these goals.

d.   What do you perceive to be the lesson of this Shadow, i.e. what has your experience of this Shadow (and your new knowledge of it) taught you? What do you perceive to be the gift of this Shadow, i.e. what does it give to you, what power does it bestow?

☐ SHADOW 8: FRANTIC–DESTRUCTIVE (F-D)
'What's the point? We all die anyway!'

KEY ISSUE: *Self-destructive thoughts and behaviour based on experiences of abuse and abandonment; desperate need for self-control, and terror of losing control.*

CAUSE: *Based on the core fear that will lose control and kill yourself.*

The name of this Shadow is rather scary, and it's quite shocking to hear such a label of yourself. Before you run away, please keep in mind that resolving this Shadow is truly simple and, when achieved, the positive effects are dramatic. Before we discuss resolution, let us first describe this Shadow.

You fluctuate between feelings of being out of control (frantic) and trying to control pain by inflicting it on yourself (destructive). This Shadow manifests itself in many ways, including socialising with people who cannot be trusted, exposing yourself to dangerous activities, high-risk ventures, drug and alcohol dependencies, and ensuring that there is always someone around who can be depended on to abuse you. Feelings of desperation often emerge when you are alone. In the extreme, suicide attempts are made in the effort to control death, or because you have reached a point where nothing works and living no longer seems a viable option – it is too out of control and painful. It should be clear that the fear that fuels this Shadow is that of being out of control or losing control. Taking positive control of your life, health and body is essential to your wellness.

You don't understand the point of living because, for you, life has become translated into pain and loss. The lack of social and familial law and order in your life has created a lack of personal boundaries and respect for your life, health and body. In turn, this has probably been one of the causes of your illness. You've given up believing in God (or a higher being), because *'God gave up on me.'* After all, *'if there was a God, why would there be so much pain in the world? You just have to look around you to understand what I mean?'*

People dominated by this Shadow tend to involve themselves either with people led by the same Shadow (who encourage erratic and extreme behaviour) or those scoring high with the *Apologising–Failure* Shadow (who are prepared to subjugate their own needs through love and sympathy).

A typical behaviour is evidenced with those who attach themselves to some religious movement. They are either expelled from the group because they perceive the principles of the religion as an attempt to control them and, therefore, they set about undermining those principles, or they endure abstinence or some other form of suffering for the sake of 'salvation'. There is little joy, peace or serenity in religion for people with high scores in this Shadow.

People led by this Shadow can be detected by two key characteristics. First, they have intense and desperate eyes. Second, there is little concept of personal boundaries and frequent invasion of other people's personal space without permission and a blatant ignorance of cues in this regard. Therefore, other people tend to be repelled in the unconscious act of trying to re-establish their personal space while you experience another sensation of rejection and abandonment, although this is, unwittingly, all your own doing. The only people who do not have a problem with this invasion of personal space is, of course, other people led by this Shadow, who support and reinforce the pattern of self-destructive, inappropriate behaviour. In the end, they are the only people left.

How does this Shadow develop?

- **Abuse – physical, emotional or mental:** This Shadow is the consequence of having to cope with overwhelming and painful circumstances for which you were ill equipped at that time – physically, emotionally or mentally. On rare occasions, it is the consequence of some catastrophic event such as rape, assault, torture or a disaster of some kind. At the same time, you felt alone, powerless and abandoned. Altogether, the result is a set of self-destructive behaviours and inclinations. You feel stranded in this world, with no clear sense of what it all means, and why all this pain exists.

  It is also important to understand that abuse can be non-physical, such as being shouted at, accused, degraded or humiliated for no apparent reason.

- **The abuse was senseless:** The abuse and punishment made no sense to the child, such as being hit *'Just to remind you that the world is a hard place'*, or was completely out of proportion to the misbehaviour (if any). This is a key aspect of the formation of this Shadow. As a result, all sense of fairness and structure was either destroyed or damaged. Another consequence of this abusive treatment was that, as a child, you were unable to develop a sense of personal boundaries and personal space, simply because these were often violated without reason. Essentially, you couldn't form a clear idea of where you fitted, of your 'place in the world', and the world itself made no sense to you.

- **Belief that 'I must be bad and must be punished'.** These experiences of abuse and emotional or physical neglect and abandonment lead to beliefs such as: *'I'm alone in the world, the world is a scary place, and I'm too small to fix any of it.'* Because no one took care or control of the environment around you, you developed a sense that no one is in control and, consequently, the belief that there is no structure in the world. In other words, everything is random and usually painful.

  Children have an inborn sense of cause-and-effect. To justify this kind of treatment, you concluded, *'There must be something fundamentally wrong or bad about me.'* The sense of helplessness is profound, as you could not do anything to stop the abuse or neglect. You often sensed your life was in danger, either through physical actions against you, or emotional threats to this effect.

- **Decision that 'To control the pain, I must take the role of the abuser'.** As a child, you could not tolerate such lack of structure indefinitely and you had to strive to find some way to restore a sense of control and meaning. The only meaning you could perceive was that you were bad and had to be punished, as this is what the world (people) apparently communicated to you.

The only logical way to control the abuse and pain was to take over the role of the abuser, and begin to punish yourself. At least in this way, you could regulate the pain and abuse. It is at this moment that the *Frantic–Destructive* Shadow emerges – the (frantic) method of regulating and controlling pain and abuse as your response to a world that is out of control.

This Shadow regularly slides into the *Never Enough* Shadow. When you 'hit rock bottom' – which is nothing more than reaching the point of having challenged death and survived (a perceived control over death) – you become totally energised and want to tackle the world.

During this stage, you become almost manic in your attempts to absorb and 'have' as much 'life' as possible, usually with little concept of what it involves – time and effort. The inevitable 'crash' leads to a slide back into the self-destructive Shadow. This see-saw pattern of intense glee and depression is another key characteristic of this Shadow.

Dealing with people dominated by this Shadow

In dealing with people who score high with this Shadow, the maintenance of boundaries and personal space is crucial. However, unlike most personal interactions, these boundaries need to be stated clearly and repeatedly, so that the person led by this Shadow begins to establish some sense of stability and certainty. Therefore, working with these people demands a high level of clarity regarding your own personal boundaries and values – what works for you, and what doesn't work for you – and the ability to state these without fear of rejection or need for approval.

Considering the abusive experiences underlying this Shadow, most people's initial reaction is to step in and rescue the victim, out of sympathy. However, for reasons already stated, this can have disastrous effects. Instead, a firm 'tough love' approach is the most likely method of assisting these people in dealing with their issues. It is essential that people dominated by this Shadow discover that there is at least someone who somehow has managed to get control of himself or herself, and who has a clear sense of what this whole thing called 'life' is about, even on a limited scale. In many respects, this 'someone' will serve as an anchor and reference point.

However, it needs to be understood that your clarity and firmness are not arbitrary or random. The rules and reasons of interaction need to be stated, and they need to be rational, fair and serve both parties' interests.

The stated approach works to protect the person affected by the Shadow and the person working with him or her. It is very common for a person to use self-destructive behaviour in interactions with others, such as failing to arrive for important appointments, not doing assignments and similar behaviour.

It is crucial that the person you are helping knows where you stand, and what you will and will not tolerate. If you say that you will do something, then back it up with action.

The resolution of this Shadow lies in establishing and clarifying a sense of personal integrity, which was prevented by earlier events and abusive people. Those with this Shadow have looked outside for guidance, meaning a sense of order and justice, and found little evidence of it. Based on what they have experienced, there is indeed very little meaning to life. However, the fundamental lesson to be learned is that integrity (self-truth – who I am, and where I fit in) is found inside, not outside.

This is not some glib catch-phrase: it is a challenge to people with the *Frantic–Destructive* Shadow to stop wasting time trying to control the uncontrollable, and begin forming their own personal framework and structure of justice, honour, love and meaning. Just as the *Never Enough* Shadow focuses only on what is missing in his or her life, this Shadow views life from the perspective of what is wrong, painful and unfair. It is time to turn this around, and use these painful experiences as references to define yourself.

■ ASSIGNMENTS FOR THE FRANTIC–DESTRUCTIVE (F-D) SHADOW:

Step 1   Immediate tasks

    a. After reading about how this Shadow develops, write a page on how this Shadow developed in your own life. Who abused you? Who do you believe neglected or abandoned you, either physically or emotionally? Remember to view this in terms of the child's mentality, and not in terms of the adult you are today.

    b. Identify at least three recent events in which you felt out of control and desperate, wondering why you should bother with this thing called 'life'.

    c. List three important values or principles that have pulled you through difficult times. Where did you learn these values and principles?

    d. List at least three qualities you bring to this world that make the world a better place to live in.

    e. Write a page about your understanding of God and when you stopped believing in a higher being. How would you reintroduce spirituality (not to be confused with religion) into your life?

    f. Write a paragraph regarding the difference between human justice and divine justice.

    g. Regarding your present health condition:

    ■ Identify three occasions when your perversity and defiance helped you to deal with medical authorities and situations.

    ■ Identify three occasions when this same sense caused a problem in this area, such as refusing help and support, or not recognising that there were health professionals who cared about what they do and who would not neglect or abuse you.

    h. List three specific people who, without question, value you and respect your integrity. If this is difficult for you to answer, spend some time giving it deep and careful thought – these people do exist.

Step 2:   Issues to start thinking about (to be addressed in subsequent sessions)

    a. Identify five fears you have in terms of never knowing the meaning of your life. Just identify these fears and be specific. A subsequent chapter will show you how to deal with these fears.

b. Can you think of a time when you felt happy and that all was right in the world? How long did that feeling last?

c. What future goals and desires do you have that will provide you with a sense of purpose and also allow you to be sufficiently flexible to adapt as the situation changes? Ensure these goals provide ongoing focus and application and give you the feeling that you're in control.

d. What do you perceive to be the lesson of this Shadow? In other words, what has your experience of this Shadow (and your new knowledge of it) taught you? What do you perceive to be the gift of this Shadow? In other words, what does it give to you, what power does it bestow?

DEALING WITH FEAR

Fear is the greatest obstacle to healing. We believe it is also at the root of all the various issues you will need to deal with, including stress, expressing what you feel, and finding a sense of purpose and passion for the future.

The power of confronting fear

In 1990, Sue Weidenfeld and colleagues *[1]* conducted a study of the effects on the immune system of confronting fears. A group of 20 people with an irrational fear (or phobia) of snakes were individually taken through a series of three two-hour sessions over three weeks, in which they confronted this fear. The results were astounding and important. After the intervention, there was an increase in the number of helper T-cells, of 132 on average, and an average decrease in cortisol levels of about 30 percent. These results were maintained for months after the intervention. As the average range of helper T-cells is somewhere between 600 and 1200, this represents a 10 to 20 percent change in this aspect of the immune system, purely through psychological technique. Very few drugs can accomplish the same result.

There was an important twist to this experiment. A small group (25 percent) of the subjects did not benefit from this process. In fact, their immune system got worse during the experiment, and then returned to previous levels after the experimental intervention was completed. When the researchers looked at the psychological profiles of the people who responded negatively to the intervention, they found that they all had the lowest scores on self-determination (the sense of '*I can*') before the intervention.

This is an important finding, because it indicates that issues of low self-worth need to be addressed before embarking on other processes to boost the immune system, otherwise they may sabotage the process and cause increased stress. For assistance on this issue, refer to Chapter 5 (page 78), under the heading *Response–ability: Yes, I can.*

As a whole, however, the experiment clearly demonstrated the dramatic immunological benefits of confronting fear.

The impact of fear on the immune system should not be underestimated, either for its direct effects (increasing levels of cortisol or adrenaline), or for its indirect effects (causing its victim to give up, feel hopelessness, apathy, depression, failure to seek support, and many other consequences). We would go as far as to say that fear is the single most overlooked important factor in mind–immune conditions.

Types of fear

There is a wide range of emotions – mild to strong – that fall into the general category of fear: worry, anxiety, concern, phobia, panic, terror, apprehension. These are all forms of fear.

All forms of fear are started by the thought '*What if …?*', whether this concerns something that is actually happening to you, or something you think might happen. The effect is the same.

The biological mechanisms behind fear

Why is fear such a powerful force in our lives? Why is it that, even when logically we know better, we still feel afraid of certain things? The simple answer is that fear is neither logical nor reasonable. Do you remember the story of our ancestor Trog in Chapter 3 (page 47) regarding how the SAM and HPAC systems developed as a means of survival?

The brain's fear mechanism developed similarly, solely to protect you from danger. Also, as with the SAM and HPAC systems, the problem is that the dangers that were once outside of ourselves – wild animals, for example – are no longer there, and most of our human reactions are based on perceived dangers, which are inside ourselves. The problem is that your brain does not know the difference!

For example, until a few hundred years ago, if people were rejected by their tribe or family, they faced the real possibility of dying due to attack from wild animals or other tribes, or starvation. Therefore, rejection by the family, loved ones or society was literally a death sentence. In those days, individuals needed the group or tribe to ensure physical survival. When you say '*I would just die if he (or she) left me!*' you are essentially tapping into the genetic memories of this bygone era, and although 'logically' you know better, it still feels like a death sentence.

So, when there are situations in which your brain perceives that your survival is at stake – such as perceived loss of control or failure to control a situation – it activates and dominates your behaviour, regardless of your 'positive' thoughts. It is as if our physical existence has moved beyond mere physical survival, but our emotional states are still trapped in that faraway time.

When dealing with issues of fear, you are essentially dealing with the primitive parts of your brain, not the more sophisticated thinking (logical) parts of your brain. Techniques that work wonderfully for the 'thinking brain' simply do not work for the 'primitive brain'. Our understanding of positive thinking and affirmations is that they are thoughts and concepts of the 'thinking brain', and the intention is that, by repetition, these thoughts and concepts will filter down into the more primitive parts of our brain. That is why positive thinking programmes encourage you to feel a thought, so that it can step into the more basic brain areas. However, if you have fears regarding those thoughts, or fears that contradict them, these emerge from the 'primitive brain' and override the 'thinking brain'.

FEAR PRINCIPLE 1

Fear can – and will – override more sophisticated thoughts and feelings.

Confronting fear needs to be directed at updating our primitive emotional and mental responses, to take the present reality into account. It is totally useless to tell someone (or yourself) '*Stop being silly – there is nothing to worry about!*' The fact of the matter is that the 'primitive (survival-focused) brain' believes there is danger, even although your logical 'thinking brain' says otherwise. You have to deal with the reality of all levels of your brain and mind.

FEAR PRINCIPLE 2

Believing you are in danger feels exactly the same as the real thing.

It is important to understand the fact that the intention
and purpose of the 'primitive brain' is a positive one,
namely to ensure your survival. It is your ally –
not what you would consider an 'intelligent'
ally – but one that will get you
through situations of danger.
One way of looking at the 'primitive
brain' is as your watchdog – it will
growl and bark until it believes
the danger is over.

*Danger!
I must protect
my master*

To understand fear, and how to deal with it effectively, this analogy of the
watchdog is useful. When you are afraid, your mind races and your thoughts
and feelings are dominated by the fear – the watchdog is jumping up and
down, barking and growling at the 'danger'. This happens 24 hours of the
day, even while you are asleep. It is indeed a chronic low-grade stressor! If
the situation is resolved, the fear stops, just as a watchdog lies down when
the danger is over. However, if the situation is chronic and long-term, the
watchdog will growl and bark constantly.

FEAR PRINCIPLE 3

**Unresolved fear will keep your unconscious mind activated 24 hours a day.
Fear does not go away when you sleep.**

Fear activates the emotional parts of the brain, specifically the hypothalamus.
The hypothalamus then proceeds to send out its chemical messages, which
results in chronic activation of the SAM or HPAC systems, depending on the
situation. This occurs 24 hours a day until the fear is resolved, and the results
can be devastating to the immune system.

FEAR PRINCIPLE 4

There are two and only two things to do with a F.E.A.R.

F.E.A.R. = **F**orget **E**verything **A**nd **R**un!
(avoid and deny it)

or …

F.E.A.R. = **F**ace **E**verything **A**nd **R**ecover!
(deal with it)

In other words, you have the choice to deal with your fears and move beyond them, or try to ignore them, deny them and pretend they are not there.

A fear indicates that you believe a certain outcome is probable. This automatically removes choice from the situation. Confronting fear removes the emotional energy from the fear and shifts it from a probability towards one of many possibilities, inserting choice into the situation.

When we ask people what they think 'fear' is all about, they say various things, all illustrating uncertainty and concern about something happening again or for the first time.

FEAR PRINCIPLE 5

Fear is nothing more and nothing less than the unanswered question: *'What if … ?'*

Think about it – every worry, concern, terror or anxiety you have ever experienced can be summarised as the thought *'What if this-or-that happens?'* Furthermore, as far as the 'primitive brain' is concerned, the real question is: *'How can I survive (control the outcome) of this situation?'*

Until this question is answered, the 'primitive brain' will jump up and down, barking and growling, demanding some action.

Fear Principle 6

The sole purpose of confronting fear – including the fears of your own death – is to increase your sense of being alive.

This principle is illustrated by an old Buddhist parable:
Two monks were on a journey to a distant monastery. The journey was a long one, and they walked for many days in complete silence, because they belonged to a sect that required them to stay silent from dawn until sunset.

Early one morning they arrived at a river. The river was running quite fast, but not too fast for the monks to cross. However, there was also a young woman wanting to cross the river who was too afraid to cross. One monk quietly picked her up, carried her across, and gently put her down on the other side. The other monk followed, and neither said a word until the sun went down at the end of the day.

'How could you touch the woman? It is forbidden!' said the one monk. *'Indeed,'* said the other monk, *'but I only carried her for five minutes, while you have been carrying her in your angry heart all day!'*

Dealing with the fear of death is the same. You confront the fear, leave it behind and move along. The alternative is to carry the fear all day, every day, causing great harm to your body and peace of mind.

Fear Principle 7

When dealing with feared possibilities, always put as much energy into desired possibilities.

In other words, when you confront your fears of death and take steps to settle your unfinished business, i.e. deal with the possibility of your death and dying, you also need to deal with the possibility of living, at the same time (or soon thereafter). So, when you do the suggested actions, make sure you refer to the goals you have set for yourself in Chapter 6 (page 92).

We like to imagine that this process is like shifting money from one bank account into another. When you confront your fears, you withdraw money from your Death Account. When you have done this, you need to reinvest it into your Life Account, where it can gather interest, and fund more pleasurable things.

In Assignment 1, you are asked to take specific actions to deal with your fears of death and dying. This is an example of how we propose you do it: Set a date to discuss funeral arrangements. As soon as you have made the appointment, make another appointment – on the same day, after the appointment with the funeral director – with a travel agent to book the trip to Bali that you have always wanted to take.

Common sense required

We human beings have not eliminated all real physical danger from our world. There are still a number of threats present, such as rape, murder, assault, hijacking, car crashes, aeroplanes falling out of the sky, fires, floods, earthquakes and so on.

To be afraid of these threats is normal. But the chances of them happening are generally not high (depending on where you live), and some are quite remote possibilities. However, normal preventive measures are appropriate for all these situations. So, when you do the exercise on confronting fear, please do not be deluded and think: *'Oh well – I confronted the fear of rape, so I don't have to be careful when I go out alone at night.'* That would be silly. Certainly, confront the emotional aspects of such threats, but please ensure you take logical and physical measures to reduce the chances of them happening as well!

The illusion of safety

No matter how securely you are settled into your comfort zone, you cannot escape risk. Crossing the road is a risk. Falling in love is a risk. Marriage is a risk in which you may face failure and disappointment. Even life itself is a sexually transmitted terminal disease! If you try to limit and control risk, you will be less vulnerable to it but you may also sacrifice excitement, new experiences, surprise and fun for 'ho-hum' predictability.

Paradoxically, trying to avoid risk is one of the biggest risks you can take. You risk never getting that terrific job, never exploring your talents to the full, never driving in a sports car with the warm wind in your hair.

Why take a risk? Because a life lived in fear is a life only half-lived! Taking a risk is a good thing, and one which we associate with impressive people. Being bored can motivate you to take a risk in the hope of making life more stimulating and satisfying – but only if the changes you hope for are realistic.

Unattainable hopes become an excuse not to bother taking risks. The biggest excuse not to bother, though, is fear. We are all sometimes reluctant to move forward because we're scared of what might happen. *'It's OK for him,'* we think, *'but I'm not like that. After all, I'll probably do it wrong and everyone will laugh at me.'* These reactions are normal, but not helpful.

When we do unfamiliar things, we tap into our fear and experience a very primitive biological response – the 'primitive brain' kicks into motion. In scary situations, our fight-or-flight instinct is triggered, leaving us feeling anxious and defensive. Also, fear of something going wrong reminds us of things that went wrong previously. You stand up to make a speech at work and it reminds you of the time you stood up to talk to your class and you made a fool of yourself. Years later, you can still feel that embarrassment. A bad risk-taking experience usually makes us more cautious. It needn't even be our own bad experience – seeing your father risk and lose his business can make you resist starting one of your own, even if you clearly have what it takes.

We also feel it is important to realise that there is a very big difference between 'putting your life at risk' and 'taking risks in your life'. Some people confuse the two.

Levels of fear

The fear of breaking a fingernail or of having your new hair-do wrecked in the wind is not the same as being afraid of dying painfully. Although some people might argue about this – especially the part about your hair – common sense and experience seem to indicate that there are different levels and intensities of fear.

The fears of death and dying

It is ironic that the one issue that is constantly on your mind – the possibility of dying in pain and the possibility of death – is the one that everyone avoids discussing, insisting that 'this will upset you' (which it will), and that it is 'negative thinking'. Yet it may be the effects of this chronic fear that destroy the remainder of your immune system!

No amount of clever and abstract 'thinking brain' reasoning can override the reality that dying painfully is a fundamental 'primitive brain' fear. Furthermore, no amount of positive thinking has the power to diminish this fear. The only thing that denial-based positive thinking can accomplish is to suppress this potent fear until it is too late to do anything about it. However, at least you can die believing that everyone else believed your nonsense about 'being perfectly OK with dying'. Get real – ask your body if it wants to die painfully!

Therefore, when dealing with a chronic, potentially life-threatening illness, the first fear on which to focus is the possibility of dying. Ignoring it will not make it go away.

Furthermore, before you start the argument that 'thinking about dying' is 'negative' – which is an argument invented by terrified people who do not have a clue about what fear does to the immune system – remember that the point is to move through the fear and not dwell on it endlessly. The irony is that people who refuse to talk about death end up obsessing about it, and they never get to move beyond this fear.

The fear of death itself is a relatively easy one to deal with. Regardless of your religious or spiritual beliefs, or the total absence of any such beliefs, the issue of death boils down to one of two things. Either there is something after the death of the physical body, or there is absolutely nothing at all. Logically, if there is a life after death, then the only time you will know this for a fact will be when you are physically dead. Until then, it is a matter of belief.

If you have any concerns about exactly where you will go after death – for example, heaven or hell – then do something to increase your chances towards reaching the more desirable location. For example, go to your priest and make a confession, or write letters to all the people you think you have harmed, and apologise. If, on the other hand, there is absolutely nothing after physical death, then you will literally switch off at death, so there is no need to be concerned about any of this. Case closed.

In our experience, people are not so much disturbed by death as they are by the possibility of dying in pain, lonely, dependent, blind or helpless. This is a tricky situation, as your religious beliefs and morals can determine your practical options in terms of confronting this specific fear.

It takes enormous courage to confront the fears of dying and death, as there is always the nagging thought in the back of your head: 'Am I doing this because I believe I am going to die? Is this admitting defeat?'

The answer is this: it depends on whether you are doing all this *and* taking active steps to create an exciting future.

Here is a useful affirmation to remind you of the true motive of confronting the fears of death and dying:

I am alive right now.
As long as I lessen the energy I invest in my fears
and increase the energy I invest in living
I will continue to live
in increasing health and happiness.

This is the key to leaving the fear of death and dying behind you. At the same time as you write your will, enquire about pain-killers, and talk to friends about who will care for the kids, ensure that you plan the trip you have always wanted to take, enrol in the college course that you have always wanted to do, and start on some of the goals and projects you have delayed until now. If you remember David's story, he bought his coffin and organised his funeral service on the same day as he bought a house with a 30-year mortgage.

When you deal with your fear and take the necessary steps to get your affairs in order, your life – and your death – become freer and much more peaceful.

Yes, it is possible that you could still die, even if you do all the various exercises in this book to strengthen your immune system. However, the quality of your life in the period of time that you are alive is what is important.

The worst that can happen if you follow the instructions about the fears of death and dying is that you have a good death, versus entering the dying process unprepared, frightened, with so many things undone and unsaid. There is enormous power in taking control of the quality of your life, and this includes how it will end. There are a number of practical options you can implement right now to deal with this fear:

■ ASSIGNMENT 1:
CONFRONT YOUR FEARS OF DEATH AND DYING

STEP 1   Draw up a living will.
Think about whether you are willing to be kept alive with machines, such as an artificial respirator or similar machines that are used when your basic bodily functions have collapsed. If this is something you want, then tell your closest family member about it, or write it down and ensure that your physician is aware of this.

However, if you do not want to be kept alive with machines, ensure that your doctor is informed – preferably in writing – as well as your closest family member. Informing a friend will not work, as a friend has no legal rights in this situation. If necessary, write down your wishes in this regard, sign the document, have it witnessed, and ask a friend or family member to keep it for you in case it is ever required. There are complicated laws regarding this issue.

STEP 2   Plan your own funeral.
Decide which hymns you want sung, what flowers you want, what you want said at the service, and who you want to attend. If possible, save some money to pay for this eventuality, so that your family does not have to be burdened with the costs. Get this over with so that you can focus on living.

STEP 3   Get your finances and will in order.
Ensure that your will is current, and that you have done this legally. Get it done and over with. Make space for living.

STEP 4   Express your feelings and thoughts.
Speak to friends and family about the possibility of your death. They will be very upset initially, but assure them that all you want to do is ease your mind and sort things out so that you can turn your attention to healing your body.

Discuss who you want to care for your children and pets, and start to hand over certain household duties to other family members. After all, you need the time to focus on your healing, don't you? Be very aware of the fact that friends and family will think you are preparing to die. However, keep reminding them that you are simply doing an emotional house-cleaning so that you can concentrate all your energy and attention on more important things – your health, and creating a compelling future.

STEP 5   **Pain management**
Some people do not mind enduring pain until the body dies naturally. However, many people fear this. There are several options – some legal, and some illegal, depending on which country you live in. For example, in some countries it is legal (and in some countries it is illegal) to use marijuana (dagga) to ease the pain of serious illnesses. There is also a legalised capsule form of this herb.

One person's pain threshold is different from another's. Some people can endure pain and others prefer to take pain-killing drugs. Most hospitals and hospices ensure that patients are kept pain-free. Ask your doctor about this, and discuss your fears regarding pain with her or him.

STEP 6   **Self-deliverance options**
Finally, there is one other option: self-deliverance, also known as suicide. Before you recoil in horror, please keep in mind that some people might prefer to die when the quality of their life is beyond repair. This all depends on the individual, his or her religious beliefs, and the laws of the country she or he lives in. Several countries have legalised assisted self-deliverance (or assisted suicide). If this is something you are willing to consider, then please think carefully about the method you will use, as certain methods are rather messy and can traumatise friends and family members. Probably the most effective methods involve drugs. However, please do some homework on this beforehand.

In this regard, it is important to remember that the greatest trauma caused to family and friends is what is called 'unfinished business', namely not saying goodbye. Please ensure that you give each person who loves you an opportunity to say goodbye, or at least write each one a special '*I know you love me and I love you*' letter, explaining your reasons for your actions. Include all the people with whom you have had arguments and conflict.

The fears of your Shadows

Once you have confronted your fear of dying, it is time to deal with the underlying fears of your strongest Shadows (refer to Chapter 8, *Effective and Ineffective Coping Methods*, page 141). Briefly, these are:

SHADOW	CORE FEAR
Obstinate–Inflexible	People will take away my choices.
Passionless–Reasonable	Risk, loss and pain (again)
Control–Distance	Losing control of your 'image', which will lead to criticism for not being perfect (fear of being vulnerable). Public humiliation (severe form of criticism).
Apologising–Failure	Being rejected for failure. Not meeting others' expectations (failure). Success raises expectations. Fear of success.
Impatient–Restless	Running out of time. Failing to achieve everything you must do.
Blaming–Shaming	Being trapped and helpless. Rejection for being needy (being unloved).
Never Enough	Dying unfulfilled. Being abandoned (again). Failing to get what you 'need' to be happy.
Frantic–Destructive	Losing control and killing yourself. Believing there is no meaning to life at all.

These are powerful fears, and they drive most of your behaviour. They are all derived from past experiences in which something happened to you and you now fear something similar may happen again. That is why they are chronic – i.e. they operate almost all the time – and this has a major impact on your immune system and therefore your illness.

Any successful Applied PNI process must involve confronting these powerful fears on an ongoing basis.

The first step is always to identify the fear and recognise that you have it. Then follow the instructions for confronting fears, described below:

▥ THE CONFRONTING OF FEARS METHOD

STEP 1 **Be specific about what you are truly afraid of.**
The 'primitive brain' does not deal with – or understand – abstract thoughts and concepts. It deals with – and understands – only concrete things (who, where, when, how much). The first step involves being quite specific about who, where, what and how your fear is focused on.

Examples:
'I am afraid that Bob will leave me because I am sick.'
'I am afraid that my boss will fire me if I make a mistake in the year-end report.'
'I am afraid that, if I listen to the doctor, he will think I am weak, and make me do things I don't want to do.'
'I am afraid that if I try this Applied PNI stuff, I won't do it properly, and then I will die.'
'I am afraid that if I get better, I won't get the attention I get now.'
'I am afraid that if I get really sick, I won't be able to get the diploma in garden design I always wanted.'

STEP 2 **What is the worst imagined situation?**
Try to imagine what your primitive brain is thinking. It tends to exaggerate the fear and creates a 'worst-case' imagined situation. So what is that exaggerated worst-case situation? Describe it.

This is typically where most people stop. They imagine the worst-case situation of their fear, and then frantically try to block it out. Don't block it out: go immediately to step 3 when you have uncovered the imagined worst-case situation.

STEP 3 **Make a practical plan of action to deal with it.**
Your first impulse may be to try to think of a way to reverse or prevent the worst-case scenario. For example, if your fear is of being rejected by someone, you may want to think of ways to get back at him or her. This does not work, in terms of releasing the fear.

Treat the imagined worst-case scenario as a 'done deal' – i.e. it's happened, you can't reverse it, now you have to face it.

If this worst-case situation happened – and you cannot reverse it – what is the very first thing you would do in that situation? Be realistic – you know yourself well enough – about how you would react. Would you cry? Would you go home and get drunk? Would you tell a friend? What exactly would you do?

An unacceptable answer is '*I don't know*', or '*Well, I'll just be positive and trust the process*'. Do you think the primitive brain would accept that as an action? Of course not – it wants to know what you will do. Crying is a 'doing'. Walking to a friend's house is a 'doing'. So is getting blind drunk, and so is throwing a tantrum, eating too much ice-cream, taking a pill and going to sleep. What would – and could – you do, first?

For how long? And then what would I do? These are critical questions in moving through the fear process. If your first step is to cry, then how long would you cry for? And then what would you do? And then? And then? …

There are important considerations in this 'And then?' method:

- **The actions you describe must be realistic for you.** You can't fool the primitive brain – it knows what you can and cannot do. If it thinks you are being unrealistic, it will not accept the solution and the fear will remain.
- **It is not about what you would like to do – it is about what you could do to get through the imagined worst-case situation.** This may involve doing things you don't particularly want to do, such as asking for help from someone you don't want to ask, or doing a job you don't like for a while.
- **Keep going until it's over.** You continue describing, step by step, what you would do to get through the worst-case situation. This does not mean that you 'fix' the worst-case situation. Instead, it means that you simply survive it – get through to the other side – till it's over.

The following example illustrates this process:

> *'I am afraid of rejection.'*

Rejection by whom?
> *'Oh, anyone.'*

Sure, but whose rejection do you fear the most right now?
> *'My husband John.'*

What do you imagine as the worst-case situation?
> *'I know this is silly, but … I sometimes worry that he will leave me and get a younger girlfriend.'*

Describe an imagined worst-case scenario in which this happens – imagine the actual worst-case situation.
> *'Well, I suppose the worst-case situation could be that I come from home one day, it's raining hard, and as I get to the front gate of our house, I see my suitcases on the lawn. When I try to open the door with the key, I realise that the lock has been changed. I walk around to the front window, and there I see John, with his arms around a young woman, laughing at me. I try to talk to him, and he just laughs at me, and kisses her instead. Then he opens the window a little, and tells me that he doesn't want to see me again. He also tells me that he has transferred all our joint savings into his name, as well as the house and car. I have nothing, except the clothes in the suitcases on the lawn. Then he closes the window, and draws the curtain closed. It is still raining hard.'*

What is the very first thing that you do?
> *'Well, I am shocked. I am wet. I cry – I can't believe this is happening.'*

How long do you stand there, crying?
> *'Only a few minutes – I am getting more and more wet.'*

And then? What do you do next?
> *'I collect my suitcases, and stand on the pavement for a minute, trying to think of what to do next.'*

And then? What do you do next?

> 'I cross the street and go to Mrs Brown, who lives across the road. I
> don't really know her, but she seems like someone who would help
> me.'

And then? What do you do next?

> 'I ask her if I could use her phone, and I phone Jenny, my best friend.
> I ask her if I can stay at her place for the night, till I figure out what
> to do.'

And then? What do you do next?

> 'Then I wait for Jenny to fetch me with her boyfriend's car. While I
> wait, Mrs Brown makes me a cup of tea, and I cry again.'

And then? What do you do next?

> 'Well, when Jenny arrives, I burst into tears again. Then she takes me
> to her place, and we talk for a long time. I cry a lot.'

And then? What do you do next?

> 'The next morning I ask my boss if I can take the day off. He probably
> asks me why. Although I hate to tell him about my private life – he's
> such an arrogant arsehole – I have to, so that I can find a lawyer and
> go to the bank to check if all the money is really gone.'

… etc., until she feels that she has survived the worst-case situation.

When you do this process, several things become clear. First, that
there are indeed specific things you can do to lessen the practical
aspects of the worst-case situation. In the previous imagined situation, it became obvious that the rejected wife had made herself
vulnerable to being left with no financial resources. This made
coping with the fear more difficult. We suggested that she immediately open up a savings account and put a little money away each
month, for her 'Worst-Case Fund'.

In the above example – a true one – the fear of rejection was
relieved substantially. When we spoke to John – the husband – it
became apparent that his wife had been afraid of being rejected by
him for quite some time, which resulted in her feeling insecure. He

understood this, but was becoming more and more distant because of her constant need to be reassured. In fact, he said, if she hadn't dealt with this fear, he probably would have left her because of the behaviour it caused. Ironically, the fear itself was leading to the actual manifestation of what was feared. After she had reduced the fear, their relationship healed considerably. She still, however, kept adding to her 'Worst-Case Fund', as a reminder of needing to deal with her fears in a realistic way.

■ PRACTICAL GUIDELINES

- Your fears will not instantaneously disappear when you do the process of confronting them. It takes an hour or so for the emotions to settle a little, so please do not be surprised if you are a little upset during and after the process.
- Do not just do steps 1 and 2, and then stop because 'it is too upsetting'. It is step 3 that ends the fear, and steps 1 and 2 simply make it possible to focus the fear specifically enough to deal with it properly. If you start the process, ensure you complete all steps.
- Confronting a specific fear is not a guarantee that it will not happen. The process is strictly designed to reduce or eliminate the emotional distress caused by a fear, which has a negative impact on the immune system. As you will discover, the objective of the process is to ensure that you will get to a point of knowing how you will deal with the feared event, if it ever happens.
- Use your common sense in your plan of action for dealing with a specific fear. If there are preventive measures you can take, such as self-defence training if you are afraid of being attacked, then do so. Often, when dealing with fears of being trapped in a car, a lift or some place where no one can help, the fear can be dealt with partially by carrying some communication device with you at all times, or alternatively always ensuring that there is someone with you in such situations. You may even choose to notify someone beforehand that you are entering such a situation, and ask them to check that you arrive safely.
- When dealing with a phobia – which is an irrational fear of something like spiders, heights or confined spaces – please consult a psychologist or professional therapist for assistance. The method described here can be used in such circumstances, but certainly not without professional supervision.

- It is easier to work with someone else, especially when you have no idea of what you could or would do if a specific situation arose. Other people may provide suggestions for you to consider, although you do not have to accept such suggestions.
- Above all, do not let anyone belittle your fears. If you feel afraid of something – even something you have dreamed about – it is a legitimate fear and needs to be treated accordingly.
- It has been explained in this chapter that your mind can operate at various levels, including logic, emotions and the irrational. Fear and anxiety are not always logical or rational. Does that make your fear less real? Of course not! Even if you know full well that your fear is unrealistic, deal with it as a legitimate fear. If you feel it, it is real enough to you. Do not tell yourself that you are being 'silly'! Even nightmares contain legitimate fears.
- This process works best when the fear is real to *you*. If someone else says you should be afraid of something, and you are not afraid of it, then there is no point in working through the process on their fear!
- Finally, fear is a feeling, not a thought. Do not intellectualise this process – just deal with your feelings. Furthermore, if you are inclined to intellectualise things, then draw your fear instead of writing about it. You cannot 'think' this process – it needs to be expressed, by speaking out loud, writing or drawing.

■ ASSIGNMENT 2: CONFRONT YOUR SHADOW FEARS

STEP 1   Select your strongest three Shadows.
Read the descriptions carefully. Pay attention to the typical effects they have on your behaviour, relationships, health, creativity and spirituality.

STEP 2   Choose what you are going to do with the released energy.
If you are going to withdraw energy from a fear, where are you going to invest it afterwards? In other words, what 'good' thing are you going to do for yourself afterwards? Be specific. Keep your word with yourself.

STEP 3   For each of the three Shadows, identify the basic fear that causes you to behave according to that Shadow. Write this down.

STEP 4 Read the instructions and guidelines described in *The Confronting of Fears Method*, pages 220-4.

STEP 5 Apply the three steps in the method, for one fear at a time. Make absolutely sure you are being specific – who, what, where, when – when describing the fear. There may be several cases (e.g. people you are afraid will reject or criticise you). Deal with each one separately.

STEP 6 This process is open-ended, i.e. you will need to use this method many times, over a long period of time, as fears arise. Shadows do not disappear – they simply weaken. If nothing else, repeated application of this method will gradually increase your sense of 'I can' (self-efficacy), which positively affects all areas of your life.

Fears concerning illness

This category of fears concerns issues of the effects of the illness. Here are some examples:

> What will people think/say/do if they find out about my illness?
> Will I lose my job?
> Will people treat me differently?
> Will my hair fall out from chemotherapy?
> Will my husband/wife/lover reject me, including sexually?
> Will I be able to achieve my goals if I get too weak?
> Will I be abandoned to die alone?
> Will surgery leave me disfigured?
> What if this PNI stuff does not work for me?

Please remember that worry is a form of fear, as is anxiety. Worry and anxiety have a direct impact on the immune system. Do not dismiss them as small things – deal with them directly as they arise:

■ ASSIGNMENT 3: DEAL WITH FEARS CONCERNING YOUR ILLNESS

STEP 1 Identify at least one real fear that you have regarding your illness, and the possible effects it is having, or will have, on your relationships and abilities. Write these down.

STEP 2   For each fear listed, decide where you will invest the released energy, i.e. what 'good thing' are you going to do for yourself after confronting the fear.

STEP 3   Read the instructions and guidelines described in *The Confronting of Fears Method*, pages 220-4.

STEP 4   Apply the three steps in the method, for one fear at a time. Make absolutely sure you are being specific – who, what, where, when – when describing the fear. Deal with each imagined or actual feared situation separately.

STEP 5   This process is open-ended, i.e. you will need to use this method many times, over a long period of time, as fears arise.

Fears concerning getting well again

If PNI therapy – or any change process – were as simple as deciding whether you wanted to do it or not, and then doing what needed to be done, it would be an incredibly rapid process. However, this is certainly not a typical situation or outcome.

Whether we like it or not, we all have reasons – usually unconscious – for holding on to pain and problems and resisting change, even when we consciously want to change the situation. This is often an overlooked source of anxiety and can be the cause of slow recovery, or even an unconscious sabotage of the healing process, whether medical or other types.

This type of fear – and the behaviour that goes along with it – is called secondary gain. Essentially, there are indeed benefits to being ill, and there are fears about losing those benefits.

For example: I get attention when I am ill. I don't get it when I am healthy.
I can avoid doing things I don't want to do (duties, work, seeing specific people) by being ill.
People who are normally not nice to me, have to be nice to me because I am ill – i.e. I gain attention and sympathy by staying sick.

So-and-so cannot leave me, because he (or she) would feel guilty for abandoning a sick person – i.e. being ill allows me to keep people and avoid being abandoned.
I can avoid dealing with my real problems by staying ill.
I can manipulate people with guilt, using my 'problem'.
Will I lose all my friends from my support group?
Will the kids take me for granted again when I am better?
If I am well, what will I talk about when someone asks me how I am?
Will I have to go back to my boring job if I am well again?
What if I cannot find a job again? Isn't it better to stay ill?

It is not easy to identify and admit to such fears. However, it helps to realise that the benefits of being ill are often learned in childhood, when love and special attention are given to you when you are ill. Other benefits include avoiding school, especially tests, exams and bullies. Being sick – even with just a slight fever or upset stomach – may be an excellent way to get the attention of a father or mother who is normally too busy. Guilt is a superb method to get – and keep – someone else's attention.

No, there does not have to be some hidden fear about getting well again. However, it is always a wise idea to find out first if such fears exist. How? It is useful to employ a technique called the Square Analysis, so that you can discover if you have any fears of losing any benefits of being ill. This is basically an exercise in identifying advantages and disadvantages of being healthy and sick.

■ ASSIGNMENT 4: SQUARE ANALYSIS

SQUARE ANALYSIS	
Being well: Advantages	**Being well:** Disadvantages
Being sick: Advantages	**Being sick:** Disadvantages

STEP 1   Define desired goal
       'I want to get well again.'

STEP 2   Define the opposite of the goal (or the absence of action)
       'I want to stay sick.'

STEP 3   Advantages and Disadvantages of BOTH

a. **Get well = benefits:**
If I get well again:
Who will love me more?
Who will give me more attention?
Who will continue giving me love and attention?
Who would approve?
What will I be able to do that I can't do now?

b. **Stay sick = benefits:**
If I stay ill:
Who will love me more?
Who will give me more attention?
Who will continue giving me love and attention?
Who would approve?
What duties and problems will I continue to avoid?

c. **Get well = fear:**
If I get well again:
Who will love me less?
Who will leave me?
Who will give me less attention?
Who would not approve?
What duties will I have to deal with?
What problems will I have to face again?

d. **Stay sick = fear:**
If I stay sick:
Who will love me less?
Who will give me less attention?
Who would not approve?
What goals will I not be able to achieve?

■ ASSIGNMENT 5: Fears of being sick and well

This assignment is simple, but not easy. Identify five advantages and disadvantages of being sick and of getting well again.

(+) **BE WELL AGAIN** What will I gain or keep, or what duties and problems will I avoid if I get well?	(–) **BE WELL AGAIN** What am I afraid of losing, what problems will I have to face, what unpleasant duties will I have to deal with, if I become well again?
1. .... 2. .... 3. .... 4. .... 5.	1. .... 2. .... 3. .... 4. .... 5. ....
(+) **STAY SICK** What will I gain or keep, or what duties and problems will I avoid if I stay sick?	(–) **STAY SICK** What am I afraid of losing, what problems will I have to face, what unpleasant duties will I have to deal with, if I stay sick?
1. .... 2. .... 3. .... 4. .... 5.	1. .... 2. .... 3. .... 4. .... 5. ....

Once you have completed the previous exercise – which is quite a challenge to your honesty – write down the strongest fears you have to becoming well again:

1. ....
2. ....
3. ....

Now take each fear of getting well and process it using the three-step *Confronting of Fears Method*, pages 220-4.

Fears related to necessary changes

In the course of reading and working through this book, you may come to realise that certain behaviours – such as not saying what you think and feel, or starting to do things that give you joy – need to be changed in order for you to recover and remain well thereafter. However, because the people in your life – friends, family and community – not only expect you to behave in a certain way, but have also become accustomed to your behaving in a certain manner, there may be legitimate fears regarding the effects such necessary changes will have on your relationships.

Consider the following examples:

> If I start saying what I truly think and feel, I will be rejected, and lose my loved one(s), or my job.
> My husband/wife/lover will leave me (abandonment).
> I will lose my identity – I will no longer fit in with 'people like us'.
> I will be criticised and humiliated.
> I will be beaten until I go back to my old behaviour.
> How will I control the people around me if I am honest?
> How will I keep my job if I am no longer stubborn, impatient, etc.?
> I will lose respect from the people who look up to me.
> My old friends will think I am strange, and stop talking to me.
> What would people say? (Think of specific people.)

As you can gather, change is not a straightforward process! It should also be obvious that fear can block many things, including your intentions and actions to heal your body.

Whenever you become aware of a fear that is blocking your progress in terms of doing what you need to do to get well, use the three-step *Confronting of Fears Method*. It works!

Additional Suggestions

Practise with small risks: Stretch yourself gradually – speak out in a meeting or join an evening class. Small achievements are satisfying and build confidence for bigger challenges.

Have a contingency plan: Think of your action plan and realise that if it doesn't work out, it is not the end of the world – what other options do you have?

Grin and laugh: If worst comes to worst, tell yourself, '*At least I tried!*' Don't see it as proof that risks are not worth taking. After all, risks are, by definition, a case of win some, lose some.

Conquer fear: Use the '*What If?*' technique, recognising that the fear of doing something is often worse than the fear of actually doing it. Push yourself into something you're dreading and it's likely you will end up wondering why you were so reluctant.

GET IT OUT OF YOUR BODY!

The suppression of emotions – keeping your feelings bottled up inside – has been shown to suppress the immune system, and the expression of emotions has been proved to improve immune functioning. The research in this area is extensive, and applies to cancer, AIDS, and many other conditions *[1, 2, 3, 4, 5]*.

In Chapter 7 we introduced the use of writing to release emotions from past loss events. In this chapter, we continue with this principle and expand on methods of expressing emotions safely, short-term methods that you can use when an emotion surfaces, as well as methods to switch off some of the recurring reactions that are problematic for you.

What are emotions?

Emotions are mental–physical–chemical actions that are generated inside your body, based on what you perceive or experience.

EMOTION = Energy in MOTION

Each emotion has something to say about where you are at that moment in time. Emotions are re-*actions* to something you think, see, hear, taste, experience. It is a mistake to view any emotion – including anger – as something bad. When we discussed the mind–immune connections in Chapter 3, we stated that the adrenaline-producing SAM system and the cortisol-producing HPAC system were designed for good reasons, such as providing the chemical motivation to fight, run away or heal wounds. Emotions originated in the same scenario, and are part of this system.

Anger, for example, is always an indication that something has hurt you (physically, or an aspect of your identity) or is going to hurt you. Therefore, anger is an important action-oriented message, based simply on a survival motivation.

Do something with your emotions!

When you do something with emotions – act out, talk, write – all the chemicals stimulated by the emotional reaction find a way out of your body through sweat, tears or urine and your body returns to normal. However, if you do not express the emotion in some way, these emotional chemicals do not leave your body, causing problems because your body cannot return to normal.

If you do not express the emotion you are feeling at that moment, it is stored away in your body, waiting for another opportunity to be heard. Even if your 'thinking brain' believes the emotion is silly, stupid or bad, your faithful 'primitive brain' watchdog protects the value of your feelings on your behalf. It knows more about what is good for you than the 'thinking brain', particularly when it comes to your survival.

Let's clear up one simple point. It is wonderful if you understand your anger, for example. But did you get it out of your body?

You will find that you cannot really be objective about why you feel what you feel, until you release the emotional energy itself.

Suppressing emotions

The problem with suppressing emotions is that it requires effort to keep them from surfacing and this mental effort acts as a low-grade chronic stress. For example, if you are angry or sad about something someone has said or done, and you do not express that feeling, then your mind has to ensure that that feeling does not pop out the next time you see that person.

Remember – the emotional chemicals are still floating around inside your body. Instead, you hold yourself back, smile and say: '*Nothing is the matter!*' Strictly speaking, this is a lie – something is the matter! But why would you lie about how you feel? For one thing, you probably think you will hurt that person's feelings, right? By the end of this chapter, it is possible you may have another view regarding this belief.

If you believe the ability to control and hide your emotions is an indication of how strong you are, then you obviously have not considered how illogical and silly that belief is! If you are suppressing your emotions because of fear of ridicule or rejection, then logically such an attitude indicates a lack of courage, not the presence of strength. It takes courage to be vulnerable and allow other people to see that vulnerability.

Have you ever considered how fundamentally dishonest and deceitful it is to smile and say '*I am fine*', when, in fact, you feel angry, sad or upset? Oddly enough, many people use this absurd justification for suppressing their emotions.

Our definition of 'fine' is:

False **I**ndication (of) **N**o **E**motion

In other words, 'fine' is a catch-all phrase for all the emotions you're experiencing but do not want to express!

Yes, it is true that the random expression of emotions can sometimes be destructive. However, this becomes even more so when you bottle them up over time, and then just explode one day. We have encountered many people who would literally rather die than tell someone how they really feel. The fear of rejection, and the need to be accepted, is very powerful indeed.

It is quite possible that the protective 'primitive brain' sometimes believes that if you were to say exactly what you think and feel, the consequences would be bad for your survival. At a deep level, fears of rejection and humiliation are often experienced as a fear of death – '*I would just die if he (or she) left me!*' Therefore, for some people it is relatively safe and appropriate to just say what they feel. However, for other people, this is almost incomprehensible, and they 'would rather die' than risk saying what they really feel. Where do you stand with this? Be honest, because the issue of perceived safety needs to be taken into consideration when thinking of ways to express what you feel.

The price of being 'nice'

Are 'nice' people honest people, where a 'nice' person is defined as someone who will smile sweetly and tell you everything is fine, even when she or he is angry and hurting inside? We do not think so. Based on our experience, such nice people die faster. This is largely because 'nice' people – not to be confused with genuinely caring people – suppress their emotions, mainly their anger.

We define 'nice' as follows:

Never **I**ndicates **C**oncealed **E**motions

The reason is simple. So-called 'nice' people cause enormous damage to their immune systems by suppressing their feelings.

The fear behind being 'nice'

The major fear most people have about being honest about their thoughts and feelings is that it can be destructive in relationships. And yes, when expressed without responsibility, it can prove destructive. If you did not care about the consequences of your words and action, then there would be no problem in terms of your personal expressions. However, if you do care about relationships, you will be aware that there are always consequences for every word and action.

So here is the dilemma. If you are in the habit of suppressing your anger and other 'not too nice' feelings, then you are probably doing so because you do not want to hurt anyone's feelings, because you want their love, approval and acceptance. You fear rejection. However, it is this very suppression of emotions that may be a major contributing factor in your immune system being suppressed, and this could possibly cause your death.

If you began to say exactly what you felt, then you could lose the love of the people you want to be in a relationship with. If you don't do this, you could lose them anyway, through death. Seems like a no-win situation, doesn't it?

Escape from the 'nice' trap

There is a way out of this no-win situation, however. For a moment, put aside what you assume it means to express emotions, and pay attention to the exact words of the following:

In order to experience the immune benefits of expressing your feelings, you need to get those feelings outside of your body.

Does it say '*Tell someone*' anywhere? No, it doesn't! Most people assume you have to tell someone, but this is not necessary – speaking is only one way of expressing emotions. If you wrote an angry letter that you burned immediately afterwards, this would be just as effective, in terms of your immune system. In fact, most PNI studies that show just how beneficial expressing emotions is, used writing as the method of expression.

This leads us to the first of the important principles in applying PNI research for your health:

EMOTION PRINCIPLE 1

Expressing emotions means getting it out of your body

This is all that is required. There are many different – and safe – methods to do this, discussed later in this chapter.

EMOTION PRINCIPLE 2

Thinking is not feeling

You need to find a way of actually expressing what you are feeling. Thinking about it does not help at all. There is no way around this fact, at least not in terms of health and your immune system. So, you cannot expect any benefit from sitting and thinking about what you are feeling. The feelings actually have to exit your body in some way or other.

There are probably people who genuinely do not ever feel upset or angry and they are usually nominated to sainthood at some point. However, the rest of us – including you and I – get angry, irritated, upset, sad, confused, miserable and a whole range of other emotions, all in one day. This is part of the human condition.

However, if you are dominated by the *Control–Distance* or *Passionless–Reasonable* Shadows, you wouldn't know an emotion if it jumped up and bit you! Yes, we understand – you're detached from these things called emotions, aren't you? '*Well*', you're thinking, '*It's not that I'm detached from them but, rather, that I just have control over them!*' News flash! Just like the rest of us, you have emotions, except you have shut off your awareness of them. You are disconnected from your body. This is dangerous, from an immune health perspective.

Some people (e.g. those with strong aspects of the *Control–Distance* coping strategy) are so skilled at suppressing emotions that they honestly do not know what is happening in their body anymore. If you were to give them a psychological anxiety test, they would score very low. However, if you were to attach a monitor to their skin, the monitor would show high anxiety levels. Are these people lying in the psychological test? No, not at all. All that has happened is that they have mentally controlled their emotions for so long that they are no longer aware of feelings and emotions happening in their own body.

Those of you who are led by the *Passionless–Reasonable* Shadow – Mr and Ms Emotionally Numb and OK – you're doing the same thing. Just because your head denies these things called emotions does not mean your body does!

'*So what?*' you ask. Well, in previous chapters we discussed the primitive and thinking aspects of our brains. Fear, terror, rage and similar primitive emotions are the domain of the 'primitive brain'. We have already explained how emotions have a direct physical link to the immune system, via the hypothalamus and the SAM and HPAC systems.

The biological reasons for this are complicated. Needless to say, various stress hormones and chemicals are secreted when emotions are suppressed. When those emotions are expressed later, these chemicals are released from the body and the hormones return to normal levels.

EMOTION PRINCIPLE 3

Facts aren't feelings

Talking about the facts of a situation makes no difference to your immune system. However, talking about your feelings about a situation makes a vast difference to the immune system. This is where people led by the *Control–Distance* Shadow get into trouble. They analyse the situation, intellectualise it and then present a logical report of what happened. This does not help the immune system at all.

This creates one of the greatest ironies. The person who is most likely to want to understand and analyse all the intricate details of PNI is the same person who is least likely to benefit from Applied PNI methods, unless she or he simultaneously makes an effort to connect and work with her or his emotions and feelings. This may seem like a rather cruel thing to say, but it is a warning to those who think they can intellectualise the healing process by replacing emotions with abstract thoughts. **Your body simply does not care about facts. It cares about what you feel about those facts.**

Therefore, for the next few days, weeks or months, we strongly urge you to give yourself permission to think less and feel more!

Dumping (or releasing) emotions

Dumping emotions means that the intent – purpose – is simply to release emotions safely. The intention is not for someone else to understand why you feel this way, nor to get revenge.

It is important to understand the difference between expressing emotions for the sake of releasing them, and expressing emotions (or thoughts) for the sake of being understood or acknowledged by someone else.

The most important thing to remember is to **get the emotion outside your body. That is the primary objective.**

Talking: Talking to someone else is only one form of expression. Non-threatening methods include talking to an object, such as a stone or tree. It sounds silly, but it works simply because these methods also get the feelings and thoughts outside the body.

Writing: For those of you who find it extremely threatening to talk about your feelings, writing them down is probably the best method – as long as you get your feelings out.

Physical release: Some people play active sport, such as bashing a ball around a squash court. If sport is something you like, we suggest you imagine the face of the person who has hurt you on the ball and then bash it to your heart's content.

Another very active method is to use a punch-bag or a pillow and hit it with all your might, again imagining that you are hitting the person who has angered or upset you. Keep doing this until you feel complete. Please note that we suggest you focus on one person's face – this keeps the exercise controlled. You may find other people's faces popping up, and then you do the same for them. Notice that you are getting all your anger and hurt out and no one else is getting hurt.

For those who believe that this is sending out bad feelings into the universe, please remember that these 'bad feelings' are already inside you and the purpose of expressing these feelings is to bring them to the surface and release them so that they can dissipate. Keeping them inside your body simply means you continue to radiate these 'bad vibes'.

If you can ensure total privacy, try to scream and shout at the same time, saying everything you want, while doing all this bashing! Be as irrational as you like – you can say all the nasty things you have always wanted to say but were too embarrassed to state publicly! How about screaming into a pillow, which will muffle the sound?

A friend of ours drives out into the middle of nowhere, turns up the volume of the music, closes all the car windows, and then screams and shouts to his heart's content. It works! Another method is to roll up a thick newspaper until it's the size of a baseball bat, and then beat a wall or some solid object. It can actually be quite fun!

What do you do if you're with other people and an emotion overwhelms you? You can do various things. You could excuse yourself and go to the toilet. Grab a cushion on your way out. Lock the toilet, flush it and scream into the pillow. Then wash your face and hands and, when you feel better, return to the gathering. They may think you are a bit odd, but what the heck! Until they pay your bills, do not be too concerned about what they think!

If this is not possible, then find a way to get the feelings out of your body as soon as possible, when you go home. It is OK to hold onto the feeling for an hour or two but, after that, you need to let it out when you feel safe to do so.

Many people prefer to sit down somewhere, once their children and partner are asleep, and write a letter to the person who angered or upset them. This is an excellent method for dealing with day-to-day emotions, as well as emotions from your past.

Guidelines for dumping emotions safely

There are certain things to remember about dumping emotions:

- It takes a while – probably a few minutes to an hour – for your body to settle after letting go of the emotion. If you can, allow yourself a few minutes to just sit and breathe calmly. After letting go of very intense emotions, a bath or shower goes a long way in helping the body to settle. Drink water, to flush the emotional chemicals out of your body.
- When you express the emotion, be honest. Do not try to apologise or justify the way you feel. Just let it out, as it is, with all the anger, rawness and swearing. Give yourself permission to be unreasonable. After all, emotions are not intellectual! You'll find that the emotion 'hangs around' if you've not said exactly what you wanted to say. In our workshops, we give delegates a list of people to whom they must write letters, and we ask them to say exactly what they want to these people. The letters are destroyed afterwards – they're never mailed. Many of our delegates report a sense of lightness and having had a deep, peaceful sleep afterwards. Others say they had a restless night and feel tired the next morning. If the latter occurs, know that you have not said everything you wanted – there is more you need to say. Write it all down – get it over and done with. Some people refer to this as 'getting it off your chest'. In Africa, it is referred to as 'coughing it up' or 'taking it out of the body'.
- It is astonishing how most cultures have found ways to accomplish the same objective, namely the releasing of pent-up emotions. Some cultures do it with sport, as participants or as observers. Notice the roaring, shouting and venting in audiences at well-attended soccer matches or boxing contests. Some African traditional healers advise people to go into the bush on their own, dig a hole, pour muti (medicine) into the hole, and then scream all the anger into the muti. When all the anger is out, they are instructed to cover the hole with soil, turn around, and never return to the same spot. Alternatively, a stone is selected, and the person is instructed to scream at the stone, bash it and then throw it away when all the anger is gone.
- An important key is to pretend you are confronting the person who angered or upset you. Do not edit what you want to say to them. Stop

being so nice! Say what you think and be as irrational and emotional as you need to be. Remember, you are doing this for you, not them!

- The content of what is expressed is important. The facts of the situation are not nearly as important as the expression of the feelings. When two groups are asked to write about a traumatic event, and one group is instructed to stick only to the facts while the other writes only about the emotions, it is the second, emotional-content group whose immune systems benefit. This is important to remember if you are inclined to be analytical and reasonable about your feelings. It does not help your immune system or you to be reasonable and analytical. 'Thinking brain' processes may assist afterwards, but not in the initial 'dumping of emotions' process.

When you really have to say it to someone

There are certain things that may arise out of the exercises in expressing your emotions, which you simply need to tell someone else. This is quite common. Often, it is related to something that the other person has said or done which needs to be cleared up – you need to tell them.

There are three parts to doing this as safely as possible:

1. **Write down** – or use any of the suggested safe techniques for expressing your feelings – exactly what you are feeling. Ensure that you express all the anger, resentment, swearing, and similar feelings. Let this settle for an hour or so, and then check to see if there is anything else you need to express in the letter. This part is important, as it reduces the emotional rawness of what you need to say, which reduces the likelihood of an emotional argument.

2. **Have a look at your fears concerning the consequences of telling the person how you felt about what they said or did.** Using the three-step *Confronting of Fears Method* from Chapter 9 (pages 220-4), confront your fear about saying what you need to to this specific person.

3. Claim responsibility for your emotions. This means that you do not say '*You made me so angry ...*' Instead, say '*I felt angry when you said/did ...*'

■ ASSIGNMENT 1: EMOTIONAL HONESTY

In your day-to-day activities, notice how often you say what you feel. Do you say you are 'fine' or 'OK' or 'alright' as a habit, without thinking? Begin to become aware of what upsets you and notice what you do with that emotion – do you say or do something, or do you say nothing?

■ ASSIGNMENT 2: BODY AWARENESS

This assignment is particularly important for people dominated by the *Control–Distance* or *Passionless–Reasonable* Shadows:

Get back in touch with your body and its multitude of sensations. This may involve a body massage, playing sport or doing any physical activity in which you become more aware of what is happening in your body.

■ ASSIGNMENT 3: DUMP SOME ANGER

Think of something which or someone who has recently angered you, and dump that anger using one of the suggested safe methods. You do not have to choose a deep anger – any mild irritation will do. The point is to experience what happens in your body during and after dumping a real emotion. You won't know what it feels like until you do it!

■ ASSIGNMENT 4: CLEAR CLOSE RELATIONSHIPS

STEP 1 **List four or five significant people in your life.**
These are people in your life right now, with whom you regularly interact.

1. ....

2. ....

3. ....

4. ....

5. ....

STEP 2   Write a one-page dumping letter to each person.
In this letter, let them know exactly what you feel – good stuff and
bad stuff with no regard for politeness or justification. Make sure
you say everything you want to say, as if you were talking to them
face to face.

STEP 3   Burn the letters.

STEP 4   When you speak to them again, notice the difference in what you
say and how you feel towards them.

■ ASSIGNMENT 5: PROCESS SHADOW EMOTIONS

STEP 1   Select your three strongest Shadows.

STEP 2   Write a dumping letter – minimum of two full pages each – to the
person specified below.

Please ensure you have privacy while you do this dumping process.
Also ensure that you drink plenty of water during the process, to
release the stress chemicals from your body.

If one of your top three Shadows is:	Then write to:
Obstinate–**I**nflexible	The person – in your distant past, probably childhood – who took your choices away, or who would not allow you to make choices.
Passionless–**R**easonable	The person you cared deeply about, whom you lost. This could be through death or separation.
Controlling–**D**istant	The person who criticised you for being vulnerable, imperfect (according to them) and sometimes emotional.
Apologising–**F**ailure	The person whose approval you desperately wanted as a child, but who gave you the impression that nothing you did was ever good enough.

Impatient–Restless	The person who seemed to love you only when you achieved something, but who either did not give you any attention or rejected you when you did not achieve anything.
Blaming–Suffering	The person who hurt you unfairly and unjustly, and whom you need to forgive.
Never Enough	The person who abandoned you – physically or emotionally – as a child.
Frantic–Destructive	The person who abused you physically or emotionally.

STEP 3 When you have expressed (dumped) every emotion you feel towards that person, shower or bathe, or wash your hands and face.

STEP 4 Check that you have said (written) everything you wanted and needed to say. If you find it difficult to sleep afterwards, this is because there is more to be said or written.

STEP 5 Burn the letters.

A LITTLE TALK MIGHT HELP ...

During the early 1990s, when we were doing our initial research into PNI – specifically focusing on AIDS and cancer – we interviewed 22 HIV long-term non-progressors – people who, despite having been infected for more than 10 years, had shown little or no clinical progression from being HIV-seropositive to symptomatic AIDS.

Our findings seemed to confirm most of the dominant research regarding the attitudes and coping styles associated with a strong immune system, such as the ability to express emotions, having dealt with major fears (especially the fear of dying and death), hardiness, engagement in exciting and challenging activities and goals, and healthy levels of self-esteem.

However, there was a rather odd phenomenon which appeared to be unique to these long-term survivors, and which we subsequently also found in people who have turned their cancer around using PNI-styled approaches. It was quite a simple thing. All these people had, in some way, shape or form, for a multitude of reasons, talked to their disease, and did so on a regular basis.

A dialogue with your disease

At that time, we did not know whether this was simply a random phenomenon, until we encountered another researcher's work in AIDS, namely that of Dr Jon Kaiser [1], in which he describes how he combines orthodox medical treatment and complementary holistic methods.

He describes how several of his patients began to write letters to their virus, and how, using imagination, the virus 'wrote back'. He also includes the immune effects of this technique, using case studies. The effects seem to coincide with what we have found with the long-term survivors we interviewed. Either an increase in the number of helper T-cells (CD4 cells) or a stabilisation of these cell numbers.

Quite frankly, there is little or no PNI research into exactly how this process has this effect, and we can only assume that the dialogue with the virus or cancer reduces the emotional distress associated with having an invader inside your body. However, based on the case studies, we consider this process sufficiently relevant for inclusion as a possible immune-system strengthener.

We have also noticed that the effectiveness of the dialogue with your disease depends on the nature of the disease itself. For example, with HIV – which is an external virus that 'invades' the body – the most effective dialogue appears to be directed at establishing some kind of mutually compatible agreement, or what can be called a 'truce'.

With diseases such as cancer – which are your own cells that have refused to co-operate within the normal 'rules' of how cells should behave – a more aggressive dialogue seems to be more effective. However, even in such illnesses, people have reported good results with the 'ceasefire' approach to the cancer cells.

There are dynamics that operate with such a dialogue which are quite intriguing. First, you have to assume – and know – that you are indeed able to kill the disease, if you wanted to. How is this possible, when you consider that some diseases are supposedly 'incurable'?

David said that when he had his first talk to the HIV in his body, he told it that he could kill himself and that this would automatically kill the virus too. He told the virus that, if the virus made him so ill that his quality of life was beyond repair, he would kill himself and end the whole thing. He then asked the virus if it wanted to live. The virus said, *'Yes! Of course!'* David then told the virus that he was well aware of the power of the virus to kill him, and that he respected that power. All he was asking the virus to consider was that he also had that kind of power of life and death. He then discussed ways in which he and the virus could operate with mutual respect, from within the same body. He clearly told the virus that, if the virus got out of hand, he would have no hesitation in taking whatever drugs were necessary to bring it back under control. The virus agreed that this was fair, and that it would keep itself under control.

Twenty-one years later (2004), he – David Patient – is healthy, and has the same discussion with his virus, at the same time every year.

Writing to Mr Cancer

Another person said that, when she discovered that her cancer had spread throughout her body, and that surgery was no longer possible, she initially became very angry at the betrayal of her body. She wrote a letter to 'Mr Cancer', and told 'him' in no uncertain terms how angry she was at 'him'. She then put the pen in her other hand, and she simply wrote down whatever came into her mind, intending that this was 'Mr Cancer' speaking to her. She was shocked at what he had to say! 'He' told her, in no uncertain terms, that she had spent her entire life listening to everyone else, and that 'he' was simply fulfilling her wish of wanting to escape from all the unhappiness and boredom. She then wrote back to 'him', asking whether he would agree to stop spreading throughout her body for three months, while she started sorting out all these emotional issues. He agreed, on condition that she finally did the work. She then said that she felt somewhat trapped by this agreement, as it was 'he' who was dictating all the terms of the agreement! '*So,*' he said, '*what do you want to do about that?*' After careful thought, she told (wrote to) 'him' that she wanted to be able to have an ongoing talk with him, so that 'he' could tell her how she was doing. Also, she wanted to be able to take some time off from the 'work' he said was necessary, and suggested weekends for this rest. 'He' agreed. Furthermore, she insisted that he recognise the reality that she could take full control of the situation by simply killing herself, and that she reserved the right to do so if 'he' got out of control.

Six months later, after many such discussions and modifications of the initial agreement, her cancer had stopped spreading and had begun to retreat. Two years later, the cancer was in full remission.

We should make it clear that all the people who have used this method successfully also did other things to maintain their health, including many of the methods described in this book. Therefore, this method of talking to your disease is not in and of itself a solution – it is part of an immune-empowering programme. Try it.

To do this fascinating process you need to have an idea of what the biological cause is of your illness. With conditions such as HIV, it is relatively simple – it is a virus. With cancer, it is your own cells. With autoimmune conditions, such as rheumatoid arthritis, multiple sclerosis and lupus, it is your own antibodies, although there may be other factors. If you have done your homework in finding out as much as you can about your disease (see Chapter 4 page 66), you will know the answer to this question.

■ ASSIGNMENT

TALK TO IT

STEP 1   Say what you want to say to it.
Take a pen and paper, and write a letter to your disease. Give it a name if that makes it easier. Write down exactly what you feel – all the anger, fear, questions, and whatever else you can think of.

STEP 2   Listen to what it says back to you.
Now clear your mind, and pretend you are the disease itself, and write a letter back to yourself, in response to your own letter. This is not a process of guessing or logic. In fact, the easiest way to 'listen' without interfering is to use your non-dominant hand to write the response, i.e. if you are right-handed, then write the response from the disease with your left hand.

STEP 3   Come to an understanding or agreement of some kind.
Ensure that you come to some agreement regarding how you see yourself in terms of your power to do something about this illness, and recognise the power of the disease as well. Maintain this dialogue over time.

The following two case studies are largely as the person told us, with a little editing.

DOUG – Cancer

'I was born and raised on a dairy and sheep farm. Apart from a year working in the accounts department of an oil company, university for five years and boarding school, I have spent most of my 60 years on this farm.

My eldest brother was grandfather's golden boy and a prefect at school. As a result, he thought he was the next best thing to Christmas and bossed my brother and me around from an early age.

This middle brother, who was closest to me – and who was the thickest of us all – was the life and soul of a party. He decided from an early age that he wanted to be a motor mechanic and ended up being one, and an alcoholic as well. I pulled him out of the gutter some 25–30 years ago, rehabilitated him, and lost him as a brother and friend in the process.

My oldest brother convinced me to come back to this farm straight after university and effectively prevented me from furthering my education. After a year or two of getting me locked onto the farm, he made his planned escape with his family to New Zealand. He left me to look after the farm which he was going to inherit, until my father died in 1990 and the estate could be wound up. He died of a brain tumour in Australia last year in November, about two months after diagnosis.

So, in effect, I was in a situation where I operated a farm that I did not own, and was not expecting to inherit. The result was that I lived for some 28 years in a negative state of waiting for my father to die as the rest of the family refused to help me out of this situation.

Trying to arrange finance for overdrafts, electrification, switching from industrial milk to fresh milk was a nightmare without collateral and very expensive. I was also married with two kids. My wife and I were constantly fighting for dominance, so I swung violently from the occasional *Control–Distance* Shadow to mostly the *Apologising–Failure* Shadow.

With my *Apologising–Failure* and *Blaming–Shaming* Shadows – and my misguided striving for security and being able to care best for my family in the environment I knew and felt safe in – I dug in in spite of a no-win situation and rode it out.

I was diagnosed with multiple myeloma in July–August 1997 after various other ailments. I decided to go to a specialist physician who, luckily for me, was one of the few around who had worked with myelomas for years, and therefore recognised the symptoms, as it is a pretty rare form (1 in 400,000).

An X-ray and blood tests – the latter showing the typically elevated myeloma IgG spike – and a spinal bone-marrow tap confirmed the diagnosis 100 percent. My doctor referred me to a close associate of hers who had worked with her on myelomas some years ago. By September 1997, I was on a chemotherapy protocol of one week on, three weeks off, for six months.

My initial reaction to the diagnosis was '*What on earth is myeloma?*' and an immense feeling of relief that at least I knew what was wrong with me. Even if I didn't know what it meant, the doctors seemed to know what they were doing and I was being 'treated'.

Fortunately for me, I have a good friend who is a professor who made me a member of the International Myeloma Foundation, quite the most fantastic source of info and specialist support for anyone with my type of cancer. This resulted in making me more in touch with my disease than the local doctors were!

Chemotherapy is another story and, like childbirth, best forgotten. There were a couple of tricks I learned – a set of earphones with a Louise Hay tape was one of them, in the early hours of the morning when the drug reactions hit. I remember very clearly dreading going back each month to put myself through it again. When I got to the sixth session, I decided that I had had enough.

So I survived as I knew I would – I figured that, if I can survive the drought, what else is new? In the meantime, I was studying the disease via the Internet, and investigating alternative medicine. I had always held the belief that this disease came in through the immune system and, by God, I was going to push it out the same way.

I was sent off to Cape Town after finishing my chemotherapy treatment, with a view to a possible bone-marrow transplant using my own stem cells, which they collect from the bone marrow. So I spent two separate days lying on a bed with my blood going out of one arm through a dialysis-type machine and back into the other arm. This was after giving myself injections daily for a week to mobilise my stem cells into the bloodstream. The next step would have been the total sterilisation of my body and bone marrow (in other words, no more immune system) with hefty doses of drugs and radiation. Then, they would 'rescue' me with my stored stem cells and hope to regenerate my immune system back to 100 percent. They said that the success rate for this procedure was about 35 percent. I said 35 percent was not good enough odds for me to put myself through intensive care for six months. Having done my homework via the Internet and weighing up my options, I declined the bone-marrow transplant.

It was almost like signing my death warrant, as I was, according to the professor, a 'good candidate'. But I really didn't believe that destroying my immune system was the way to go – it works for lymphomas and leukaemia up to 90 percent because these cancer cells are mobilised in the system, not buried in the recesses of the bone marrow to regenerate, as in myeloma.

So, having made the decision to go my own way (I have always followed my instincts), I researched the immune system and my wife picked up a report about PNI. She brought it to my attention and we spent the next few weeks tracking down the coordinators, who suggested I do the Applied PNI Empowerment (APE) workshop course in December 1997. The rest, as they say, is history.

APE turned me around 180 degrees. I discovered my Shadows – and my purpose – which I had carried all my life without being aware of it. I had made the shift that other PNI workers write about, and I knew without a shadow of a doubt that I was on my way, and anyone who stood in the way was going to have to like it or lump it.

The statistics make interesting reading. My myeloma state is monitored basically by blood tests every two months. When I finished my chemotherapy, I was tested in April 1997, and my IgG count (Immunoglobulin G, which fights infection) was 9g/L (the normal range is 9–15g/L).

I was told that if I could keep the IgG count below 20 or so within a year, I would not have to go for more chemotherapy. However, they were expecting me back, cap in hand, to beg for the bone marrow transplant at least within the year.

My IgG tests have run as follows:

April 97	09.5 g/l
May 97	15.1
July 97	17.1
September 97	15.4
November 97	14.9
January 98	17.3
March 98	16.5
May 98	16.5
July 98	14.1

My full blood counts have returned to normal; in other words, the white cell counts, red cells, etc. The lytic spots (holes formed in the bones) on my ribs are stable and one appears to have disappeared (although it may have been missed in the X-rays).

My Shadows assessment (in December 1997) showed that my highest scores were in the *Apologising–Failure*, *Blaming–Shaming* and *Impatient–Restless* Shadows. This changed by February 1998 to the *Obstinate–Inflexible*, *Control–Distance* and *Impatient–Restless* Shadows.

I am a lot more at peace, and I know where I am going. I have sold my farm, bought a house in the city, and have done most of my unfinished business. The high *Impatient–Restless* Shadow score is because I just can't wait to get on with the rest of my life!

My immune system has been initially supplemented with immune boosters, carotenoids and sterol/sterolins.

I will not allow myself to be in any kind of negative situation or be with negative people. I will remove myself or do damage control. I relax with music and conduct my own taped truce dialogue with 'Mike' (the visualised cancer) every afternoon. I now believe that he was sent to teach me a lesson that I cannot disregard my body.

I used to say *'If my body can't take a joke, it's bloody well going to have to learn,'* and I just punished it a bit more. If I had not got cancer I would still be messing up my life and everyone else's in the process.

In terms of the process, what has saved my life has been Shadow awareness, coping style and decisions made, the dealing with my death fears, the unfinished business letters, and the truce dialogue with my disease. Above all, the process opened me up and put purpose and passion back into my life.

SHARRON – Chronic Fatigue

Sharron was 44 when she was diagnosed with CFS (chronic fatigue syndrome). No one could have been more surprised. She'd never been ill. She'd led a full and hectic life as a mother of two children, with a career in advertising, surviving a dying marriage and coming to grips with divorce and single parenting. She worked hard and played hard. Friends marvelled at how much she juggled, seemingly successfully. One said she was 'driven'. Sharron took it as a compliment. She had also been referred to as opinionated and a bit defensive.

Occasionally, she'd spend a whole Sunday in bed, reading, eating and sleeping to recharge her batteries. Relaxation was a glass of wine or more with friends but she exercised regularly and felt her diet was pretty good and had never been overweight.

Four years before her CFS diagnosis, Sharron's lower back ached and continuously went out of alignment. At one point she was getting a chiropractic adjustment every three days. Finally after her saying *'This is ridiculous'*, the chiropractor suggested she take Vitamins E and B-complex three times a day. Within 10 days her back was fine, but she didn't understand why and stopped taking the vitamins.

About two years before being diagnosed, small changes started happening in Sharron's body. She'd get a dry spot in the centre of her throat that no amount of water would dispel. An ear-nose-throat specialist told her it was nerves. There were no suggestions other than to 'Live with it, and don't worry'. Little warts, most of them flat, appeared – on her legs, arms, back and face. She went to a dermatologist, who said they were nothing to worry about. Two were burnt off her back and she was sent home. White spots appeared on her legs, back and shoulders after she had been in the sun. This was diagnosed as a viral condition but the doctor couldn't explain why or how this happened, and spreading an anti-dandruff shampoo over the area for 20 minutes on three consecutive days was the suggested treatment.

White streaks showed up underneath her fingernails. She had slowly gained about 7 kg even though she ran and swam every day. Sharron's body wasn't metabolising fats well anymore and she drank too much wine. Her thighs became lumpy and she kept getting sores in her mouth. Her first cold sore appeared halfway through a holiday in Greece three years before diagnosis. Her gums were often swollen, bleeding and began to recede. The dentist said it was gum disease. Although she'd never suffered from allergies or sinus congestion, Sharron's sinuses became clogged. Her eyes began watering all the time. She cried in movies and, if she was talking with someone, her eyes always watered. Should there be any anger or accusation in the conversation, tears streamed uncontrollably.

She began to jump at sudden noises, and was easily annoyed and even angered. Her driving was frenetic. She shouted and swore at anyone who got in her way, including, and sometimes especially, little old ladies who drove slowly.

At the end of 1990, Sharron married the man she loved. He had three daughters who didn't live with them but visited often, and Sharron went out of her way to make them feel welcome and loved. Christmas that year went from the usual three or four people to ten, and she wanted to make it perfect. On 26 December she collapsed in the hammock, truly exhausted.

But the tiredness wouldn't go away. She gained more weight, developed swollen glands, arthritic fingers and sore throats. Her muscles became weak and her circulation system slowed – she was cold on the warmest of days. Her brain wasn't quick anymore and she had difficulty remembering things.

What finally caught her attention was that when she became so fatigued she actually dragged her feet and there was a pit in the centre of her body: she had no more 'go', no reserve, no energy whatsoever. She could barely move. Still she refused to give in, thinking it was just the empty-nest syndrome or something.

Finally in April 1991, after coming out of an aerobics class shaking, she went to a doctor. Blood tests showed a rampaging Epstein-Barr virus. All she was told was that it was the virus that caused mononucleosis (sleeping disease). Her limbs felt like lead, she got headaches for the first time in her life, and she became hypersensitive to bright light and noise. It felt best to sleep. Fortunately, marrying had forced a move to another city and she wasn't yet working. She couldn't fight it, so she slept.

For a year, Sharron stayed in bed, shuffling downstairs occasionally to huddle in front of the television. Her body had bad reactions to alcohol, coffee, tea, meat, cheese, sugar, white bread or rice, giving her gas, pimples, weakness in the limbs, sinusitis or just putting her to sleep. She was either hot and sweaty or shivering. Reading was impossible as concentration and memory had gone.

She maintains that it was her husband's humour that saved her life that first year. There was also a strange phenomenon they noticed. Whenever Sharron's husband said there was a business trip on which she could come along – to the States, the Orient, even Cape Town – she perked up and functioned quite normally. She still couldn't drink or eat those things to which her body was sensitive, but the fatigue seemed to dissipate in the face of the adventure. When she returned home, the fatigue overwhelmed her again and she dragged herself through the days. They joked about it and Sharron felt silly. As hard as she tried to maintain the 'holiday' energy level after returning home, it faded completely within two to three days. She returned to what she called 'a vegetable state'. Sitting in the sun was out of the question. More than 10 minutes' exposure caused swollen glands the size of golf balls. She couldn't go down the stairs into the garden she loved so much.

After 15 months, Sharron went for another blood test to see if the virus was still there. The results showed that the Epstein-Barr virus had abated but the Coxsackie virus was now showing in great numbers.

Confused, Sharron started to feel like a victim. The only defence she knew was to learn more about viruses and about strengthening the body. There was even more confusion when she learned that both the viruses that plagued her were so common that it was highly unusual for anyone not to have these in their bodies by the age of 30, because they were everywhere and were readily picked up through breathing or touch. Suddenly there was no enemy to rail against. Without an enemy, how could she fight?

For the next nine months, she just took it easy. She became a movie fan and bought more magazines. She walked slower, talked slower, ate less and watched her body intently for reactions to everything. She still slept for two or three hours in the day. And she thought a lot. Many thoughts led to feelings of guilt that she could have been a better mother. She cried a lot, feeling terribly sorry for herself for months. Then she decided there was no future in that, and that she had cried enough. So she apologised to her son and daughter and swore to herself that she would be a better mother from now on, even though her children were now adults. The only thing she could control were her actions, now and in the future.

In analysing how she became so ill, Sharron realised that the chronic fatigue syndrome didn't happen overnight. In fact, it had taken a long time to wear down her body's systems.

When she tried to trace back to where it began, she kept going back another 5 or 10 years. Sharron remembers thinking, '*Well, I had that trouble with my last job. Oh no, I guess it started with the divorce. Or perhaps a bit earlier when I got into retail advertising.*' She learned that the body doesn't differentiate between good stress and bad stress – stress is stress. So the great fun she'd had at the first manic advertising agency had been taking its silent toll. This didn't make much sense since, if that were the case, she reasoned that everyone under any stress would end up with chronic fatigue, but they didn't. They were still happily skydiving and bungee jumping, playing the stock market, buying, selling and starting businesses, and mountain climbing, but she had come down with chronic fatigue. She began to recognise that it must be more about her reaction to stress than the stress itself.

The important lesson that came out of this exercise was that it had taken her a long time to become really ill. Her immune system hadn't 'crashed' as she had thought, but rather it wore down like a rock that has water flowing over it for years and years. On realising that it had taken over 20 years to become weak, she was able to accept that it was going to be OK if it took five years to regain strength. This was important. It allowed her to relax and be gentle with herself.

At the end of the second year, more blood tests were taken and the viruses had flip-flopped, putting the Epstein-Barr virus ahead again. That was when Sharron's anger exploded! She decided she'd had enough of this 'nonsense' and she would now actively find a solution. She tackled it head-on by booking appointments with a naturopath, a homeopath and going to a hydro for a week of fasting.

She bought books on fasting, diet, herbal cures, on Bach remedies, on aromatherapy oils and treatments. She made up her own treatment oils, face creams, even mosquito repellent. She rejected any food with preservatives, colouring, artificial flavouring or chemicals of any kind. She refused drugs and headache tablets. She became obsessed. She was a sponge, soaking up information from any source about how to clean up the body and create vibrant health.

Although the doctor who pinpointed her problem couldn't give her any solutions or any information about what was then maddeningly called 'yuppie flu', there were a couple of books coming out about it. In Britain, it's called ME for 'myalgic encephalomyelitis' and considered a brain disease. In America, it was called chronic fatigue syndrome or yuppie flu, and now chronic fatigue immune deficiency syndrome (CFIDS).

She felt thankful to those authors because they provided her with the only information available on the disease, giving her a start at making decisions that would not only rid her of the illness, but also make a complete change in her life.

For the first time in her life, Sharron put herself first. In her mind, it was like life or death because the life she'd lived for the past two years was more like the step before death. If there was a confrontation with family, she had walked away. When a local hostess served only meat and fried chicken for a dinner party, she had taken a spoonful of gravy to avoid hurting the woman's feelings and been sick for three days. She declared war on doing anything that would harm her body or state of mind in any way. She stopped watching the news on television because she felt helpless to do anything about the needless murder and violence all over the world.

She refused to spend time with people who drained her energy. She learned to feel the difference. She attended only one meeting of an CFIDS/ME support group because she believed the members felt sorry for themselves and she didn't see how wallowing in self-pity could lead to better health. She stopped worrying about what people thought of her.

She bought a Tai Chi videotape and began learning, even though initially she couldn't remember what exercise she had just completed. Still, she felt better. It took her four years to learn the 20-minute sequence. Weekly massages became a ritual. She signed up for a correspondence herbal course. Whenever she found a good book on self-development and positive thinking, she bought it, read it obsessively and talked about it for months with anyone who would listen. Her son teased her: *'You're obsessing, Mom.'* Talking about it helped her remember and it also reinforced the theories in her mind. She stopped the power struggles with her husband, deciding that what she thought was winning wasn't winning anything. Rather, it usually sent her back to bed for a couple of days. It wasn't worth it. She knew what she knew.

She was who she was. And so was he. They loved each other, cared about each other and respected each other. That was enough. She stopped criticising herself. She stopped telling herself she couldn't do things – like drawing. Instead, she got a length of cloth and painted a tablecloth. Everyone asked her where she'd bought it.

One day, about four years after being diagnosed, she saw an advertisement in the newspaper for a part-time copywriter. She'd written all the copy for the clients she had had in a consultancy she ran from her house just after the divorce years ago. She'd taken three years of night classes on creative and professional writing. She got the job. She had some fun until taking on a project that proved to be too hectic, and there was fighting with her co-workers about how it should be done. They made up, the job was successfully completed but Sharron realised she'd reacted badly, again, to the first bit of stress. She retreated to the quiet sanctuary of her home, dedicating her life to the comfort and happiness of her enlarged family and deciding that she really didn't like advertising anymore.

Sharron's health was much improved. As long as she didn't eat or drink anything toxic or spend time with toxic people, she didn't have relapses. She drank healing herbal teas each day and occasionally had a tiny espresso, her only downfall, after which she'd wait an hour before taking 2000 mg of Vitamin C, knowing the caffeine had depleted it. She kept the balance and was ever watchful. She found a physiotherapist who worked on the parasympathetic nervous system, thus eliminating the last of the severe muscle aches she had down her sides in the night. Taking barley green and many vitamins and minerals was the first order of the day.

By year six, Sharron's body had responded well to the improved regimen. Physically, her eyes sparkled, her skin had never been so clear and healthy-looking, and her hair shone. She still had some extra weight but she was in her fifties and reasoned that most women that age struggle to lose weight. She consulted a dietician and reduced her fat intake. She was able to do aerobic exercise again – a major victory. And now she needed to figure out what to do with the rest of her life.

In quick succession, from October 1997 to April 1998, the answers came. First she took a Reiki healing course. Participating in the Reiki workshop, she released incredibly deep sorrow about the father she'd never known. She signed up for a PNI course, knowing it was along the lines of where her interest now lay – in healing and health. It involved the immune system, which she had come to understand quite well. Following the training she went to an APE (Applied PNI Empowerment) workshop, unearthing deep-seated feelings of unworthiness. The last two courses helped Sharron understand how the decisions she had taken over the past six years had helped her step out of the shroud of ME. Early in 1998, she completed Reiki II, another Reiki workshop, and travelled to California to complete studies on a technique that focused on the heart as an aid to de-stressing.

Today, Sharron can drink with the best of them again, but chooses not to. She counsels people in the Applied PNI protocol and is setting up workshops for Heart Focus. She's kicked the disease physically and, for the most part, mentally, but she has also rekindled her passion for life. Now her passion is passing on all that she has learned so that others do not have to slog through looking for information on how to combat illness. She plans to continue learning nutrition and ultimately become a naturopathic doctor and author.

CHAPTER 2: What is PNI?

1. Ader, R, Felten, D, & Cohen, N, 1991, *PsychoNeuroImmunology* (2nd ed.), Academic Press: San Diego.
2. Candace B Pert, 1997, *Molecules of Emotion*, Simon & Schuster: London.
3. Black, PH, 1995, 'PsychoNeuroImmunology: Brain and Immunity', *Scientific American*: Science & Medicine, Nov/Dec 1998, pp. 16-25.
4. Daruna, JH, & Morgan, JE, 1990, 'Psychosocial Effects on Immune Function: Neuroendocrine Pathways', *Psychosomatics*, 31(1), pp. 4-12.
5. Kiecolt-Glaser, J, & Glaser, R, 1992, 'PsychoNeuroImmunology: Can Psychological Interventions Modulate Immunity?', *Journal of Consulting and Clinical Psychology*, 60(4), pp. 569-575.
6. Martin, P, 1997, *The Sickening Mind: Brain, Behaviour, Immunity & Disease*, Harper Collins: London.
7. Ader, R, & Cohen, N, 1975, 'Behaviorally conditioned immunosuppression', *Psychosomatic Medicine*, 37(4), pp. 333-340.
8. Kiecolt-Glaser, J, et al., 1985, 'Psychosocial enhancement of immunocompetence in a geriatric population', *Health Psychology* 4(1), pp. 25-41.
9. Zachariae, R, et al., 1990, 'Effect of psychological intervention in the form of relaxation and guided imagery on cellular immune function in normal healthy subjects', *Psychotherapy and Psychosomatics*, 54, pp. 32-39.
10. Spanos, NP, Williams, V, & Gwynn, MI, 1990, 'Effects of hypnotic, placebo, and salicyclic acid treatments on wart regression', *Psychosomatic Medicine*, 52, pp. 109-114.
11. Smith, GR, & McDaniel, SM, 1983, 'Psychologically mediated effects on the delayed hypersensitivity reaction to tuberculin in humans', *Psychosomatic Medicine*, 45(1), pp. 65-70.
12. Rider, MS, & Weldin, C, 1990, 'Imagery, Improvisation, and Immunity', *The Arts in Psychotherapy*, 17, pp. 211-216.
13. Green, ML, Green, RG, & Santoro, W, 1988, 'Daily relaxation modifies serum and salivary immunoglobulins and psychophysiologic symptom

severity', *Biofeedback and Self-regulation*, 13(3), pp. 187-199.

14. Martin, RA, & Dobbin, JP, 1988, 'Sense of humor, hassles, and immunoglobulin A: Evidence for a stress-moderating effect of humor', *International Journal of Psychiatry in Medicine*, 18(2), pp. 93-105.

15. Pennebaker, JW, & Beall, SK, 1986, 'Confronting a traumatic event: Toward an understanding of inhibition and disease', *Journal of Abnormal Psychology*, 95(3), pp. 274-281.

16. Pennebaker, JW, Hughes, CF, & O'Heeron, RC, 1987, 'The psychophysiology of confession: Linking inhibitory and psychosomatic processes', *Journal of Personality and Social Psychology*, 52(4), pp. 781-793.

17. Pennebaker, JW, & Susman, JR, 1988, 'Disclosure of traumas and psychosomatic processes', *Social Science & Medicine*, 26(3), pp. 327-332.

18. Pennebaker, JW, Kiecolt-Glaser, JK, & Glaser, R, 1988, 'Disclosure of traumas and immune function: Health implications for psychotherapy', *Journal of Consulting & Clinical Psychology*, 56(2), pp. 239-245.

CHAPTER 3: Mind–Body Connections

1. Levy, JA, 1993, 'HIV pathogenesis and long-term survival' *AIDS*, 7, pp. 1401-1410.

2. Sheppard, HW, Lang, W, Ascher, MS, Vittinghoff, E, & Winkelstein, W, 1993, 'The characterization of non-progressors: long-term HIV-1 infection with stable CD4+ T-cell levels', *AIDS*, 7, pp. 1159-1166.

3. University of Pennsylvania study, April 1995, regarding RU-486, reported in the *Pretoria News*, May 24, 1995, in the article entitled 'New hope for AIDS victims'.

4. Markham, PL, Salahuddin, SZ, Veren, K, Orndorff, SS, & Gallo, RC, 1986, 'Hydrocortisone and some other hormones enhance the expression of HTLV-III', *International Journal of Cancer*, 37, pp. 67-72.

5. Kasl, SV, Evans, AS, & Niederman, JC, 1979, 'Psychosocial Risk Factors in the Development of Infectious Mononucleosis', *Psychosomatic Medicine*, 41(6), pp. 445-466.

6. Drehler, H, 1995, *The Immune Power Personality*, Chapter 6, Plume/Penguin: New York.

7. Pelletier, KR, 1992, *Mind as Healer, Mind as Slayer*, Dell Publishing: New York, p. 63.

8. Knapp, PH, Levy, EM, Giorgi, RG, Black, PH, Fox, BH, & Heeren, TC, 1992, 'Short-term immunological effects of induced emotions', *Psychosomatic Medicine*, 54, pp. 133-148.

9. Moss, RB, Moss, HB, & Peterson, R, 1989, 'Microstress, mood, and natural killer-cell activity', *Psychosomatics*, 30(3), pp. 279-283.

10. Cohen et al., 1984, cited in Ader, R, Felten, DL, & Cohen, N (eds.), 1991, *Psychoneuroimmunology* (2nd ed.), p. 1092, Academic Press: San Diego.

11. Keller, SE, Schleiffer, SJ, & Demetrikopoulos, MK (1991), 'Stress-induced Changes in Immune Function in Animals: Hypothalamo-Pituitary-Adrenal Influences', *Psychoneuroimmunology* (2nd ed.), pp. 771-787, by Ader, R, Felten, DL, & Cohen, N (eds.). Academic Press: San Diego.

CHAPTER 5: Small things that matter

1. Kobasa, SC (1979), 'Stressful life events, personality, and health: An inquiry into hardiness', *Journal of Personality and Social Psychology*, vol. 37, pp. 1-11.

CHAPTER 6: Life: why bother?

1. Siegel, BS, 1986, *Love, Medicine & Miracles*, Arrow Books: London.

2. Beck, D, & Beck, J (1987), *The Pleasure Connection: How Endorphins Affect Our Health and Happiness*, Synthesis Press: San Marcos, California, pp. 113-120.

CHAPTER 7: Releasing stress from your past

1. Guyton (ed.), 1981, *Textbook of Medical Physiology*, 6th ed.

2. Pelletier, KR, 1992, *Mind as Healer, Mind as Slayer*, Dell Publishing: New York, p. 63.

3. Baker, GHB, 1982, 'Life events before the onset of rheumatoid arthritis', *Psychotherapy and Psychosomatics*, 38, pp. 173-177.

4. McClary, AR, Meyer, E, & Weitzman, DJ, 1955, 'Observations on the roles of the mechanism of depression in some patients with disseminated lupus erythematosus', *Psychosomatic Medicine*, 17, pp. 311-321.

5. Slawson, PF, Flynn, W, & Kollar, EJ, 1963, 'Psychological factors associated with the onset of diabetes mellitus', *Journal of the American Medical Association*, 185, pp. 166-170.

6. Engel, GL, 1973, 'Ulcerative colitis', in AE Lindner (ed.), *Emotional Factors in Gastrointestinal Illness*, (pp. 99-112). Excerpta Medica: Amsterdam.

7. Grant, I, 1987, *Life events and onset and exacerbation of symptoms of multiple sclerosis*, abstract presented to the Symposium on Mental Disorders,

Cognitive Defects, and Their Treatment in Multiple Sclerosis, Nov 18-21, Odense, Norway.

8. Glaser, R, Kiecolt-Glaser, JK, Speicher, CE, & Holliday, JE, 1985, 'Stress, Loneliness, and Changes in Herpes Virus Latency', *Journal of Behavioral Medicine*, 8(3), pp. 249-260.

9. Kemeny, ME, Cohen, F, Zegans, LS, & Conant, MA, 1989, 'Psychological and immunological predictors of genital herpes recurrence', *Psychosomatic Medicine*, 51, pp. 195-208.

10. Silver, PS, Auerbach, SM, Vishniavsky, N, & Kaplowitz, LG, 1986, 'Psychological factors in recurrent genital herpes infection: Stress, coping style, social support, emotional dysfunction, and symptom recurrence', *Journal of Psychosomatic Research*, 30(2), pp. 163-171.

11. Cohen, S, Tyrell, DAJ, & Smith, AP, 1993, 'Negative Life Events, Perceived Stress, Negative Affect, and Susceptibility to the Common Cold', *Journal of Personality and Social Psychology*, 64(1), pp. 131-140.

CHAPTER 8: Effective and ineffective coping

1. Baum, A, Fleming, R, & Singer, JE, 1983, 'Coping with victimization by technological disaster', *Journal of Social Issues*, 39, pp. 117-138.

2. Wilson, JF, 1981, 'Behavioral preparation for surgery: Benefit or harm?', *Journal of Behavioral Medicine*, 4, pp. 79-102.

3. Suls, J, & Fletcher, B, 1985, 'The Relative Efficacy of Avoidant and Nonavoidant Coping Strategies: A Meta-Analysis', *Health Psychology*, 4(3), pp. 249-288.

4. Costanza, R, Derlega, VJ, & Winstead, BA, 1988, 'Positive and Negative Forms of Social Support: Effects of Conversational Topics on Coping with Stress among Same-Sex Friends', *Journal of Experimental Social Psychology*, 24, pp. 182-193.

5. The Shadows questionnaire is derived from J Steven's *Transforming your Dragons* (1994, Bear & Company, Santa Fe). The 14-item Dragon questionnaire was completely rewritten after statistical analyses on a sample of several hundred people. Based on this original analysis, weak items were deleted or reworded, others added, and further statistical analyses were performed on the transformed questionnaire, to arrive at the present 7-item Shadow questionnaire. We have also added one more Shadow (*Blaming–Shaming*) to the original seven, and rewritten the descriptions of the other seven, based on our therapy experience and discussions with clients. The original scoring procedure has also been revised in order to

attain greater accuracy of measurement. We express our gratitude to Jose Steven for providing the initial framework and concepts for the Shadows Assessment.

CHAPTER 9: Dealing with fear

1. Weidenfeld SA, et al., 1990, 'Impact of perceived self-efficacy in coping with stressors on components of the immune system', *Journal of Personality and Social Psychology*, 59(5), pp. 1082-1094.
2. Jeffers, S, 1991, *Feel the Fear and Do It Anyway*, Arrow Books: London.

CHAPTER 10: Get it out of your body!

1. Mendolia M & Kleck, RE, 1993, 'Effects of talking about a stressful event on arousal: Does what we talk about make a difference?', *Journal of Personality and Social Psychology*, 64(2), pp. 283-292.
2. Orr, NM (1994) *Coping with HIV-seropositive status: A Psychoneuro-immunological perspective*, unpublished Master's Thesis, Univ. Cape Town, Dept. Psych.
3. Pennebaker, JW, Kiecolt-Glaser, JK, & Glaser, 1988, 'Disclosure of traumas and immune function: Health implications for psychotherapy', *Journal of Consulting and Clinical Psychology*, 56(2), pp. 239-245.
4. Pennebaker, JW, & Susman, JR, 1988, 'Disclosure of traumas and psycho-somatic processes', *Social Science and Medicine*, 26(3), pp. 327-332.
5. Solano, L, et al., 1993, Psychosocial factors and clinical evolution in HIV-1: A longitudinal study, *Journal of Psychosomatic Research*, 37(1), pp. 39-51.

CHAPTER 11: A little talk might help ...

1. Kaiser, JD, 1993, *Immune Power: A Comprehensive Treatment Program for HIV*, St Martin's Press: London.